THE GUIDE TO
MYSTERIOUS
ABERDEENSHIRE

THE GUIDE TO
MYSTERIOUS
ABERDEENSHIRE

GEOFF HOLDER

The
History
Press

*To Ségolène Dupuy, chauffeuse extraordinaire.
Baby, you can drive my car.*

First published 2009

The History Press
The Mill, Brimscombe Port
Stroud, Gloucestershire, GL5 2QG
www.thehistorypress.co.uk

British Library Cataloguing in Publication Data.
A catalogue record for this book is available from the British Library.

ISBN 978 0 7524 4988 3

Printed in Great Britain

CONTENTS

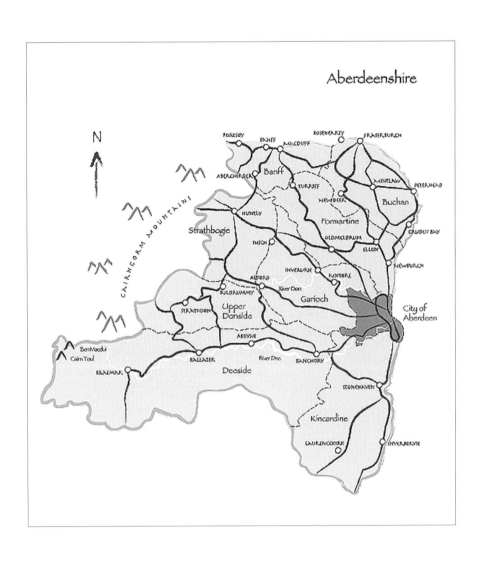

ACKNOWLEDGEMENTS

Thanks go out to: Mark Keighley of Archaeolink Prehistory Park; Dr Geoffrey Gill, chairman of the Garioch Heritage Society; Jason Schroeder of Sacred Ways (www.sacredway.co.uk); historian George Swapp; Joan Johnson, trustee of Delgatie Castle; Helen Chavez and Hazel Weeks of Aberdeenshire Heritage; and Jenni Wilson for designing the map. Special thanks are extended to the various anonymous drivers who stopped to give me lifts along remote roads.

The photograph of Meriorie Elphinstone's gravestone on page 50 is copyright of, and is reproduced, by kind permission of the Garioch Heritage Society. The image of the Wickerman on page 57 is copyright of, and reproduced, by kind permission of Archaeolink Prehistory Park. The photographs on pages 15, 48, 67, 125 and 127 are by Ségolène Dupuy. All other photographs are by the author.

This book is part of an ongoing series of similar titles. If you would like to share any stories of the weird and wonderful, or wish to find more information, please visit www.geoffholder.co.uk.

INTRODUCTION

Oddities and wonders,
Intiquities [*sic*] and blunders.
Omens dire, mystic fire,
Strange customs, cranks and freaks.
With philosophy in streaks.
Frank H. Stauffer, *The Queer, the Quaint, the
Quizzical: A Cabinet for the Curious* (1882)

Of Brownyis and of Bogilis full is this Beuk.
William Grant Stewart, *The Popular Superstitions and Festive
Amusements of the Highlanders of Scotland* (1823)

This is a guide to all things magical, mysterious, and otherwise marvellous in Aberdeenshire. Herein can be found archaeological mysteries, strange literature and legends, historical horrors, contemporary tales of UFOs and big cats, along with much in the way of magic, witchcraft, folklore and superstitions. Castles and stately homes interweave with haunted hills, graveyards, warlock rocks, stone circles and holy wells. There are bizarre beliefs and strange behaviours, sites associated with dragons, ghosts or bodysnatchers, and encounters with the fairy folk and naked ape-men.

Mysterious Aberdeenshire is organised geographically. Everything peculiar and paranormal associated with a town or village is collected together in one section, with the text then moving on to the next location, making exploration easy. The 1:25000 Ordnance Survey Explorer maps (382, 395-6, 405-6, 420-1, and 424-7) are essential for hard-to-find sites, and National Grid References are given throughout. Cross-references between locations are shown in SMALL CAPS. The book covers the whole area of the modern county of Aberdeenshire, including the historic county of Kincardineshire and those parts of the historic county of Banffshire within the current county boundary. Much of West Aberdeenshire is within the Cairngorms National Park. The City of Aberdeen will be covered in a later book, *The Guide to Mysterious Aberdeen*.

THINGS TO SEE AND PLACES TO VISIT

Stone circles, standing stones (menhirs) and other prehistoric monuments – the ritual and ceremonial remains of lost beliefs.

Pictish stones – wonderfully carved images from the Dark Ages; many include naturalistic or abstract symbols, the meaning of which still cause arguments among the experts.

Castles – Aberdeenshire has superb examples from the twelfth to the nineteenth centuries, many of which are open to the public. Ghosts, legends and curiosities abound.

Churches and churchyards – as the centre of life and death within communities, churches are frequently the home of ghoulish tales and strange customs. Aberdeenshire is rich in seventeenth- and eighteenth-century gravestones sculpted with symbols of mortality (skulls, femurs, coffins, hourglasses, death bells, gravedigger's tools, and the Grim Reaper) and immortality (winged souls ascending to Heaven, and trumpeting Angels of the Resurrection).

Holy wells – wells or springs associated with saints and/or healing.

Museums – containing everything from archaeological finds to stuffed squirrels duelling with swords (see BANCHORY).

Mountains, forests and lochs – associated with myths, magic and murders, many of which provide the excuse for a splendid coastal or hill walk.

Grotesque decoration – this typically features monstrous faces, demons, and humans or mythical creatures transforming into something else, usually foliage; one specific sub-category of foliaceous beings is the Green Man, a face either composed of leaves or spewing vegetation from the mouth, nose or eyes. See CRATHES and DALGETIE castles in particular.

Modern sculptures – strange and wonderful contemporary objects in the landscape.

Secret tunnels – every castle has one, but strangely enough no one can ever find it.

MAGIC AND THE SUPERNATURAL – KEY CONCEPTS

This book is filled with folk rituals that are 'apotropaic', which means 'that which protects against evil'. The use of fire, silver and holy words are commonly noted, and many of the charms prescribed by healers and witches were apotropaic in nature.

'Liminality' is another key concept – it means that which is betwixt and between, a threshold that is neither one thing nor the other. Hallowe'en is the typical liminal time when the border between this realm and the other-world is temporarily relaxed. Witches, suicides and other tainted people were frequently disposed of at the boundary between two properties, a liminal 'no man's land'. Liminal places also make acts of magic more powerful.

Thirdly there is the notion of 'sympathy', in which items once connected physically are forever linked magically. Thus, to bewitch a cow you do not need the whole animal, just a few of its hairs. The bones of a holy man can work miracles because, through the action of sympathy, they still contain the saint's power.

WITCHCRAFT

Witchcraft became a capital crime in 1563. Despite a few cases here and there, the law was wielded widely for the first time only in the 1590s, largely through the actions of the witch-obsessed James VI. A Royal Commission was set up in Aberdeen to try witches, and several ministers throughout the county obediently rounded up some of their more unconventional parishioners for trial. Around twenty-four 'witches' were executed, although the evidence for some of the others accused is ambiguous as to their fate.

A fine example of Pictish carvings on the Craw Stone, Rhynie, with images of a salmon and the enigmatic 'Pictish beast'.

Symbols of mortality: the skull, bones, and banner reading *MEMENTO MORI* ('Remember Death' or 'Remember you shall die'). St Mary's graveyard, Banff.

Symbol of immortality: the winged soul ascending to heaven. Strathdon parish church.

Symbols of mortality and immortality: the trumpet-blowing Angel of the Resurrection (helpfully labelled 'ANGEL') holding hands with the Grim Reaper, who is sporting a loincloth. Strathdon church.

The voluminous trial records were collected in *The Miscellany of the Spalding Club Vol I*, edited by John Stuart in 1841 (referred to as *Spalding* from hereon). Two years later Stuart edited *Extracts from the Presbytery Book of Strathbogie*, containing details of a number of witch trials outside Aberdeen. Thanks to these and similar works we have a reasonably detailed record of some of the Aberdeenshire witch trials, although many other cases are woefully incomplete.

The standard process was for the 'witch' to be first investigated by their own Kirk-Session or Presbytery. Both of these localised church bodies had the power to inflict punishments such as fines and forced repentance during Sunday worship, dressed in sackcloth and paraded before the entire congregation. For more serious crimes – such as magical murder – the Church, having established initial guilt, had to hand the miscreant over to the civil authorities, who alone had the power to condemn a person guilty of witchcraft to be tied to a stake, 'worriet' – strangled to death – and then burned.

Towards the end of the eighteenth century judicial scepticism regarding the reality of magic meant there were fewer and fewer successful prosecutions. The last witch burning in Scotland was in 1722; thirteen years later witchcraft ceased to be a crime – it had gone from a capital offence to something that, in the new Enlightenment thinking, did not exist at all. Belief in witches persisted in some parts until the First World War. Many of the episodes in this book concern nineteenth century village disputes between neighbours which revolve around magical ill-will – typically, stealing the 'goodness' of milk or crops, cursing butter-making equipment or enchanting livestock. In one case, in GLEN GAIRN, it was a man's gun that had been bewitched.

THE GOODMAN'S CROFT

In May 1594 the General Assembly of the Reformed Kirk noted: 'In the district of Garioch the Kirk resolved to apply to Parliament for an Act anent the horrible superstitioun used in Garioch and diverse parts of the countrey, in not labouring ane parcell of ground dedicate to the Devil, under the name of the Goodmans Croft.' (*The Booke of the Universall Kirk of Scotland*.) Garioch was the heart of this custom, but it was also widespread elsewhere, with packets of untilled land called Halyman's Croft, Goodman's Fauld, Gi'en Rig, Deevil's Craft, Clooties Craft, and the Black Faulie. The Church thought they were dedicated to Satan, although later writers have wondered if the offering was to a less specific spirit of the land or a vaguely-conceived nature deity. In the end an Act was not passed, and individual Sessions had to combat the Goodman and his Crofts on a case-by-case basis. It took almost two centuries, and increasing land hunger, for the unlaboured pockets of land to disappear.

THE HORSEMAN'S WORD

The Mason's Word was the password of the Scottish seventeenth-century secret society of the same name that evolved into Freemasonry. Then, partly in imitation, came the Miller's Word, essentially an eighteenth-century 'closed shop' society that restricted entry into the prestigious and profitable trade of grain miller. Partly to obscure its restrictive practices, and partly because there's no point in belonging to a secret society unless you can have a bit of sport with outsiders, members spread rumours that the Word granted magical powers over mill machinery, such powers having a diabolic price. Initiations became scary ordeals, with the candidate having to supply gifts of bread and whisky at midnight, undergo an interrogation by a mock minister at a fake altar and provide specific answers, and at the end be blindfolded to shake hands with Satan, usually a heated spade or bullock's hoof. And then the whisky was consumed. The Miller's Word was an all-male society that developed into an excuse for a boozy party away from wives and domestic duties, with the added frisson of mocking the shibboleths of institutions like the Church.

Also in the eighteenth century changes in agricultural practices brought heavy horses to most farms. Horse-handling skills were in demand, so in imitation of the millers' group the Horseman's Word was formed. Its initial purpose was to restrict access to much-sought-after jobs by selecting only those who had the real ability to work with horses. Inevitably there had to be an initiation, which again was borrowed wholesale from the millers – mock catechism, blindfold, Satan's paw and everything. At the end of the ceremony the initiate was given the 'Word' itself, said to grant almost mystical power over horses. A master horseman could 'reist' (arrest the movement of) a horse, control difficult animals and call horses from a distance. To an outsider it looked like magic. McPherson's *Primitive Beliefs* goes further, reporting claims of horses being set on fire without them being burned, and ploughs made to work without man or horse. He also suggests charms for mastering horses included the use of dead toads.

Let's not forget the whisky the candidate had to bring. At one level the Horseman's Word was a ritualistic self-preservation society for skilled workers in a changing world. At another it ensured horses were properly cared for and high standards were maintained. And at another it was a boys' club, a place of sexual boasting, alcohol consumption and wild, anti-establishment behaviour. Horsemen were reputed to have magical power over women (a good rumour to spread if you are on the pull). In later years the ritual seemed to have degenerated into petty sadism. In *Secrets, Stories, Skeletons and Stones* Bernard Maitland Balfour states that when his stepfather was initiated he was struck across the back of his hand with a trace chain, and bore the mark for the rest of his life. Others have hinted at hazing-type humiliation rituals and sexual abuse.

A key aspect of the ritual was an oath of total secrecy. In 1908, from the safety of London, 'A Buchan Horseman' revealed the oath. It begins, 'I of my own free will and accord solemnly vow and swear before God and all these witnesses that I will heal [hide], conceal and never reveal any part of the true horsemanship which I am about to receive at this time'. It then goes on to detail all the people who cannot be given the Word, including 'a farmer or a farmer's son ... a fool nor a madman ... nor to any womankind'. After much more in the same vein it concludes: 'If I fail to keep these promises may my flesh be torn to pieces with a wild horse and my heart cut through with a horseman's knife and my bones buried on the sands of the seashore where the tide ebbs and flows every twenty-four hours so that there may be no remembrance of me amongst lawful brethren so help me God to keep these promises. Amen.' The text is very similar to the Masonic Oath, from which it is clearly borrowed, flesh-tearing and bone-burying punishment included. This version of the Horseman's Oath was republished in 1972. A thorough treatment of the various secret societies is in Ronald Hutton's *The Triumph of the Moon*.

Probably the most knowledgeable modern writer on the subject is Billy Rennie, who joined the society when he was fifteen. On 14 January 2003 *The Times* reported that Mr Rennie, now the last surviving man with the Horseman's Word, was breaking the 300-year-old tradition of keeping women out, and passing the secrets on to his 10-year-old granddaughter.

BIG CATS

There are several notions concerning the many sightings of big cats in Aberdeenshire. Basically they are: 1) the cats are a non-native species, probably released former pets or otherwise introduced animals; 2) some of them are a hitherto unrecognised native species; 3) they are simply feral domestic cats; 4) they are paranormal members of the 'Phantom Menagerie' (see BEN MACDHUI). Given the current state of evidence – acres of sightings, some inconclusive video clips, a number of footprints and livestock kills, but no DNA and no physical specimens – it is possible that the range of phenomena represents all four suggestions.

The lynchpin of the sightings is the online catalogue maintained by the Big Cats in Britain organisation. The *Sunday Times* for 31 December 2006 reported the official response to BCIB's request under the Freedom of Information Act for details of all exotic animals kept in Scotland, excluding those in zoos or safari-parks. Aberdeenshire's score was forty-one North American bison, a pair of squirrel monkeys, an Asian leopard/domestic cat hybrid, twenty Bengal cats, and two leopards.

THE CONTEXT – ARCHAEOLOGY AND HISTORY

The Physical Environment

Aberdeenshire's folklore is often rooted in experiences deeply shaped by geography and history. The physical environment ranges from an extensive coastline – with fine harbours, peninsulas suitable for fortification and sand dunes that have overblown several communities – to rolling lowlands which centuries of labour have converted from wasteland to fertile farmland, and finally a sub-Arctic mountain tundra. The Cairngorm Mountains form a great mass to the west, with a finger of hills reaching the coast north of Stonehaven. This, the Mounth, acts as a natural barrier to the south of Deeside – travellers, from prehistoric axe traders to Roman legions, medieval kings, armies and modern users of rail and road, have to cross the Mounth by passes whose routes lead to fords and bridges over the Dee, with their attendant settlements. The Dee and its fellow river the Don have been both barrier and highway; and the origins of their names have distant echoes of water divinities. As late as the nineteenth century, drownings were referred to as the due sacrifice demanded by the river spirits. The isolated hills that poke out of the lowlands – such as BENNACHIE, DUNNIDEER and TAP O'NOTH – seem to have been regarded as sacred hills.

From Prehistory to the Romans

In the Neolithic period (from around 3800 BC onwards) farmers built burial cairns, henges (circular earth-banked enclosures) and stone circles. More circles and standing stones were erected in the Bronze Age (from about 2500 BC onwards).

Aberdeenshire contains about 10 per cent of the total number of known stone circles within the British Isles – well over 100 are still extant in the county, although many are badly damaged. For some unknown reason the peoples here developed a local variant – the Recumbent Stone Circle (abbreviated as RSC in the text). RSCs have a massive horizontal stone – sometimes weighing over fifty tons – framed by two tall upright stones called flankers, the entire arrangement sometimes looking like an upended vampire's dentures. The recumbent and flankers are always oriented towards the south-west part of the sky, and the other stones in the circle are graded in height away from the recumbent. Good RSCs can be easily visited at SUNHONEY, EASTER AQUHORTHIES and TOMNAVERIE, and many other places. Although the majority of Aberdeenshire stone circles are RSCs, there is a significant minority of other styles: excellent examples include CULLERLIE and THORAX.

A number of stones have prehistoric rock art such as cup-marks. These markings are completely enigmatic because we cannot read their 'language'. They could have mundane purposes – agricultural tallies? signposts? population counts? – or they might be anything from star maps to imagery from shamanic journeying.

Space restrictions mean that not all of the hundreds of prehistoric monuments can be included (although plenty are). Those mentioned in the text are either worth visiting for their own sake or have interesting folklore or stories attached to them. Many of Aberdeenshire's antiquities are on the Stone Circle Trail; if you see the Trail's sign you know there is access.

Tomnaverie, a typical Recumbent Stone Circle (RSC), with two upright pillars flanking the huge recumbent stone. The 'frame' looks to the south-west. (Photo: Ségolène Dupuy)

Cup-marks on one of the stones in Thorax Stone Circle, Finnygaud.

The Trail also includes other classes of monument, such as hillforts from the Iron Age (from about 800 BC).

In AD 84 a Roman army comprehensively defeated a confederation of Caledonian tribes at the Battle of Mons Graupius. There are approximately fourteen suggested locations for the battlefield, including BENNACHIE and KEMPSTONE HILL. Another major Roman incursion took place along the east coast around AD 211, but the Romans left no permanent presence in Aberdeenshire.

The Dark Ages

By the end of the ninth century Aberdeenshire was entirely Christian; a legacy of 400 years of work among the Picts by missionaries, largely from Galloway and Iona. Many of these holy men are remembered as saints who founded churches and settlements (such as St Ternan at BANCHORY), but often they are shadowy figures, with few reliable biographical details. It is not uncommon for one ancient source to claim that a certain holy man lived in the fifth century, while another authority categorically states that the saint was active 300 years later. Some saints may never have existed at all, which, along with the miracles attributed to them or their relics, all adds to the fun.

The Middle Ages

Early medieval Aberdeenshire was split into a number of Celtic provinces such as Mar, Formatine, Garioch, Buchan and Strathbogie, each ruled by a Mormaer. Around 1120 these became feudalised, with the Mormaers either adopting the new political and economic system themselves or being ousted by incoming Anglo-Norman families, who often intermarried with the Normanised Celtic aristocrats.

Boundaries of mountain and sea have sometimes made Aberdeenshire a redoubt of resistance to central authority from the south, but its relatively open routes to Moray to the north-west have also ensured it has many times been both military highway and battleground. Most of the major clashes of arms in Scottish history had an Aberdeenshire dimension. Edward I of England invaded during the first War of Independence. William Wallace captured DUNNOTTAR CASTLE in 1297. In 1308 Robert the Bruce annihilated the Comyns, the Bruce family's rivals for the Scottish throne, and implemented a scorched earth policy in the Comyn homeland of Buchan. Few popular renderings of Bruce the patriotic hero, victor over the English at the Battle of Bannockburn in 1314, seem to mention this vicious destruction of his fellow Scots.

In 1411 Alexander Stewart, Earl of Mar, supported by the burgesses of Aberdeen, checked the expansionist Donald, Lord of the Isles at the BATTLE OF HARLAW. Many saw the conflict as an expression of the enduring enmity between Lowlanders and Highlanders, English-speakers and Gaels. Lowland contempt for Highland raiders, who seem to have regarded Aberdeenshire as their larder, is summed up in a ditty in the *Bannatyne Manuscript* of 1568, charmingly titled 'How the First Hielandman was Made by God of ane Horse Turd':

> God turned owre the horse turd with his pykit [spiked] staff,
> And up start a Hielandman black as ony draff [dregs].
> Quod God to the Hielandman, 'Where wilt thou now?'
> 'I will doun in the Lowland, Lord, and there steal a cow.'

The Great Families

The various landed families tended not to opt for a quiet life. As John Grant put it in *Legends of the Braes O' Mar*: 'Among them flourished perpetual broils, petty strifes, thefts, depredations, burnings, and battles, the consequences of rivalry and vainglory.' The internecine blood feuds, often lasting generations, account for the large number of fortified tower houses to be found around the country – a report from 1670, printed in the *The Harleian Miscellany* in 1809, states: 'All the gentlemen's houses are strong castles, they being so treacherous one to another, that they are forced to defend themselves in strongholds'.

The Sixteenth and Seventeenth Centuries
The vendettas were only made worse by the political and cultural ramifications of the Scottish Reformation in 1560. Protestantism was made the state religion, and Catholicism outlawed – so attacks on Catholic nobles were now legitimate. How convenient for their enemies. Aberdeenshire was a holdout of Catholic resistance, and played a major part in the religious wars. In the seventeenth century there was more sectarian conflict between the Episcopalians (supporters of 'top-down' Church government by bishops, the bishops being appointed by the king) and the Covenanters (followers of the 'bottom-up' Presbyterian Church organisation, with church officials chosen by their congregations).

The Jacobite Rebellions
The failed Jacobite risings of 1688, 1715 and 1745 furthered clan enmities, with some nobles opting simply to declare for the side opposite to that chosen by their enemies. In 1745 some families hedged their bets by sending sons to both the Jacobite and Government armies – that way they would be sure of being on the winning side. After the '45 the price paid by the losers included imprisonment and the confiscation of their estates. Another consequence was that feudal jurisdiction was abolished. Up until this date, local barons, under the powers of 'pit and gallows', had the right to imprison, prosecute and execute their feudal subjects – which is why there are dozens of Gallows Hills scattered around Aberdeenshire. Those hanged were often buried on the site.

Agriculture and Royal Patronage
From 1770 onwards agricultural improvement was the watchword. Fields were enclosed, new crops introduced, and farms and farming methods changed. Landowners set up 'new towns' to 'civilise' the previously uninhabited wastelands of moss and heather. From this time can be dated the origins of what is now the familiar Aberdeenshire agricultural environment. In 1848 Queen Victoria made her first visit to Aberdeenshire. The Royal Family subsequently purchased and rebuilt Balmoral Castle, thus creating 'Royal Deeside'.

Language
Up until the fourteenth century most of Aberdeenshire was Gaelic-speaking, but pressure from English- and Scots-speakers pushed the language west into the mountains, where it survived as a native tongue until the 1970s. Ninety per cent of the place names of Aberdeenshire are Gaelic in origin, and while in Upper Deeside many place names are still recognisably so, in the lowlands the occasional tongue-twister is the legacy of anglicised Gaelic. EASTER AQUHORTHIES, for example, is a mixture of the Scots word 'Easter' (meaning east or easternmost) and the Gaelic 'Aquhorthies' (possibly meaning Field of Prayer or Field of the Pillar Stone). Many natives converse in Doric, a distinctive north-east dialect of Scots with its own vocabulary and vowel sounds.

KEY SOURCES

All books, articles, newspapers, websites and other media referred to in the text are listed in the Bibliography. Key among the sources are J.M. McPherson's *Primitive Beliefs in the North-East of Scotland* (1929), Peter Anson's *Fisher Folk-Lore* (1965) and a plethora of works by the prolific nineteenth-century folklorist Walter Gregor, minister at PEATHILL. His classic work is *Notes on the Folk-Lore of the North-East of Scotland* (1881). Much use has been made of the multi-volume *Old Statistical Account* and *New Statistical Account* (1791-1799 and 1845 respectively) hereafter referred to as the *OSA* and *NSA*. The various illustrated architectural guides published by RIAS have been at my side throughout.

FINDING OUT MORE

For more – much more – on archaeological sites, combine the sober but essential Canmore website (http://canmore.rcahms.gov.uk/) of the Royal Commission on the Ancient and Historic Monuments of Scotland (RCAHMS), and Aberdeenshire Council's Sites and Monuments Record www.aberdeenshire.gov.uk/Archaeology/ with the free-spirited user-generated www.themodernantiquarian.com. Much of the data on witchcraft is collated at the Survey of Scottish Witchcraft (www.shc.ed.ac.uk/Research/witches/). The best work on the county's agricultural heritage is David Kerr Cameron's *The Cornkister Days: A Portrait of a Land and its Rituals*. For more general works on Aberdeenshire, you cannot go wrong with anything by Robert Smith or Fenton Wyness, and Norman Adams' works will satisfy the ghoulish (for all, see Bibliography).

   Happy exploring.

1

DEESIDE

MARYCULTER – BANCHORY – BALLATER – BRAEMAR

BANCHORY-DEVENICK

In 1607 Isabell Smith of Cove was investigated for using a woollen thread to diagnose illness. Later she was accused of causing the death of Jonet Jack (although it appeared she simply did not prevent her death, as other than the use of a thread there is nothing mentioned about witchcraft). The case was continued indefinitely and, like so many, simply drops off the records. In 1732 the Kirk-Session found two men guilty of firing pistols during a marriage ceremony. Discharging guns at weddings was a popular way of driving away evil spirits; in 1839 the same Session had to forbid all gunfire at marriages.

Nineteenth-century St Devenick's Church (NJ90670248) replaced the medieval kirk built, supposedly, on the site of the tomb of the Dark Ages St Devenick. The graveyard has a watch-house and an iron mortsafe; the proximity of the site to Aberdeen meant it was often targeted by bodysnatchers.

BLAIRS MUSEUM

(Open 1 April-30 September, Saturday and Holiday Mondays 10 a.m.-5 p.m., Sunday 12 noon-5 p.m., admission charge, full wheelchair access.)

The Museum of Scotland's Catholic Heritage, housed in part of the former St Mary's College seminary, tells the story of Catholicism in Scotland both before and after the Reformation, with Jacobite items and a copy of Mary Queen of Scots' death warrant. St Mary's Chapel is a vast neo-Gothic Victorian space with beautiful detailing.

MARYCULTER

Tree-grown and only foundations-high, the old parish kirk, enclosed within a high boundary wall, retains a secluded, even spiritual, atmosphere (NO84439999). It is in the grounds of Maryculter House Hotel so ask permission at reception before visiting it. This was the site of the chapel of the Preceptory of the Knights Templar built in 1221-1236. A preceptory was a Templar regional headquarters; some of its stones form the cellars of the hotel.

The immediate area is now Templars' Park, owned by the Scouting movement. A large hollow in the otherwise smoothly rolling parkland is the Thunder Hole, site of a persistent local legend given in John Henderson's *Annals of Lower Deeside* (1890). A Templar Knight, Godfrey Wedderburn of Wedderhill, was wounded on a Crusade in the Holy Land and was nursed back to health by a Saracen woman. She presented him with a charm, a precious stone set in a gold ring, which would protect the pure of heart from the perils of disease and war. The woman – who is never

Knights Templars this way. Maryculter.

named in the narrative – followed Godfrey back to Scotland. The Templar Grand Master (or, more realistically, the head of the Preceptory) accused Godfrey of breaking his vow of celibacy. Enraged, Godfrey struck the Preceptor and was sentenced to death; as a matter of honour he was allowed to take his own life. The distraught Saracen woman appeared just as he died. She too killed herself, cursing the Preceptor and flinging the charmed ring at him in contempt. In response, the false accuser defiantly threw the charm round his neck: 'a blinding light flashed from heaven, and a blue bolt of fire struck deep down into the earth.' The Preceptor was vaporised, and the Thunder Hole was born. When Godfrey's body was lying in the chapel, those keeping vigil saw an angel in the form of the woman hover over it and kiss his lips. The tragic pair were buried by the Corbie Linn. Godfrey's armoured ghost gallops over the hill of Kingcausie and the woman's spirit sings in the woods by the Linn. She has also become a kind of psychopomp, guiding the souls of the dead: Watchers by the bed of the sick have often seen the dark and beautiful figure, with tear-dimmed eyes and blood-stained robe, enter the room and beckon to the sick one, and they have thereby known that the last farewell must soon be spoken.

As for the gold ring: The Templars, fearing to keep the charm, cast it out into the fields, where yet, at midnight, once a year, on the date of the woeful tragedy, it shines with a pale blue light, and he who finds it may wear it, and live scatheless from all disease, but let him be mindful that it brings not a blessing, but a curse to the breast that is not warmed by a pure and noble heart.

And this is the tale that generations of Scouts have told around the campfire at night in Templars' Park.

DRUM CASTLE

(National Trust for Scotland. Open 1 May-30 June and 1-30 September, daily except Tuesday and Friday 11.30 a.m.-5 p.m.; 1 July-31 August, daily 11.30 a.m.-5 p.m. Admission charge, guidebook, disabled access to ground floor. Grounds: all year, daily. NJ79620049.)

The Victorian chapel in the grounds has reused medieval head corbels and a great silver statue of the Virgin Mary. The wonderful vaulted library is visually dominated by an enormous self-portrait of Hugh Irvine (1783-1829) as the Angel Gabriel, a painting for which the word 'homoerotic' could have been invented.

Metal owl sculpture on a house at
Kirkton of Maryculter.

KIRKTON OF DURRIS

Archibald Watt's *Highways and Byways Round Kincardine* identifies the Green Lady of Durris
House (NO79819686, private) as the wife of the Laird of Durris. Driven to despair when the
Marquis of Montrose razed the house to the ground and killed the livestock, she drowned
herself in the stream. Occasional sightings of her – by men only – were reported into the
mid-twentieth century. John Henderson's *Annals of Lower Deeside* states that a 'pedagogue'
plagued his neighbours by impersonating Satan, on one notable occasion appearing among
the rafters of the church disguised as a horned ox with glaring eyes; the attendees at the
evening meeting were nearly terrified out of their wits. The minister of Banchory-Ternan
was asked to go to the kirk to lay Auld Horny; apart from a bit of irrelevant repartee it is
not recorded what happened, although presumably the impostor was exposed, else how
would the story be known? A suicide is buried on the north side of St Comgall's Church
(NO77229652); no one would allow the corpse to be brought through the gateway in the
usual way, so it was taken over the wall. The detached roofless Fraser Aisle holds an iron
mortsafe.

Watt gives a custom associated with the cairn in Cairnshee Wood (NO74049373; 'cairnshee'
means 'cairn of the fairies'). Each midsummer's eve herdsmen set a huge bonfire to exorcise
evil spirits and ensure the safety and prosperity of their flocks. In 1787, in remembrance of
the ceremony during his own childhood, Alexander Hog donated money to ensure the ritual
continued. The spectators came from all over and consumed bread, cheese and ale. The custom
finally lapsed in the 1930s. A 1926 article on the folklore of stone circles by James Ritchie
describes how a farmer removed some of the stones from the Cairnfauld RSC (NO75359406)
and in return had his cattle devastated by disease. A large natural boulder at Upperton
(NO73899213) had the name 'The Sutor's Mither', but what the shoemaker's mother had to do
with it was unknown.

CRATHES

Afore the fire folk couldna' sit for fear,
For peats and clods cam' bunging ben the flear;
The Parson cam' and sained the house wi' prayer,
But still the clods were thuddin' here and there.

An iron mortsafe, designed to foil bodysnatchers. St Comgall's Church, Kirkton of Durris.

The spoons an' dishes, knives an' forks,
They frisked aboot as light as corks,
And cups and ladles joined the dancing,
An' thro' the house they a' gaed prancing.

William Walker,
The De'il at Baldarroch (1839)

For two weeks in December 1838 the inhabitants of Baldarroch Farm – and their neighbours, and the gentry – witnessed a 'clodding', an Aberdeenshire version of a poltergeist attack. Sticks, stones, and clods of earth rained down; cutlery and crockery flew from room to room and out of the chimney; and much of the mundane world seemed to be in unnatural motion. As the story spread it became exaggerated, with tales of dancing hayricks and sightings of the Devil, but the core phenomena were amazing enough. If, that is, they were accurately reported: the main description is in Charles Mackay's *Memoirs of Extraordinary Popular Delusions* (1852) which does not quote a single first-hand witness or written source. If we take Mackay as being a faithful record, then the clodding was all the work of two servant girls, whose love of mischief played off the credulity of all concerned; when, having been observed dexterously faking some moving items, the pair were incarcerated, the phenomena ceased. Several later commentators thought it unlikely that the duo could have caused so much mayhem, especially with the thrown items, so it may be another example of what is a classic poltergeist trope – the original 'high-end' phenomena inspire one or two people into 'low-end' imitations, the copyists are caught, and the case is 'solved'. As Charles Fort has commented, 'There never was an explanation that didn't itself require a second explanation'.

One of the fascinating things about 'The Baldarroch De'il' is the way it sucks other folklore into its orbit. Fenton Wyness' *Royal Valley* says the farmer called in Adam Donald, the 'Wizard of Bethelnie' – who actually died more than fifty years before the events (see OLDMELDRUM). This may be a distortion of the reported action of the Baldarroch farmer, who travelled 40 miles to persuade a wise man called Willie Foreman to remove the enchantment. McPherson's *Primitive Beliefs* suggests the clodding was caused by a woman who had illicitly been given the Horseman's Word. It only stopped after an extraordinary meeting of horsemen had been convened to stop it.

In 1976 one of the most significant Neolithic structures in Britain was found just west of Balbridie Cottage on the South Deeside Road (NO73359590). It was a timber hall 79ft (24m) by 39ft (12m) in size that had been used both for the storage of a large amount of grain, and for some ritual purpose (possibly with the ritual and the domestic functions being intertwined). This is the largest structure of its kind in Britain. There is not a whit of anything to see now, but the ground plan is laid out at ARCHAEOLINK PREHISTORY PARK.

CRATHES CASTLE

(National Trust for Scotland. Open June, 10.30 a.m.-4.30 p.m. daily; July and August, 10.30 a.m.-5.30 p.m. daily; September and October, 10.30 a.m.-4.30 p.m., Saturday-Thursday. Admission charge, guidebook, no disabled access. Gardens and Estate: 9 a.m.-sunset all year.)

Exterior
Several eroded gargoyles, numerous false cannon spouts, heraldic panels (including the Horn of Leys – see below), a human figure on a turret finial, and a pair of unicorns dehorned by the elements. Norman Adams' *Haunted Valley* (1994) relates a tale from 'many years ago'. A horse-drawn hearse arrived at the main door, but the butler could see no coffin. The hearse then just returned down the drive. Kate Greig, a cleaner at Crathes, told Adams that staff

A carving of the ancient (or is it?) Horn of Leys on the exterior of Crathes Castle.

returning from late-night dances were frightened by footsteps following them along the path (although the most likely explanation here is not a supernatural one).

Main turnpike stair
The original sixteenth-century finial figure, Laird Alexander Burnett, in doublet and hose, holding a sceptre and sitting on a decorated orb.

Great Hall or High Hall
The fireplace has a pair of caryatids and two griffons, wyverns and serpents are worked into the fruit and foliage design on the Cordova leather screen, and within four roundels on the Victorian oak cabinet are portraits of the laird and his wife, and a unicorn and dragon. The main item of interest is at the core of Crathes' legendary past – the jewelled ivory Horn of Leys, supposedly a gift from Robert the Bruce in 1323, granting the Burnetts their lands and privileges. In recent years this provenance has been questioned, the main arguments being ably summed up in Robin Jackson's 2004 article 'The Horn of Leys: Fact or Fiction?' in *Leopard* magazine: 1) The horn first appears in the castle inventory of 1890 and not in the previous detailed cataloguing of 1760. The 1890 inventory describes the item as 'Oak case with ribbon and ivory horn' and gives it the value of £1 1s, a surprisingly low figure for a supposedly priceless heirloom. 2) The horn has a stylistic similarity to Afro-Portuguese ivories carved in Sierra Leone in the late-fifteenth and early-sixteenth centuries. 3) Visual evidence suggests it is hippopotamus ivory. 4) Sir James Burnett, the 10th Baronet, did not believe in the great age of the horn and in a catalogue prepared for an exhibition at the Scottish Society of Antiquaries in Edinburgh in 1856 he suggested the Burnetts acquired it when they obtained the Forestership of Garioch from the Blackhall family in the seventeenth century – and the Blackhall coat of arms contains a hunting horn. Bruce may indeed have granted a symbolic horn to the Burnetts – it is possible, however, that the Horn of Leys on display is not the original, but a much later item.

The Laird's Bedroom
The four-poster bed is elaborately carved with human figures, stags, dragons, unicorns, bulls, boars, grotesque faces, winged heads, and a pair of strange prancing winged horses. The wardrobe is topped with two griffons.

Room of the Nine Nobles
Here we first encounter Crathes' wonderful painted ceilings. A transcription of the Biblical quotations and moralising proverbs on the beams is available from reception. Michael Bath's *Renaissance Decorative Painting in Scotland* (2003) makes the point that the figures were meant to be inspirational, and the improving texts were there to be learned by heart. The iconography of the Nine Worthies (or Nobles) was established by the thirteenth century. They comprised three pagan figures (Hector of Troy, Alexander the Great and Julius Caesar); three Biblical warriors (Joshua, King David, and Judas Maccabaeus, who led the Maccabean Revolt against the Seleucid Emperor Antiochus); and three modern heroes (King Arthur, Charlemagne and Godfrey de Bouillon, one of the leaders of the First Crusade). In every case the biography of the Nobles has been exaggerated or invented. Alongside these men in their medieval armour can be seen solar faces, flowers, a black wyvern, a two-headed foliaceous beast, and a demon with bat wings, round head, collar, lion feet and curled tail.

Long Gallery
Good ceiling bosses with animal motifs, including a monkey and a toothy golden-winged head.

Green Lady's Room
The painted ceiling glories in grotesqueries, with fierce faces, a pair of griffon heads, a staring bull, and monstrous triple-headed female foliaceous figures. In the eighteenth century,

Alexander the 4th Baronet was famously afraid of ghosts, which is when the Green Lady started making her appearance. Her most common description is of a young woman carrying an infant; about 100 years after Alexander's death, a child's skeleton was discovered under the hearthstone. Inevitably, a tale was woven of a tragic servant made pregnant and abandoned. Watt's *Highways and Byways* gives the Green Lady a different story: a distant French relative of the Burnetts, she took refuge in Crathes during a time of war and became attracted to the baron, so the matriarch of the house poisoned her. The third version is that the ghost is the murderess herself, Lady Agnes. I suppose it is possible that there is not one Green Lady, but three. Norman Adams states that overseas visitors with no foreknowledge of the haunting have refused to enter the room, and that an invitation to attend the opening of a 1992 community arts project was sent to the Green Lady; she did not attend.

The Muses Room
The seven Cardinal Virtues and the nine Classical Muses make this room a centre of female power. This is the most striking of the painted ceilings, its weird decoration including: three winged female figures with their breasts on their shoulders; four Green Men; a fierce, grotesque face spewing vegetation; two griffon heads; triple-lion-headed monsters with a column for a body and squatting legs; a triple-headed female bust; a human figure bound to a post over two Green Men; a double-headed dog-like monster wearing a dancer's costume; a goat-like dragon looking backwards; a fierce female head; triple sheep-heads each holding a ring; a regal bald female head; a triple-headed male torso; a female face in vegetation; and a truly freaky headless male dancer with a large hole in its neck. 'Wisdom' is shown holding a dragon-headed serpent and standing over a five-pointed star. The wall frieze has two unicorns, a grotesque face, a winged soul or angel, and a woman with evil bat wings. The best way to study this astonishing display of bizarre imagery is to lie on the floor and look up, not an action that generally achieves favour in NTS properties.

BANCHORY

Banchory Museum (free, wheelchair friendly, check www.aberdeenshire.gov.uk/museums or 01330 823367 for opening hours) has three unmissable examples of the Victorian art of 'shock taxidermy': a snake strangling a very surprised-looking monkey; a pair of squirrels duelling with swords, one giving the *coup de grâce* to the heart; and a cat and hare boxing, with Puss-in-Gloves delivering the KO.

The museum has a brief display on St Ternan, the fifth-century missionary whose well in Banchory is said to have performed miraculous cures. Celtic saints often had magical bells; Ternan's 'Ronecht' followed him all the way from Rome. It was lost after the Reformation but in 1863 an old bronze bell was dug up in Bellfield Park; it may have been the Ronecht. After much subsequent voyaging it now hangs in East Church on North Deeside Road. Sadly Ternan's embalmed head, kept as a relic until at least 1530, has not turned up. Opposite the church is Banchory-Ternan graveyard (NO70699574), with a small number of carved tombstones and a spectacular two-storey anti-bodysnatching watchtower. One hundred paces west of the East Church, built into the wall on the north side of the road, is a prehistoric cist slab inscribed with the details of its discovery. A worn Celtic cross is inserted in the wall directly opposite. There are vague tales of a monk haunting this part of town. The West Church in the centre has good Victorian gargoyles.

James (Jack) Stewart's *Deeside Tinkers* gives two stories from the travelling folk. One winter Jack's granny and granddad were camping somewhere near Banchory when a strong wind scared the pony away and above the tent appeared a terrifying apparition of two mounted warriors in combat. Later a local crofter woman told them that other people had seen the same vision of the Battle of Cortager. When he was young, Jack himself camped at Cortager. Late one night at

The two-storey watchtower at Banchory-Ternan graveyard, with lookout windows, chimney (for a fire to keep the watchers warm) and warning bell. Bodysnatchers beware!

Banchory, Dee Street: weathervane in the form of a hare (possibly a reference to shape-shifting witches?)

the burn he saw a man wearing a long tight-fitting tunic closed at the neck, tight trousers, long boots and a three-cornered hat. He was carrying a long spear and had a hole in his neck with blood staining his tunic. Jack told no one, but the next night a girl from another family saw the same apparition. I have been unable to trace a place or battle called Cortager.

The crannog in the treacherous marsh of the former Loch of Leys (NO70469779) is the original home of the Burnetts of CRATHES CASTLE. The Battle of Corrichie Memorial on the B977 (NJ73260140) commemorates the 1562 victory of Lord James Stewart, of the Protestant faction, over George Gordon, the Catholic Earl of Huntly. Stewart had Huntly's body embalmed, dressed in sackcloth and transported to Edinburgh so it could 'hear' the House of Gordon legally forfeited and proscribed. The two men hated each other (you couldn't tell, could you?). Traditions have grown up that Mary, Queen of Scots is supposed to have watched the battle from the rocky outcrop called Queen Mary's Chair on Hill O'Fare (NJ71860171) and drank from Queen Mary's Well (NJ71310180).

In 'Personal Experiences in Witchcraft', penned in 1896 for the journal *Folklore*, Alex McAldowie recalled meeting Witch Jeffrey when he was seven years old. McAldowie knew her reputation as a healer of diseases – and that she had bewitched five children because their father drove her off his land when she was gathering firewood. Despite his terror that Witch Jeffrey would change him into a toad or a rabbit, she simply greeted him, and later the lad accompanied young women to the witch's house where she read his palm, often consulting an hourglass. On another occasion McAldowie and his chums sneaked into a Horseman's Word ceremony at Murtle, but were discovered and ejected before they could hear anything important.

In 1644 Gellen Farm was hit by supernatural combustion: 'a fearful unnatural fire whilk kindled of itself, and burnt the bigging [building] of this town only. When the people saw this fire, they ran to quench and stamp it out, but when it was quenched in one part, it brake out in another part.' (John Spalding, *The History of the Troubles and Memorable Transactions in Scotland*, 1792.) In 1887 D.H. Edwards' book *Modern Scottish Poets*, discussing local poet Joseph Grant, mentioned that Grant's grandfather had written a manuscript called 'Medicine, or the Art of Healing', which set out a combination of modern pharmacology with witchcraft-era prescriptions on when the drugs should be administered (such as at twilight or in the dawn 'between the sun and sky') and what precautions should be taken (silence in the case of meeting anyone when the drugs were administered). Where is this manuscript now?

STRACHAN

David Rorie, writing in *Folklore* in 1914, noted an episode from Strachan about twenty years earlier. A young servant girl refused to skin a hare, saying, 'Na, na, it micht be somebody's granny!' Good stone circles can be visited at The Nine Stanes (NO72339122), Eslie the Greater (NO71719159) and Eslie the Smaller (NO72259215).

TORPHINS

A building on Beltie Road has a splendid plaque with a green griffon embracing a star and sun. There is a torii (a Japanese shrine gate) in a garden on Craigour Road. Glassel Stone Circle (NO64889966) is worth visiting, as is the Pictish stone at Craigmyle (NJ64010234), although the symbols are very faded. Demolished Craigmyle House was haunted by a lady in a silk gown, known locally as 'the ghaist wi' the sweeshin' skirt' (Fenton Wyness, *Royal Valley*). Two men saw a large black cat on the road into Torphins in 1994 (www.scottishbigcats.org).

The stone circle of Eslie the Greater, near Strachan.

KINCARDINE O'NEIL

A walk south from the Old Deeside Road just west of Craiglash Quarry brings you to the Warlock Stone (NO619984), now just a large boulder in the trees but once, apparently, the centre of the local witch-cult. The stone has been cleft in two; the standard cause given is that this was done deliberately to prevent its re-use by Satan's minions. There is, however, no record of this destruction and the break could have been natural.

The witches accused of dancing around the 'gryt stane of Cragleauche' at Hallowe'en were Isobel Ritchie, Margaret Bane (or Clerk), Margaret Og, Isobel Og, Jonet Lucas, Jonet Davidson, Beatrix Robbie, Isobel Robbie, and Helene Rogie. The musical accompaniment was provided by the Devil, who was sometimes invisible, although not so invisible that they could not kiss his posterior. He copulated with all the witches in the form of a beast (possibly a man in an animal skin?). Music, dancing, sex – it sounds like quite a party.

The main information comes from the trial records of Margaret Clerk, an old woman who confessed and named the other witches before being executed in March 1597. Clerk obviously had a local reputation – at the church door of Kincardine O'Neil, a young man said to her, 'Get fire to thee, witch carling.' She replied, 'Thous shalt be drowned before I be brunt.' He drowned watering his horses in the Don. She transferred labour pains onto attendants: the pains of the wife of Nicoll Ros, in Auchlossan, were cast onto Andro Harper, who recovered when the gentlewoman was delivered of child; but when John Jameson in Auchinhove received the pains of his wife Elizabeth Sang, he died. Isobel Ritchie was appointed Satan's special domestic servant and fourriour (quartermaster) and had to attend him at meals. She also performed two 'devilsiche dances' between Lumphanan and Craiglash. Jonet Lucas was accused of using threads for enchantment and charming and making walls shake and conjuring up the Devil in animal guises. Isobel Og enchanted cloth with a thread from a winding sheet, and caused storms by hanging a beetle from a thread and whispering words to it. Jonet Davidson used different coloured pieces of cloth, thread and 'writings' to harm; when Patrick Hunter picked up a writing he caught influenza and died. Margaret Og practiced charming and took the dew

The Warlock Stone, Craiglash Hill. Dancing witches and Satan not shown.

of the green of Bogloch to her house to accomplish 'devilrie'. Helen Rogie made a wax or clay image of a man. There is much more on all of them in *Spalding*. Most of the witches were executed in April 1597, although Jonet Lucas, Jonet Davidson and Beatrix Robbie were merely banished on pain of death.

A Headless Horseman stalked the drove-road across the desolate Moss Maud (NO6299), driving pedestrians to their death in the bogs. Potarch ferry was menaced by a kelpie keen on drowning travellers; he lost his job when the bridge was built (NO608973). The buttressed and roofless Auld Kirk in the village (NO59219964) has a few carved death symbols including an unusual winged skull. To the west at the Dess road junction stands the Gibbet Stone (NO56889978).

LUMPHANAN

'By the pricking of my thumbs, something whacky this way comes.' There is good documentary evidence that Macbeth was indeed killed here in 1057 (and not at Dunsinane in Perthshire, as claimed in Shakespeare's *Macbeth*) but everything else Macbetherised in Lumphanan is mere fibs and fables. The Peel of Lumphanan (NJ57600369, Historic Scotland, free) is an impressive motte surrounded by a huge ditch and an external bank; it is much later than Macbeth, but still sometimes gets cited as the place where he made his last stand. The king is said to have had his last drink at Macbeth's Well just past the disused bridge in the Kirkton (NJ57950390), was killed at Macbeth's Stone (NJ57500342) on the railway embankment, and, having had his head severed by MacDuff and placed on a golden platter for delivery to Malcolm Canmore, was buried in Macbeth's Cairn, actually a prehistoric burial site (NJ57820533, ask permission at Howburn Farm). I'm surprised he wasn't said to buy a pint at the Macbeth Arms Hotel.

Norman Adams' *Haunted Valley* tells of the Lost Loch of Auclessen, which has appeared and disappeared several times from the area south of Bogloch. *The Place Names of West*

The Gibbet Stone near Kincardine O'Neil. Supposedly the execution-tree was inserted into the socket.

Aberdeenshire (1899) relates a legend from this loch. It was home to a huge frog, which snacked on one cow or sheep a day. At last the beleaguered locals got the pitchforks and flaming brands out and killed the monster in its lair, which was thereafter called Achadh an Losgainn, 'Field of the Frog', corrupted into Auchlossan. In every respect apart from the identification of the creature as a frog, this is a dragon legend. John Grant's *Legends of the Braes O' Mar* (1861) relocates the Tad-Losgann (toad-frog) to the River Clunie near BRAEMAR, where it was the pet of Malcolm Canmore, King Malcolm III, who taxed the local population to feed it with their livestock. The monster was killed by a put-upon peasant, who was then sentenced to death unless, he being a skilled archer, he could split an apple placed on his child's head held in the arms of his wife … on the other side of the Dee. Did the Aberdeenshire William Tell achieve the impossible shot? Of course he did! What kind of story would it be otherwise?

Several of the witches active on Craiglash Hill were from the Lumphanan area. Others were delivered up to the Aberdeen courts by the local minister, John Ross. His inquisitorial document from 1597 makes for extraordinary reading. Elspet Strachund from Warthill charmed fevers away with threads, buried a burning coal in her yard at Hallowe'en, and bewitched a man to death. Isabel Forbes from Glenmulloch bewitched a man with parts of a spinning machine. James Og from Lumphanan performed numerous rituals to transfer the goodness of his neighbours' land and milk to himself. Agnes Frew or Fren from Lumphanan charmed cattle for good or for ill, depending on her preference. Margaret Reauch in Green Cottis caused animals to wither, killed sheep by throwing water on them backwards between her legs, passed disease to a man by 'embracing every nook' of his house, and confessed that 'the devil was in the bed between her and William Ritchie, her harlot, and he was upon them both, and that if she happened to die for witchcraft, that he [Ritchie] should also die, for if she was a devil, he was too'. No action was taken against Elspet Strachund, James Og and Agnes Frew; the others were sent for further investigation, but there is no further record of them.

A wonderfully-described sighting of a meteor on 12 December 1895 is given in R.C. Maclagan's 'Ghost Lights of the West Highlands'. The letter was sent from the Lumphanan manse at 6.47 p.m., on a night of deep snow:

The legendary Macbeth landscape of Lumphanan, Part 1: The Macbeth Well.

Part 2: Macbeth's Stone, where he was supposedly killed.

Part 3: Macbeth's Cairn, a prehistoric burial mound where he was allegedly interred.

My path was lit up as if a machine with more than usually powerful lights had come up behind me. I turned to see, so as to protect myself, when crossing the heavens in a straight line from west to east was a most brilliant meteor. Its head was, in size and shape, a doubly enlarged goose's egg. Its tail was fan-shape and fish-shape, the colour of the tail lurid. In the rear of the tail were numerous sparks like stars. It was visible for about two seconds, and seemed to drop in Aberdeen.

ABOYNE

A Pictish stone stands in the vestibule of the Victory Hall (usually open most weekdays). The stone circle of Image Wood (NO52409904) is a delight. Cuddly creatures and maniacal men adorn St Thomas's Church. The foundations of old Formaston Church, discreetly signposted from the entrance to The Lodge on the Loch, can be easily visited and offers a small selection of carved stones including a Grim Reaper and a winged skull (NJ54120014). The church once belonged to the Knights Templar. Up to the early nineteenth century pilgrimages were made to St Skeulan's Well here, with rags left on St Skeulan's Tree; as the rag decayed so would the illness. A fine modern circle and outlier stand outside the World Horse Welfare charity on the A93 to the east (NO555999). Worth the walk is St Machar's Cross (NO50329988), probably named after St Mochrieha. The saint's well (a wet patch) is adjacent but his 'chair', an artificial hollow, was broken up for building stone about 1810. The cross was once removed but miraculously returned. Machar is one of those Dark Ages saints whose doings are far more fable than fact, and may not even have existed.

In December 1626 Johnne McConnochie's wife and a woman called Helene were arrested for witchcraft but there are no more details.

The *Sun* for 18 December 2000 quoted farmer Murray Brown as having seen a UFO twice in the previous week. It hovered over his farm and was, 'the brightest white light I've ever seen, wing-shaped, like a boomerang'.

Image Wood, Aboyne; possibly the smallest stone circle in Aberdeenshire.

Above & below: Calm and crazed heads on St Thomas's Episcopal Church, Aboyne.

COULL

In 1914 David Rorie recorded in *Folklore* the recollections of 'H.R.,' a man of seventy-five. When he was young he knew a widow who whenever she bought or sold anything went to her husband's grave and explained her decisions to him. As he had been a great user of snuff she would leave a pinch on the grave, for his use until her next visit. McPherson's *Primitive Beliefs* says that in 1702 Allaster Caddell shot a huge hare as it escaped into the house of William N. That night his mother died in agony of a bullet wound. The charming and isolated church (NJ51190248) has a small number of carved stones and a substantial morthouse. A barney over bodysnatching left one man injured and was coincidentally followed by the departure of the gravedigger.

BIRSE

Robert Dinnie's 1865 *Account of the Parish of Birse* relates that the keeper at the ale-house by the churchyard held a wake for his wife, at which he treated his neighbours to refreshments on the house. When they insisted on taking extra drink and paying for it – and so breaching the unwritten rule that the bereaved supplied the victuals – the innkeeper felt obliged to rest his conscience by consulting with his wife at the graveside. She agreed to the proceedings and he happily dispensed strong liquor for the evening. Dinnie also writes of a great treasure that thwarted all attempts to find it. One man who did succeed was about to lift the gold when a voice shouted, 'The kirk and manse are on fire'. He rushed off, only to find it was a false alarm, but when he returned to the diggings the ground was undisturbed as if all his labour had been imaginary; concluding that the spirit of the treasure was mightier than he, the gold-digger ceased his explorations. This exact story is told of many locations in Scotland.

FINZEAN (PRONOUNCED 'FINGEN')

The top of Corsedarder Hill on the B976 has three monuments from different periods. The most recent is the tall monolith erected as a Millennium Stone (NO596939), dedicated on 1 January 2000 when 300 people watched it being anointed with waters from the several boundary rivers of the dispersed community. Opposite is the 'Dardanus Stone', a short block dug up in the eighteenth century and erected here in the belief that it commemorates the eponymous, if fictional, Pictish King. It may be a cist slab, and is currently held together by iron bands. To the west is the prehistoric Corsedardar Long Cairn (NO59189378), once immense, still impressive; Dardanus is supposedly buried here. Dominating the area is the tor of Clachnaben, 'Stone of the Women' (NO614865). Mr and Mrs Lucifer were hillwalking in the area one day – in his case probably not needing stout footwear, being naturally blessed in that direction – when they had what police officers call 'a domestic'. She was younger and more athletic so stomped off to the top, shouting abuse – a bad idea. Hubby lobbed a great boulder and crushed her, and she lies beneath it to this day.

GLEN TANAR

Here the landscape is imprinted with the hand of Sir William Cunliffe Brooks MP, who embraced eccentricity as only the rich can. From 1869 he set up many monuments and punning inscriptions on the estate. Here are the best:

'Welling springs make grateful brooks', just before the entrance to Glen Tanar House (NO47499596).

'The pine is King of Scottish woods / and the Queen ah who is she / The fairest form the forest kens / The bonnie birken tree', on the track along the north bank of the Water of Tanar (NO47079457).

'The worm of the still is the deadliest snake on the hill', an obvious reference to illegal whisky distilling, at Snakeswell, on the road between Glen Tanar and Tillycairn (NO47279734).

'Well to know when you are well off', drinking basin between Tillycairn and Newton (NO4627971).

'Men may come and men may go but I go on for ever', at Ever Well, on South Deeside Road (NO44649745).

'Work as tho you might live for ever' and 'Live as tho you might die today', at a drinking trough by track to Deecastle Farm (NO43799686).

Best of all, and astonishingly egocentric, are the Haunted Stag Stones, two pawn-like small pyramids topped with spheres in the open heather west of Duchery Beg (NO500939). On 9 October 1877 Brooks shot a hitherto elusive stag at the not inconsiderable distance of 267 yards (244m) so, naturally, he set up monuments to mark where hunter and hunted were at the crucial moment. One is inscribed 'The Haunted Stag', the other 'The Stag is dead. Sure bullet to its fatal mark hath sped'.

A modern standing stone in the kirkyard of St Lesmo's Chapel (NO47929605) commemorates Donald MacKintosh, Brooks' gamekeeper (d.1876). The two men often sat by this stone at its original position in the hills while out shooting, and agreed the first to die would have it as their grave marker.

DINNET

Loch Kinord has a crannog, (NO44359952), thought to be ancient and enlarged in medieval times when it was used as the prison for the adjacent Castle Island (NO43979964). The area around the loch hosts the Kinord Stone, a Pictish cross-slab covered with interlace carving (NO44009979); two complex prehistoric settlements (NJ444002 and NJ44930017); and a medieval settlement with five circular enclosures looking just like large stone circles (NJ430001). The Culblean Memorial on the B9119 (NJ435002) commemorates the Battle of Culblean of 1335 when Andrew de Moray defeated the would-be throne-grabber Earl of Atholl. Atholl made the fatal error of retreating up the Vat Burn, a narrowing chasm with no way out. In the seventeenth century the waterfall and giant pothole of the Vat sheltered Gilderoy (Patrick) MacGregor and nine other desperadoes, the original Hole in the Wall gang. They were hanged in Edinburgh and their severed heads and right hands exhibited in towns throughout Scotland.

McPherson's *Primitive Beliefs* mentions a man from Bogingore near Loch Kinord who cured his sick cow by giving it 'dead water' collected from a graveyard stream while avoiding speaking or being spoken to. Somewhere near Dinnet was the Kelpie Stone. Childless women passed through its 18in (46cm) hole to conceive. A noble lady performed the task to no avail; only when she repeated it in the same direction as the river flow did the charm work.

TARLAND

David Rorie's 1914 article 'Stray Notes on the Folk-Lore of Aberdeenshire' includes a youthful experience from 'H.R.', aged seventy-five. He was coming through the kirkyard at night when he was scared by 'something white' moving about under a table-tomb. It turned out to be a woman who regretted her conduct towards her husband and each night communed with his grave. The charming roofless old kirk (NJ48180439) has a few stones with winged souls, and,

'In the Beginning', a sculpture combining art and antiquity, Tarland.

on a musician's memorial, a fully carved fiddle. Where the B9119 exits the village to the south stands a modern sculpture called 'In the Beginning', three rugby-ball-shaped stones carved with spirals and rings that echo prehistoric rock art.

Cared for by Historic Scotland, and with the added advantage of (fairly steep) wheelchair access, Tomnaverie on the B9094 (NJ48650349) is one of the best RSCs to visit. *The Place Names of West Aberdeenshire* gives the name as 'Tuam-an-fhamhaire', 'grave of the giant'. There are several souterrains or earth-houses in Aberdeenshire but most are hard to access. In contrast the souterrain at Culsh on the B9119 (NJ505055, Historic Scotland) is open to anyone who can crawl into its atmospheric and dark subterranean passage. The general view is that souterrains are Iron Age structures designed for food storage, although some in the earth mysteries camp plump for a ritual purpose.

LOGIE COLDSTONE

Dool, dool to Blelack,
And dool to Blelack's heir
For driving us frae the Seely Howe
To the cauld Hill o' Fare
The Fairies' curse on Blelack House

The 'Dool' or Doom of Blelack is recorded in J.G. Michie's 1896 *History of Logie-Coldstone and the Braes of Cromar*. The story given is that Charles Gordon, the laird, wanted to evict the fairies from his estate before he left to fight for the Jacobites in 1745, and to this end employed the 'Fairy Doctor', a man reputed to have convivial relations with the Little Folk. This was John Farquharson, who lived at Parks, north of Logie Coldstone. The fairies refused to shift unless alternative accommodation was provided, so Farquharson indicated the Hill of Fare, near Banchory. This was too cold for the new tenants, so they cursed the House of Blelack. Consequently the Gordons suffered for their Jacobite affiliations, the estate was ravaged and the house burned after Culloden and, to further the Dool, the new house built in 1753 was accidentally destroyed by fire in 1868. Farquharson was also cursed: 'While corn and girss [grass] grows to the air / John Farquharson and his seed shall thrive nae mair.' The man, it was said, was forced by poverty to leave the country.

Well, not exactly. In *Reminiscences of Cromar and Canada*, published in Ontario probably around 1900, Donald Robert Farquharson traced his family tree, and the story he tells is different. John Farquharson and his seed did thrive, as shown in new information that Michie passed to the Canadian author. John Farquharson was born about 1700 and worked as the tacksman of Parks until 1745, when he moved to a farm near Forres in Moray. There he died, his descendants steadily moving up the social scale. His grandson was an excise officer, and later generations distinguished themselves in the Church and academia. By Donald's day, the seed of John Farquharson was spread through North-East Scotland and Canada. *Reminiscences* also gives the location of the 'Seely Howe', the Hollow of the Fairy Court. It was on the farm of Carrue, south of Blelack (c. NJ441032). John Farquharson's relationship with the fairies was well-known in succeeding generations of the family, with Donald's father telling him how the creatures frequently visited John and sang to him: 'Johnny, I lo'e ye, Johnny, I lo'e ye, Nine tunes in ae nicht will I come and see thee.'

In Logie Coldstone Donald's grandfather employed a young herdboy named Geordie Sherris. At Hallowe'en he took part in a divination game which involved carrying the coal-rake around the house at night, an action supposed to reveal a key figure in your future. Geordie returned terror-stricken, having seen a great red bull. Shortly afterwards he was gored to death by such a creature. *Reminiscences* also tells of the remorseful spirit of a murderer who haunted a neighbour. Eventually the man gave in to the ghost's entreaties and dug up the bones of the victim from 'McRob's Cairn' in the woods of Blelack and reburied them in consecrated ground. In return he asked to obtain the favour of God. 'That,' replied the spirit, 'I cannot give, for alas, I have lost it myself.'

On 10 April 1597 Kathrene Fernsche was investigated by the Logie-Coldstone Kirk-Session. She was accused of removing sickness from George Ritchie and then laying it on his sister, who died, and casting her sorcery on Alexander Welche, who also perished. She stole a man's livestock and killed some of his other animals, and gave a woman a husband-attracting pendant and ring for her daughter. Obviously her magic was not all-powerful, as she had promised her own son that her spells would protect him from harm; this he confessed just as he was about to be hanged. The charges were serious enough for Kathrene to be burned, but there is no record of what actually happened to her.

A standing stone called St Wolock's Stone lurks outside the old Logie cemetery at Kirton (NJ43640240). Wolock/Walloch is a shadowy saint – two authorities give his dates as either fifth century, or eighth century. The other graveyard at Kirk Hill (NJ43240565) contains an early Christian cross-marked stone. The recently-restored Poldhu Wells (NJ436036, track access off the A97) are two rectangular basins containing chalybeate waters much visited by health-seekers in the nineteenth century. The modern plaque mentions 'ancient springs of legendary healing powers'. The Lady's Well spring is just south of the Blue Cairn (NJ41130633), a massive cairn surrounded by the remnants of a RSC.

MIGVIE

Perhaps the most surprising sight in this area is the former Migvie Church (NJ43670684), an unassuming temple stunningly restored by Philip Astor as a combination art gallery and place of contemplation. The whitewashed walls host images of Scottish religious figures, Biblical texts and poems. The symbol stone in the kirkyard serves as the inspiration for the superb Celtic cross and Pictish symbols carved on the inner doors by Gavin Smith. A second fragment of a Pictish stone is on display. More Pictish figures, including the mysterious mounted man on the original stone, appear in the Matisse-like stained-glass windows by Jennifer Bayliss, with their bodies decorated with symbols as if they were all-over tattoos. In the centre of the space are arranged four stone armchairs decorated with more texts and symbols. On the walls can be found the occasional painted wagtail, inspired by the bird whose nest was found in the roof during restoration. Completely unadvertised, this is a special and spiritual place. Behind the church, at the garden gate beside the farmhouse, is a boulder with dozens of cup-marks, some linked to form an L-shape and a cross (NJ43740676).

BALLATER

The imposing Glenmuick Parish Church dominating the centre has excellent stained glass featuring saints despatching dragons. The *News of the World* for 11 June 2000 reported that workmen renovating the Old Railway Station had heard phantom footsteps. But was the 'dark figure' spotted outside the royal waiting room actually Queen Victoria? Or just a tabloid's attempt to link a vague paranormal-like report to royalty? The same paper (20 June 1999) noted that guests at a holiday cottage heard sneezing, banging and voices from an empty room. According to Richard Jones' *Haunted Houses of Britain and Ireland*, Ravenswood Hotel on Braemar Road is haunted by a solid-looking apparition of a bearded man in an Arran sweater.

   The remains of Tullich kirk sit in an ancient circular graveyard on the A93 east of Ballater (NO39059754). A faded Pictish stone and sixteen Early Christian cross-marked stones hint at the antiquity of the site, supposedly founded by St Nathalan in the seventh century. John Grant's *Legends of the Braes O' Mar* tells how Nathalan farmed the land here; during a famine he sowed the soil with sand and up grew corn, but just as the miraculous crop was to be harvested the river flooded the fields. Nathalan briefly cursed God; so as a penance he locked himself into an iron chain and threw the key into the Dee, in a spot still called Key Pool. On pilgrimage to Rome Nathalan bought some fish – and in it was found, still not rusted, the same key. It was the sign that God had forgiven him (the tale of an item miraculously found in a fish is told of several Celtic saints). Nathalan is supposedly buried at this site, which was a place of pilgrimage before the Reformation.

   The other story associated with Tullich is that one cold Sunday the congregation, waiting outside the church, stamped their feet to keep warm. A fiddler took up the beat, a keg of whisky was procured, and by the time the minister arrived the Tullich Reel had been invented. According to Fenton Wyness' *Royal Valley*, 'dool and destruction' was pronounced on the dancers, and every one died within the year. A winged Grim Reaper holding an hourglass and scythe perches on a tombstone, here and there are two splendid carved skulls.

   Within the old Glenmuick kirkyard at Brig o' Muick on the South Deeside Road (NO36589482) lies John Mitchell, a poacher whose gravestone says he was born in 1596 and died in 1722 at the age of 126. Just west is the Scurriestone Standing Stone (NO35789497), its name supposedly coming from sgur, 'to rub', from its use by animals, although this derivation may be contested. Knock Castle (NO35239516, Historic Scotland, free) is the site of a grisly legend set during the bloody feud between the Gordons and Forbes. In vengeance for a relative's death a Forbes killed seven Gordon brothers for accidentally trespassing on his land, and spiked the severed heads to their peat-spades. An alternative version is that one of the Gordons secretly married a Forbes lass, whose father promptly killed him and slaughtered all his brothers to prevent any repercussions. Whichever variant is given, the result is the same. On hearing the news that all his sons were murdered, Alexander Gordon fell to his death down the stairs at Knock. Not surprisingly he is supposed to haunt the gaunt ruin.

GLEN GAIRN

Amy Stewart Fraser's *The Hills of Home* gives several strange episodes. John Davidson of Balno set off to the Braes of Cromar early in the morning. At Lary he met Ally Ritchie from

Candacraig, said to be an 'unlucky foot' (a person thought to accidentally bear ill-fortune). After greeting him John knew his errand would not prosper, and when crossing over a burn he slipped and fell on his back. Cursing Ally he went home. Next morning he went over Morven to avoid meeting Ally again. On 6 January 1902 the Torran burn, normally a small stream, swept May Ritchie into the Gairn. The river was dragged daily for miles. Over three weeks later a local man had a dream that the body would be found on an islet at Cambus O'May – and it was. The long-serving Father Lachlan Macintosh, 'the apostle of Glen Gairn', died aged ninety-three in 1846. His coffin was temporarily taken to the chapel at Clashinruich for two days, 'during which time many strange visions and lights were seen prowling round the chapel'. All that remains of the chapel is a rectangular outline of stones (NJ31390116); the field below it was used to bury children who died in infancy. A second catastrophically ruined chapel sits in the wood at Dalfad (NJ31790055). Both sites are characterised by their loneliness and sense of lost times. Macintosh was interred in the cemetery at Bridge of Gairn (NO35289701), where a ruined church stands on the site of a pre-Reformation kirk dedicated to St Kentigern (aka Mungo). St Mungo's Well is just to the east (NO35409700).

John Grant gives the legend of the Cailleach-Bheathrach, the Thunderbolt Carline or Witch. The slopes of the hill of Mammie (NJ317019) were home to her Buailtean or cattle folds. In Glen Morven lies Sloc na Caillich, the Carline's den, where she tried to bite a new valley through the hills, but was defeated by the jaw-breaking nature of the rocks. Many Cailleachs inhabit the remote mountains of Scotland; most of them control the weather or shape the landscape. Gairnshiel Lodge at the remote junction of the A939 and B976 (NJ29430074) may furnish sightings of the apparition of an old woman, while marching men have been heard on the old military road outside. The Lodge private but available for exclusive hire.

Somewhere near Glas-choille, (NJ310035) was Tobar-Na-Glas-Choille, the Well in the Grey Wood. In 'Guardian Spirits of Wells and Lochs' (1892) Walter Gregor describes a small knoll nearby as inhabited by a spiteful spirit called Duine-glase-beg, the Little Grey Man. If anyone drank from the well but did not leave an offering of a pin or other metal, he would hunt them down and cause death by thirst. In 1891 Gregor gathered several pins from the well. Daldownie (NJ246009), an easy walk along the River Gairn, has An Sidhean, the Fairies' Mound, behind the farmstead. It may be an early medieval motte. The farmer here swore he heard fairies revelling at night, and saw their footprints outside in the morning.

In an article of 1889, 'Devil Stories', Walter Gregor related a tale told about Mr Catnach, a teacher in Corgarff. Hunting in the upper reaches of the Gairn (c. NO1297), he found all his shots bouncing off a particularly fine stag. He and his youthful companion camped at a shieling, only to be disturbed at midnight by a terrible noise – which turned out to be the Devil. When Catnach called out in God's name, Satan disappeared in a great flash of fire. The next day he met a woman who, upon inspecting his gun, diagnosed that it had been rendered useless by a neighbour with the evil eye. She then told Catnach to shoot at a hind that was approaching. Despite having only powder and no ammunition, Catnach casually fired – and the deer dropped dead. The woman then vanished. The story ended with Catnach saying that in case he met the Devil in the shape of a stag again, he was going to make a 'silver cross button' for his gun.

The same article has a tale from the same part of the hills, but the exact location is not given. It was told to James Farquharson by an old woman from Braemar, who died in 1843 at the age of ninety-three. A thief and murderer named Ian use na gergie, Blood John of the Fir, sheltered overnight with two companions in a shieling in a wild corrie. Very suddenly John became ill, and there came 'a sound like the croaking of thousands of ravens'. Outside, a raven larger than the hut appeared: repeated assaults showed it to be bullet-proof. At midnight (of course) John died – and cue the Devil rushing in through the door, crying, 'I claim my own!' One of the men quickly drew a circle round the body in the name of the Trinity, whilst the other made the sign of the cross over it. Satan, frustrated, summoned thirteen other smaller demons, and they all proceeded to cavort outside the circle. At dawn the infernal crew shot up through the roof, 'with a roar so terrible that it rent a hole in a rock near the shieling, which is called 'the Hole of Hell'.

CRATHIE

A. Macdonald's 'Some Former Customs of the Royal Parish of Crathie' (1907) and 'Scraps of Scottish Folklore' (1910) describe how fifty years previously the local farmers at Hallowe'en walked the circuit of their fields with lighted torches to drive away evil spirits and ensure fertility. A burning peat was placed between a newly-birthed animal and the byre-door, and left there to smoulder – again, the fire kept evil at bay. One farmer banished the disease among his livestock by replacing all his black Minorca breed of chickens by white-feathered birds. Nowadays only a modern pillar marks the site of St Manire's Chapel (NO30119620), once used for the covert burial of unbaptised children after sundown. The adjacent standing stone, possibly the sole survivor of a stone circle, was claimed by Alex Inkson McConnochie in *Deeside* (1893) to have been used as a reading desk for the chapel.

In terms of the way stories get repeated and exaggerated, Abergeldie Castle (NO28719528, private) brings together an irresistible combination of royalty and spooks. The conventional tale, as set out by several nineteenth-century authors, is that the witch Kitty Rankin revealed to the Lady of Abergeldie what her husband was currently doing on a ship many miles away – which happened to be making love to another woman. Kitty was ordered to raise a storm to wreck the ship but when news came that the laird was drowned the now-remorseful lady threw Kitty into the dungeon. When the witch escaped, an imprisoned warlock named Robert McKeiry offered to track her down in exchange for a pardon. Kitty shape-shifted into a hare, so McKeiry transformed into a greyhound. Kitty became a mouse, only to be snared by the wizard in the guise of a weasel. Kitty was burned at the stake atop Craig-na-Ban overlooking the Castle and her screaming spirit haunts the castle to this day. When Abergeldie became a royal lodging in 1848 the story gained a new dimension: celebrity. In his *Memoirs* the Duke of Windsor (later Edward VIII) noted the castle's tower was 'infested with bats and haunted, we were led to believe, by the ghost of Kittie Rankie,' a minor aside which has since cemented Kitty's reputation as a proper ghost with a royal imprimatur.

All this is very well, except that there is no record of Kitty (or Caitir Fhrangach, French Kate, Catherine Ranking or any similar name), or of the burning, or any element of the story. None of the Victorian writers could track down which Laird of Abergeldie was supposedly involved, or even the century of the alleged events. It sounds like a folk tale that has got out of hand.

In *Royal Valley* Fenton Wyness reveals that the standing stone on the lawn in front of the castle was once nicknamed Lady Portman, after one of Queen Victoria's ladies-in-waiting whom the servants found as stiff and unyielding as the stone.

In *A Queen's Country* Robert Smith investigates a cottage called Druimview at Khantore, near An Garadh in Glen Geldie, south of Abergeldie Castle (NO287938). A previous occupier was Jean Taylor, said to be a 'spooky' woman, always talking about bad omens and claiming she had heard the ghost of Willie Blair, Queen Victoria's fiddler. Her nephew Charlie Stewart lived there later and was in the upstairs room when he heard someone in the house. Distinct footsteps came up the stairs and stopped outside his room. He opened the door – but there was no one there.

BALMORAL CASTLE

(Typically open between the start of April and the end of July, 10 a.m.–5 p.m. daily. Admission charge, good disabled access, audio tour.)

Ronald Clark's book *Balmoral* enumerates several curious episodes in the history of the royal holiday home. On 28 September 1853, at the laying of the foundation stone, Queen Victoria spread the mortar with a silver trowel and struck the stone three times with a golden mallet. A cornucopia was placed on the stone and Her Majesty poured out oil and wine, all in the best

Masonic fashion. On 7 September 1855 the castle was finally ready and as Victoria and Albert walked into their new home the steward, François d'Albertançon, made sure they had good luck by throwing an old shoe after them. When Prince Albert died, Victoria kept casts of his hands in a glass case at the foot of her bed. In November 1900, when she left Balmoral for what turned out to be the last time, the Queen was too frail to leave her carriage to say goodbye to the local older women in their homes, as was her normal custom. Several said that she would never return. Later this 'prophecy' was attributed to Highland second sight, although simple observation of the aging monarch would be a more straightforward explanation. Victoria died on 22 January 1901. It was later claimed that when the bell of Crathie Church began to mournfully toll and the flag was raised to half-mast on the Balmoral tower, heavy snow stopped the tower clock at 6.30 p.m., the time of the Queen's death.

McPherson's *Primitive Beliefs* includes a piece from *Scottish Notes and Queries* written by Alex MacDonald (presumably the same MacDonald who penned the folklore pieces on CRATHIE). He describes a Hallowe'en rite often observed at Balmoral during Victoria's time:

A huge bonfire was kindled and all the clansmen were mustered in Highland garb. The interest of the promenade was centred in a trolley on which there sat the effigy of a hideous old woman or witch called the Shandy dann. Beside her crouched one of the party holding her erect while the march went forward to the bagpipe's strain … the pace was quickened to a run, then a sudden halt was made a dozen yards or so from the blaze. Here, amid breathless silence, an indictment is read why this witch should be burned to ashes, and with no one to appear on her behalf, only this *advocatus diaboli*, paper in hand – she is condemned to the flames … Then follow cheers and hoots of derisive laughter, as the inflammable wrappings of the Shandy dann crackle and sputter out. All the while the residents of the castle stand enjoying the curious rite, and no one there entered more heartily into it than the head of the Empire herself.

McPherson comments that the Shandy dann was not the name of the witch but the trolley.

On 7 September 2008 the *News of the World* reported the find of a mammoth tooth and another fossilised bone on Balmoral estate.

INVER & GLEN FEARDER

Wyness' *Royal Valley* describes how on a dark wintry night in 1767 John Davidson was working the Inver Mill (NO23259369) when the Black Han' appeared, a black hairy hand that had terrorised Glen Fearder since the 1745 rebellion. Davidson was silent on what transpired, but the next morning he went to a certain spot and dug up the basket-hilt of a sword. He hung the relic above his fireplace, saying 'Rest noo, Black Han'. The floating hand did not make another appearance.

Carn na Cuimhne, 'Cairn of Remembrance', by the A93 (NO24139419) was a martial mustering point when trouble threatened. The *NSA* states that each man placed a stone here when they departed, and removed one on safe return. The number of unclaimed stones indicated the size of the casualty list. Far up the glen the deserted Auchnagymlinn township (NO192956) once had the grave of the last giant. Sadly the 20ft (6m) long mound has, like the giants themselves, long vanished.

GLEANN AN T-SLUGAIN

John Grant tells of the legendary birth of the founder of Clan Farquharson, Finlay Mor. In a remote shieling in the glen his mother was midwifed by three magical crones who entreated her to let no mortal touch the child until they returned. Sadly the local women did handle the infant, so that one third of Finlay's 'weird' was negated when the Three Fates turned up again. They could only promise future greatness for the child and his succeeding generations.

BRAEMAR

Legends of the Braes O' Mar of 1861 is a goldmine of Braemar folklore. Among the main stories are:

The ruinous state of Kindrochit Castle on Balnellan Road is due to its destruction by cannon-fire to contain the plague within. Years later a redcoat was lowered into the deep dark cellars in the hope of finding treasure. On his return he reported an encounter with a ghastly group: 'They all sat round about as if living, with glittering ivory faces, dressed in strange garb, and silent, motionless, breathless, and dead.' When the Watson family later cleared out the ruins they were ticked off by a little old man wearing a red cap. And, of course, a secret tunnel runs from an unknown subterranean vault to the river.

At the Reformation the Catholic priest John Avignon (or Owenson) was manhandled by Beatrix Farquharson of Invercauld. He predicted the hand that had defiled him would rot 'and be cut from her shoulder before a year and a day pass'. The prophecy came true.

A man called McRoy encountered a 'rumbling fermentation' of fairies which he dispersed using the name of God. In their place was a beautiful naked woman, whom he soon married. Some time after, a drover and his young son stayed at McRoy's house and recognised the woman as their erstwhile wife and mother, spirited away by the fairies years before. Presented with the tale, she remembered her previous life, and elected to return to it.

An old woman predicted Donald Dubh would hang himself in his own garters unless he attended Mass every week. This he assiduously did until the day came the Dee was too swollen to cross to the church. An avaricious herdboy sold his 'right and title in the benefit' of the Mass in exchange for Donald's new garters – and was soon after found hanging from the byre roof, suspended by the garters. Thus Donald cheated his 'dool'.

When the Jacobite standard was unfurled at Braemar in 1715 the gilt ball at its top fell down to the ground, an accident taken as an ill omen of failure (and oh how that omen was brutally justified). A plaque opposite the Invercauld Arms Hotel marks the raising of the standard.

On 25 July 1745, Duncan Calder, the Seer of Glen Lui, reported that Bonnie Prince Charlie was landing that day at Moidart, on the coast far to the west. An incredulous laird despatched a messenger to verify this piece of second sight, but before he returned the last Jacobite Rebellion was under way.

McPherson's *Primitive Beliefs* tells of a young man who took ill after offending a witch. He waited for the right opportunity to counter-attack, tore her cap off and scratched her forehead. Having bloodied her 'above the breath', he recovered. Mackinlay's *Folklore of Scottish Lochs and Springs* (1893) reports the fate of the last kelpie seen in Braemar. He stole a sackful of meal from a mill to give to a woman he desired. The miller hurled a fairy-whorl (a holed stone) which broke the thief's leg. The kelpie fell into the mill-race and, ironically for a water-creature, drowned.

The recently refurbished Braemar Castle (NO15609237, no disabled access, irregular opening hours, check 013397 41600 or www.braemarscotland.co.uk) has four noted ghosts – the Black Colonel, John Farquharson, who torched the place; a young bride who killed herself when she mistakenly thought her new husband had left her; a piper; and a murdered baby.

Coral Lorenzen's *Encounters with UFO Occupants* has a 1958 'Close Encounter' case from the Braemar area. At five o'clock on a November morning two Territorial Army soldiers on an exercise heard a 'gurgling noise' and saw two beings over 6.5ft (2m) tall wearing peculiar suits. There was then a 'swishing' noise as a large disc swooped over their heads, leaving a sparkling trail.

On 8 June 2003 the *Sunday Mail* reported two hillwalkers had seen a big black cat on the Invercauld Estate. There had also been several sightings over the previous weeks, with others in January 1997 and 2001.

GLEN CLUNIE

John Grant related the legend that the MacDonalds of this glen were descended from a man who as an infant had been snatched by a wolf from his home. He was brought up within a family of wolves, a true 'wild child' hunting and feeding with them, and although he later returned to human society he set up home with a she-wolf. Glen Muic had a similar story, although there the MacDonalds were descended from a man raised by wild boar.

GLEN CALLATER

'We passed a green hillock, on which a man still living has seen fairies dancing, with a piper playing to them.' (William MacGillivray, *The Natural History of Dee Side and Braemar*, 1855.) This mound may be at NO165852, where there are the remains of about twenty unroofed shielings. The track leads along the source of the Callater Burn, where fantastic rock formations emerge from the river-bed. The chalybeate Priest's Well by Lochcallater Lodge at the lower end of the loch (NO17958437) was a holy well associated with the miracles of the resident officiant.

INVEREY & LINN OF DEE

All these tales are from Grant unless otherwise stated. The fragmentary Inverey Castle (NO08858927) was burned because John Farquharson took part in the first Jacobite Rebellion of 1689. Nicknamed the Black Colonel for his swarthy complexion and dark hair, on his deathbed in 1698 he ordered his body be interred next to his mistress, Annie 'Ban' or Fair Annie, in the graveyard of Chapel-of-the-Seven-Maidens just north-west of the castle (the chapel and kirkyard are now just a graveless bank at NO08668939). His relations, however, had him buried at Braemar. On three separate occasions he made his objections plain by raising the coffin out of the grave onto the grass. This was followed up with a thorough and violent haunting of all the parties, so eventually his relatives had the coffin towed up the Dee to be buried at Inverey. Fenton Wyness adds that many years later two young men digging a grave accidentally struck the Colonel's coffin, and each took a tooth as a memento. That night Farquharson appeared to both thieves and asked for the return of his goods, a request that was not refused.

Almost opposite the Victoria Bridge stands – just about – an ancient Scots pine, traditionally the Gallows Tree (NO10138952). Here the Farquharsons hanged a man called Lamont, leading his mother to curse the clan, stating the tree would still be standing after the Farquharsons had faded away. The curse was held to be fulfilled in 1806 when the direct male line of Farquharson came to an end. Many of the Farquharson lands ended up being owned by the Duffs. Much earlier, in 1653, when William Duff of Dipple was born, his father Alexander Duff of Keithmore recorded 'ane greene ladye who approached William's cradle and stretched forth her hand over it'. William Duff went on to make a fortune; possibly the Green Lady had granted him financial acumen. (Source: Wyness' *Royal Valley*.)

Tobar Mhoire, St Mary's Well (NO08458919) was miraculously relocated by a saint after a contest with a druid. It was long regarded as holy. Wyness states the well was haunted by a Grey Monk, last seen terrifying a well-known Aberdeen lawyer in the early twentieth century. When Fearchar Shaw was swept into the river and his body could not be found, his wife prayed to the

Virgin Mary all night at the well. In the morning she went to the river and her husband's body had been washed up on a low bank of sand. This is Grant's version. Walter Gregor, in 'Guardian Spirits of Wells and Lochs' (1892) gives a variation. The man was drowned below the Linn of Dee. His wife took his plaid and went to the pool below the linn, folded the plaid in a certain way, prayed to the spirit of the pool, and threw the plaid into the water, saying, 'Take that and give me back my dead'. The next morning the corpse, wrapped in the plaid, was found lying beside the pool.

South, past the Colonel's Bed – a gorge where the Black Colonel once took refuge – is Creag an Fhuathais (NO099839), 'Crag of the Spectre'. Grant tells how Father John Avignon was called upon to exorcise the 'wicked, malicious, mischievous ghost' which rolled boulders onto travellers and appeared as 'loathsome, black, shapeless, monstrous, huge'. The priest erected an altar and a large wooden cross on top of the hill, and after a Mass was conducted the evil spirit was never seen again. Grant also gives the legend of Creag Anthoin (now Tom Anthon, 099881). Anthon murdered a noted local man and fled the country. Gillespie Urrasach (Gillespie the Bold) followed and killed him, burying the head near this spot.

GLEN DEE/GLEN EY

On 28 September 1759 Sergeant Arthur Davies, one of a number of soldiers who patrolled the mountains in the wake of the 1745 rebellion, left his billet at Dubrach near White Bridge in Glen Dee and crossed the hills south-east to rendezvous with another picket in Glen Ey. He then left his companions to do a bit of hunting. Somewhere between Glen Ey and Allt Cristie Mor he was murdered and his considerable valuables were stolen. It was not until five years later that a prosecution for the murder took place in Edinburgh. Despite considerable eye-witness testimony against them, Alexander Bain MacDonald and Duncan Terig, alias 'Clerk', were both found Not Guilty. The defence had undermined the prosecution's case by concentrating on the unusual evidence given by a young man from Inverey called MacPherson. He said he had been instructed by the ghost of Sergeant Davies to go to the Hill of Cristie and bury his bones. MacPherson duly found a body with Davies' distinctive clothing. The spirit also stated that Clerk and MacDonald were the murderers. On being asked what language the ghost spoke, MacPherson replied, 'In as good Gaelic as ever I heard in Lochaber'. MacPherson and several other witnesses at the trial were Gaelic speakers and addressed the court through an interpreter. Sergeant Davies, however, was a monoglot Anglophone; he did not speak Gaelic. MacPherson's testimony was therefore undermined and, as they say in American crime dramas, the perps walked.

However, many people – including their advocate – were convinced that Clerk and MacDonald were guilty. They were in the area, they had guns, they were seen by witnesses, and at least one of them became suspiciously wealthy after the murder, with his sweetheart wearing jewellery which looked very similar to that owned by Davies. The local tradition was that MacPherson heard the shot and came over the hill to find Clerk and MacDonald robbing the corpse. Clerk gave him a choice – take some of the loot to keep silent, or be killed on the spot. MacPherson fled, his dog keeping Clerk off. MacPherson then tried blackmailing Clerk; when that failed he invented the supernatural story, knowing well that in the Highlands a ghost's instructions had to be obeyed to the letter. The case is discussed in John Michie's *Deeside Tales* (1872).

2

GARIOCH

(pronounced 'Geer-rie')

KINTORE – INVERURIE – BENNACHIE – ALFORD

BLACKBURN & KINELLAR

'Sculpture at Tyrebagger', signposted from the A96, is a series of contemporary artworks on the walking trails of Elrick Hill and Tyrebagger Wood, reachable from the car parks on the B979. Several of the sculptures are strange, evocative, dreamy, even numinous. Highlights include: a herd of life-size bison; a group of six poles supporting discs, looking for all the world like a tribute to flying saucers; a solid circle imitating the full moon on water, with references to fairy tales and the imagination inscribed on nearby trees; a bizarre severed deer's head made from bright yellow metal; and, a personal favourite, a dark circular underground chamber with a camera obscura that projects the sky and trees onto a table – as the trees move in the wind outside, so does the projected image. Kinellar churchyard north of the village (NJ82161440) hides two stones from a destroyed stone circle, one in the kirkyard wall, the other partly under it. One of the tombstones is inscribed, 'Heart, if you've a sorrow, take it to the hills'. A pair of modern standing stones are on the road east of the church.

HATTON OF FINTRAY

The ruined old churchyard (NJ84071653) has a semi-subterranean anti-bodysnatching vault for the storage of coffins. In 1845 the *NSA* made an interesting 'fertility' comment about the standing stone at Peathill (NJ82111906): 'It is remarkable that the corn grows very luxuriant around this solitary pillar to a distance of fifteen yards, and has always been eighteen inches higher than the crop immediately beside it.'

KINTORE

When Isobel Cockie, the Kintore Witch, was on trial in 1597 she had a rap sheet stretching back forty years. The list of charges ran for several pages; most of them involved disputes with neighbours. She blasted recently-harvested crops, prevented butter from churning and made cows give only water or blood. Several times she caused cattle and horses to sicken, run wild or die, simply by placing a hand on them. She reduced Alexander Chalmers to poverty by killing his sheep. She had a con going with Helen Makkie, aka Suppok: Helen would bewitch people and Isobel would then be paid to remove the enchantment. Her cures involved using threads, south-running water and potions made of certain herbs. When Catherine Smart died Isobel told no one for fourteen days so she could steal her goods. Several times she cursed men who had clashed with her or found her stealing their property. Her speciality was placing a spell on a doorway; when the victim walked through it they were struck with fever and an extreme madness that saw them trying to climb walls and roofs. Some had to be bound hand and foot and held down by neighbours. The son of one afflicted man threatened to burn Isobel, so she charmed her victim back to health. A man named Deans, 'roasting' with one of the witch's fevers, only found relief by drinking from a healing well at Dayston Farm; the well, now lost, later became much visited by health-seekers who left behind buttons or pins as offerings. Isobel was charged with the murder of Cristane Leslie; it may be significant that Cristane was the daughter of the Reader, one of the church officials. In the dung heap in the morning Cristane found a 'witch's clew' (a ball of yarn or thread) of many colours. When it was thrown on the fire it gave such a crack she thought the house would fall. She became unwell, took to her bed and died within twenty days.

Isobel was named by two other witches, Helen Makkie and Jonet Wishert (see FYVIE). One of them said that at a dance in Aberdeen Isobel did not like how the Devil was playing the jaw's harp, so she took it out of his mouth and played the instrument herself. Unlike many witches, Isobel did not confess. She was found guilty on all charges and executed in February 1597. The documents are in *Spalding*. In contrast to the comprehensive records for this case, we know almost nothing about Helen George, accused of murder by using an enchanted potion in 1671; there is no indication of a verdict, although she was probably acquitted.

The churchyard in The Square (NJ79301628) has a double-sided Pictish stone and a fair collection of carved gravestones, some most odd. Ferneybrae Standing Stone (NJ80211459) and Fullerton Stone Circle (NJ78391797, one stone left, site reused for burials in the Iron Age) are south and north of Kintore respectively.

Camies Stone (NJ76861792) supposedly marks the death-in-battle spot of a Danish leader Camus or Cambus, who was then buried in Camies Grave, a stone cist to the north-east (NJ76301809). Both battle and leader are fictional, and the monuments pre-date the Vikings by at least two and a half millennia. At his death the farmer at Braeside left *mucho dinero*; this, it was said, was because he had rifled the treasures of Camies Grave. One of the several piles of stone on the nearby ridge also conceals gold; it is the 'eastmost westmost cairn,' that is, it cannot be found. The stories are in Ritchie's 'Folklore of the Aberdeenshire Stone Circles.' Close by is Clovenstone Farm, named after a large natural boulder split in two (NJ76751778).

Bizarre figure on a tombstone in Kintore churchyard. Are the fan-like horizontal effusions supposed to be wings, sunbeams, or divine radiance?

The persistent tradition is that witches were executed here; this may be a memory of the fact that a court did judge a witch at the stone. Watt's *Extracts from the Burgh Records of Kintore* (1864, quoted in McPherson) has a 1595 case from 'This Court of ye Burgh of Kintore, holden at ye Cloven Stone'. In this instance the court acquitted two men of striking Isobel Cockie, on the self-defence grounds that she was 'in ane distemper [violent], and they were forced to put her out of doors'. This was at least a year before she was investigated for witchcraft.

On 15 June 1991 the *Daily Record* reported that a horse was badly wounded near Kintore by a large cat-like animal, and in 2003 a woman saw a sandy-coloured mountain lion at her home (*Sun*, 10 January). On 20 June 2007 the same paper mentioned a buzzard attacking a Kintore jogger, taking a chunk out of his scalp.

LEYLODGE

Several 'standing stones' in the area (for example at NJ76901309 and NJ76331290) have recently been reclassified as cattle rubbing stones. The remains of the RSC at NJ76671325 are genuinely prehistoric.

BROOMHILL

Neither ancient nor agricultural, but quite wonderful, is the Breemie Stone Circle and Labyrinth (NJ769111). In 2004 Jason Schroeder, drawn by a vision, persuaded local farmer Alan Brownie to let him build a new RSC here. A year later a Mind, Body and Spirit Festival was held at the site, and Maria Hayden and Barry Hoon designed and installed the turf and stone labyrinth, with enthusiastic participation by the festival-goers; there was also a temporary Fire Spiral. A second festival took place in 2006. Everything about the circle – its extent, the recumbent, the arc of sky it encompasses – is huge. More on the esoteric background to the siting and design of the circle and labyrinth can be found at http://mariahayden.com and Jason Schroeder's www.sacredway.co.uk. There is sometimes livestock in the field; park and ask permission at B.A. Farm Stores and walk up the hill to the east.

KEMNAY

The village name is supposedly derived from the Kembs, low hills to the south-east; they are the remains of a vast rope of sand made by a Donside witch at the behest of the Devil. Witches were supposed to congregate around the stonking tall Lang Stane O'Craigearn (NJ72381493). A lovely walk through Fetternear Estate takes you past griffon-topped gateposts to the evocative ruins of Fetternear House (accidentally destroyed by fire in 1919). High up a stone dated 1691 is carved with a small cross and 'IHS MRA', I[E]H[U]S or *Jesus Hominum Salvator*, 'Jesus Saviour of Men,' and M[A]R[I]A, *Maria Regina Angelorum*, 'Holy Mary, Queen of Angels'. This subtle message quietly proclaims that the owners were Catholic. Count Patrick Leslie picked up this Jesuit-inspired symbolism while fighting the Turks. In 'The House of Fetternear' (1971) H. Gordon Slade suggested that the symbols also had a talismanic value, that is, they provided divine protection for the house. Further east are the overgrown fragments of St Ninian's Church and graveyard with St Ninian's Well (NJ73311748) by the river. The difficult-to-visit Chapel O'Sink Cairn (NJ706189) is supposedly the remains of a chapel whose stones kept sinking into the ground (an action usually attributed to Satan or the denizens of Faery). The Ark Stone 200 paces north was once thought to be a recumbent stone (and the cairn was once thought to be a stone circle) but it is now regarded simply as a large natural boulder.

This way to the stone circle: signpost to the modern RSC at Broomhill. (Photo: Ségolène Dupuy)

Broomhill's modern RSC: big circle, big skies.

The turf and stone labyrinth constructed beside the modern RSC at Broomhill.

Bodies were definitely kept in the semi-subterranean anti-resurrectionist morthouse at the parish church graveyard (NJ73721609), but what about the coffin in the cellar? Much excitement was generated in the press in 2008 when hotelier Malcolm Edwards planned to break through a wall in the Burnett Arms to get to the bottom of a local mystery. The tradition is that a former landlady from the 1930s, Maggie Dufton, had three coffins made. One, full of rocks, lies beneath her gravestone. The other two, containing her corpse and her cash respectively, were interred in the pub. Her apparition and presence have been reported several times. There were teaser stories as an infrared probe camera was pushed through a tiny opening in the wall, revealing what seemed to be some kind of box. A séance was held, at which Maggie and her daughter Agnes were apparently contacted, saying that murders had happened at the hotel (but when? Who were the victims and the perpetrators? The spirits were silent). And then, with the event relayed live to a television screen in the bar, the wall was opened up to reveal … absolutely nothing. Mr Edwards said: 'I'm gutted.' (*Press and Journal*, 18, 23 June, 7 July 2008; *Evening Express* 19, 23 June, 2 July.)

McPherson's *Primitive Beliefs* describes the digging of two graves, one for death, the other for life. Whichever one a sick person turned to determined their fate. In 1675 Elspet Crombie presented her child to such a grave at night and said, 'God send it health or heaven.' Heaven was clearly the choice, as the sick bairn died.

INVERURIE

Inverurie's heart of strangeness lies in the graveyard on Keithhall Road, dominated by The Bass and Little Bass, natural glacial mounds that were shaped into a medieval motte-and-bailey castle. Connected once, they were separated when the Victorian cemetery was laid out. The size of The Bass has impressed itself on antiquarian and folk belief. Alexander Watt's *The Early History of Kintore* (1864) summarised the prevailing notions: it was the sepulchre of King Aoch, who died in 881; it was one of a series of signal towers when the Danes were invading; it was raised over victims of the plague, so if opened the epidemic would sweep forth to rage again; and it was the subject of a prophecy allegedly by Thomas the Rhymer:

When Dee and Don both run in one / And Tweed shall run in Tay,
Ye little river of Ury / Shall bear ye Bass away.

Although the land used to flood frequently The Bass remains solid enough. James Milne's *Twixt Ury and Don* (1947) adds that it was (of course) a treasure site, as well as a place of pagan magic and ceremonies, and that if you put your ear to the grassy slope on a certain date you could hear 'the echoes of some long bygone saturnalia'.

Perhaps the strangest belief about the site is in John Foster Forbes' *Giants, Myths and Megaliths*. Forbes was a kind of New Ager before his time – during the Second World War he visited ancient sites such as stone circles and Glastonbury, always with a psychic who would tune in to the location's distant past by touching the stones, a procedure known as psychometry. At Inverurie his psychometrist was Iris Campbell. Both Forbes and Campbell hated the feel of The Bass from the start: 'a wind both mischievous and evil sprung up making conditions very disturbed'. Campbell was drawn to a stone in the graveyard with the image of a horse, and picked up that the site had been used by evil cultists whose bodies had been grotesquely distorted by the sheer amount of earth energy needed for the performance of their dark arts. They exerted a hypnotic power over the local people, who were then sacrificed to these monsters' dark gods. The horrors only finished when the druids came with their white magic and built The Bass to imprison and disperse the evil energies. The Bass represented masculine magic and the Little Bass the feminine equivalent. It took Forbes and Campbell days to shake off the malign influence of the site.

The gravestone of Walter Innes (d.1616) and his wife Meriorie Elphinstone who 'DEPAIRTIT THE 15 DAY OF NOVEB 1622'. Meriorie was the famous 'Twice-buried Mary'. Since this photograph was taken in the 1970s, the inscription has largely mossed over. (Photo: the Garioch Heritage Society)

A Pictish stone carved with the image of a horse. In the background is the Bass of Inverurie, home of the plague, mythical kings and black magicians.

The horse image Iris Campbell referred to is on one of four carved Pictish stones in a line under the trees in the west end of the cemetery, roughly where the old church once stood (it was removed because of flooding). This horse is unique in the Pictish art that has survived. Next to these carvings is an upright, moss covered gravestone with two angels looking like fat bumble-bees. This is the grave of Walter Innes of Ardtannes and his wife Meriorie Elphinstone, or 'Twice-buried Mary' as she has become known. Having been interred in the usual fashion, she was rudely awoken from a trance-like state by the gravedigger, who had opened the coffin and was attempting to remove rings from her fingers. Saved from 'death by premature burial', she made her way home to Ardtannes, where she greatly surprised the grieving Walter and his friends. Meriorie/Marjory/Mary (she is known by all three) went on to live a full life. The episode may be true; or it may be an exaggeration, or a floating tradition that has come to rest in Inverurie. We will never know, as there are no contemporary records. This tale has been told and retold, sometimes with the events set in the time of the bodysnatchers. But this is not the case – as the photograph shows, Meriorie died in 1622 (six years after Walter passed away), thus pre-dating the resurrectionists by two centuries. There is a bodysnatching connection, however – the large coffin-shaped block nearby is a granite mortsafe, placed on the grave to prevent unauthorised access (there were several cases of bodysnatchers working in this graveyard). The smaller granite stone adjacent was placed on the coffins of children.

The area around The Bass was the site of the Battle of Inverurie on 23 December 1745, when a Government army was defeated by a Jacobite force. A memorial between the cemetery and the river describes the action. We learn that it took place at night, in moonlight, and that as the Royalists were retreating, the Jacobites fired at what they thought was a fresh army – which, come the daylight, turned out to be a ridge of ploughed ground.

Once upon a time Broomend of Crichie was one of the most impressive prehistoric monuments in Aberdeenshire, a stone circle within a henge, connected by a grand avenue of paired stones to a second circle surrounding a cairn, and thence to a cemetery of cairns and cist graves. This ritual landscape is much denuded, but there is still one avenue stone left, plus another two stones within the henge. In the nineteenth century an excellently-carved Pictish stone was found nearby and erected in the henge. The site (NJ778197) is easily accessible behind the garage at the junction of Elphinstone Road and the A96. Across the road is the Port Arch sculpture, a modern piece with images of Inverurie industries and life, along with several Pictish symbols.

Kinkell Church (NJ78581906) to the east of the river is cared for by Historic Scotland. The plain ruins house a rare but very eroded sacrament house; a metal panel showing Christ crucified, with the Virgin Mary, an angel, and several severed heads; and an excellent tombstone of an armoured Gilbert de Greenlaw, who fell at the BATTLE OF HARLAW in 1411. A recumbent stone shows an angel holding sickles, but this is hard to see in the moss.

The Carnegie Museum above Inverurie Library in The Square (open Monday and Wednesday-Friday 2 p.m.-4.30 p.m., Saturday 10 a.m.-1 p.m. and 2 p.m.-4 p.m., free) has mysterious carved Neolithic stone balls, Pictish stones and other archaeological items. The Kintore Arms Hotel on High Street has a splendidly painted coat of arms featuring two ever-so-slightly-camp armoured knights. Within a housing estate on Gordon Terrace is the Pictish Brandsbutt Stone, with two stones from a former stone circle, and good interpretation by Historic Scotland. Adjacent is a circular artwork marked with the Pole Star and the constellations of Ursa Major and Ursa Minor (not Cassiopeia as the plaque states). A short distance away on the Blackhall Road roundabout by the supermarket is a metal sculpture of a family of crows. Almost opposite is a circle of modern stones inset with coloured glass panels. Bainzie Road has another contemporary circle and a sundial supported by birds and covered with poetic quotations.

In the 1590s Isobel Strachan (aka Scudder) was active in the area. She bewitched the mill at Caskieben and hid a charm in Walter Ronaldson's barn that made him stop beating his wife. In 1657 John Mill (or Milne) and Isobel MacKie were charged with charming, and John was back in September 1658, accused of transferring a headache from a Fetternear man to a woman, who then told him to charm the pain from her or she would denounce him to the Kirk-Session. He gave her a linen pouch filled with powders and told her to hang it around her neck for nine nights and then burn it. This she did, and recovered, but John was still charged, although the trial was later abandoned. This is in P.G. Maxwell-Stuart's *An Abundance of Witches*.

McPherson relates the tale of a young man whose drowned body could not be found in the Don. A wise woman was consulted, and an ordinary soft biscuit was placed in the river at the place of the accident; the place where it sank accurately located the body. The spirit of the river, which had been keeping body in thrall, was appeased by the biscuit. Grant's *The Mysteries of All Nations* describes how the daughter of a rich farmer married the poor man of her heart after a fortune-teller told her parents that the rich suitor they preferred would end his life in poverty. Grant suspected the fortune-teller may have been paid by the daughter to achieve that result. Room 406 of the Thainstone House Hotel is reported to be haunted by the Green Lady, a daughter of the former owners who was killed in a riding accident.

West of Inverurie, Easter Aquhorthies (NJ73232079, Historic Scotland) is one of the best RSCs in Aberdeenshire. It has been suggested that the structure of the site amplifies sounds, which may have been a factor in ceremonies conducted there. To the north, a Pictish symbol stone lies in the garden wall behind Drummies farmhouse (NJ 4262350).

The Battle of Harlaw Memorial Monument (NJ75142407) marks the place where, on 24 July 1411, a feudal land dispute over the ownership of the vast Earldom of Ross in the Highlands culminated in a pitched battle between Donald, Lord of the Isles, and a Lowland army under Alexander Stewart, Earl of Mar. Around 1,500 men died, and the site was known thereafter as Red Harlaw. Although there was no decisive victory on the day, Donald's invasion was checked, so it was a strategic win for the men of the North-East. Many saw it as Lowland prosperity rescued from Highland plunder. It made a deep impression on popular culture, appearing in ballads and songs, and several local sites owe their folklore to the battle (for example, the Liggars' Stane at NJ74702488 to the north, a prehistoric standing stone that supposedly marks the graves of the female camp-followers killed at the battle). Other examples are at GARTLY and RHYNIE.

PITCAPLE & WHITEFORD

William Alexander's *Northern Rural Life* (1877) has a wonderful supernatural soap opera. In 1737 the minister, Mr Gilbert Gerard, reported to the Kirk-Session at Chapel of Garioch that he had been asked by George Watt from Bridgend Farm to come and 'converse with the spirit, who, ever since about three or four weeks after the death of his mother in the preceding February, had frequently appeared and spoken to him and his brothers without the windows of the rooms where they lay, to their great terror and amazement.' The spirit had identified itself as the deceased mother of George and his six well-to-do brothers. It revealed to them many things, primary amongst which was 'that it was the will of the great God that Geordie Watt should marry Tibbie Mortimer, because that Tibbie was now in a gracious state, and had been predestinated to glory from all eternity'. If George did not marry the servant, the seven brothers would 'be consumed with fire from heaven' and George himself would go to Hell. Not surprisingly, this concerned George, not least because he had no intention of marrying beneath his station.

So one evening the minister went out to the farm, north of Pitcaple (NJ719269). After some hours, a voice was heard at the window of the bedroom in which Geordie Watt slept, saying, 'Speak, George Watt, speak, men and minister! Come here and I will discourse you all'. Gerard ran outside and, as the Session records state:

> The appearance which first presented to his view was about the bulk of ane ordinary woman, covered with white clean linnen [*sic*] head and arms down to the middle of the body before, and somewhat farther behind. Then, willing to unravel the matter whatever the event should be, he made such a trial of the apparition as he thought agreeable to the principles of the Christian revelation and true philosophy; and by its resistance to the end of a small rod which he had in his hand, he soon found it to be a material substance … The apparition was brought flat to the ground, and then, being charged as a base impostor to speak, it was silent till he pulled the white veil from its face, whereupon (it being a bright moonshine), he clearly saw that it was the above-named Isobel Mortimer.

Tibbie was upbraided by the minister and formally condemned by the Session. But there was more to the case than met the eye. Ten months later the Presbytery convicted Ms Mortimer of not only 'acting the part of a ghost and blaspheming the holy name of God,' but also for 'fornication with George Watt'. She had to stand in sackcloth in church for several Sundays and pay a fine. George was accused of having a hand in the ghostly charade, a charge he strongly denied, and he defiantly refused the shame of appearing in sackcloth. Eventually the Session agreed to him paying a substantial fornication fine, and he was allowed to sit in his personal seat in the church while Tibbie was on humiliating show in front of the congregation. It is not recorded how their relationship proceeded thereafter.

Somewhere near the ruined Logie-Durno church (NJ70432640) was the kinker-steen well, where children with whooping cough drank from a natural rainwater hollow and left pins as gifts. Three Pictish stones are in a clearing in the woods just north of the drive to Logie House (NJ70342589). The *Evening Express* for 8 August 2007 reported that a jet-black big cat was seen the previous June on the north side of the A96 near Pitcaple.

CHAPEL OF GARIOCH

The Maiden Stone (NJ704247, Historic Scotland) is one of the tallest and best Pictish stones in the county. Both the carvings and the name have generated a slew of folklore as different generations have tried to understand the meaning of the stone. The main themes were summarised in Alex Inkson McConnochie's 1897 book *Bennachie*:

1. It is a boundary stone between Marr and Buchan, the symbols representing the fertile Garioch as the Land of Cakes.

2. In 1419 Andrew Leslie, 5th Baron of Balquhain, carried off and married Isabella Mortimer. During an argument between Leslie and her father, Isabella threw herself between the fighters and was killed.

3. The daughter of the Laird of Balquhain eloped with the son of his hated neighbour Harthill. Her father pursued them and she was killed here, the stone being erected to her memory.

4. One of the girl's rejected suitors called up Satan ('0800-DialSatanicRevenge; If you are calling about sending your ex-girlfriend to Hell, press 1. For all other options, please hold for the next available operator. Conversations may be recorded to help improve the quality of our service'). In the guise of a handsome young man, the Devil bet the maiden he could build a road to the top of BENNACHIE before she could finish her baking. He completed his task faster than a speeding bullet, so the girl fled, with the Devil in hot pursuit. At the last minute she uttered a prayer to God and was turned to stone; the missing chunk on the Maiden Stone is where Lucifer had grabbed her. Not surprisingly, this version is the preferred story. As an afterthought, the area is haunted by the maiden and her betrayers.

The two sides of the Maiden Stone, as shown in Alex Inkson McConnochie's *Bennachie* (1897). Some of the images have faded since.

EAST SIDE.   WEST SIDE.

The divine statue of Persephone, Goddess of Spring and Fertility, near the Maiden Stone.

Walk 100 paces west of the Maiden Stone and turn right through an entrance and then immediately right along a path through the trees. Here in a glade is one of the glories of Aberdeenshire, a 13ft (4m) high monumental statue of Persephone, the Greek Goddess of Spring and Fertility. The daughter of Demeter the Corn Goddess, Persephone was carried off to the underworld by Hades. She was finally released but Hades had tricked her into eating six pomegranate seeds. She could therefore only spend six months of each year above ground, her respective sunlit and subterranean sojourns thus accounting for the cycle of crops. The themes of fertility, abduction and transformation cleverly echo the Maiden Stone, and the mirror symbol from the latter can be seen in one hand, while the other is holding the pomegranate seeds. The statue – which often has an emotional or numinous effect on visitors – was created in 1961 by Shaun Crampton (his initials are on the back). In front of it is a small circular stone representing the omphalos or centre of the world.

There is a Satan's Well on Gallows Hill (NJ72822439) but I can find out nothing about it. The site can be visited from the track over the hill if the field is not in crop.

BENNACHIE

Historian W. Douglas Simpson once called Bennachie 'the Sphinx of the Garioch.' It is one of the contenders for the site of Mons Graupius, and its several peaks, especially Mither Tap, dominate the area visually and in folklore. The best place to start is the Visitor Centre (open 9.30 a.m.–4 p.m. in winter, 10.30 a.m.–5 p.m. in summer, closed Mondays) which has displays on history, wildlife and legends and details of the various walks (including trails suitable for wheelchairs) and the sculptures in the woods. Much of the area's folklore was collected in McConnochie's *Bennachie*; unless otherwise indicated this is the source for the stories given here.

The breezy summit of Mither Tap (NJ68252240) is home to beetling masses of rock and a hillfort, the impressive entrance to which forms the end of the partly-paved Maiden Causeway.

It is easy to see how this elemental landscape has generated legends. The causeway and fort were built by the Devil (see the MAIDEN STONE) or by Sir Andrew Leslie of Balquhain as a secure rape-camp for the local girls he abducted. In reality the causeway could well be the early medieval or prehistoric route to the fort. The giant Jock o' Bennachie lived here. Little John's Length to the east of Craigshannoch is his bed; assuming he slept full-length he was 600ft (183m) tall. North-west of Craigshannoch a shirt-shaped surface is where he dried his clothes. The giant threw boulders at TAP O' NOTH, especially after its resident guardian stole his girlfriend, Anne. Jock then met a strange woman he mistook for the Lady Anne; when they kissed he sank into an enchanted sleep beneath the mountain. Only when a certain woman finds the magical key will he be released. A man once found the key, but couldn't turn it in the great lock. He put his hat on the key to mark the place, and went to get help. When the party returned, key, lock and hat had all vanished.

A prophecy attributed to Thomas the Rhymer runs:

Scotland will never be rich, be rich,
Till they find the keys o' Bennachie;
They shall be found by a wife's ae [one] son, wi' ae e'e [one eye],
Aneath a juniper tree.

In recent times Jock has been seen less as a piece of folklore and more as a protective spirit of nature, the Warden of Bennachie. In September 1997 Mr J. Craig of Aberdeen told Andy Roberts about an incident that had taken place some years earlier. He and two companions were resting below the summit when they were seized with a sense of absolute terror. All three immediately fled, only stopping running when they reached the foot of the mountain. Craig was convinced he and his friends had 'met' Jock o' Bennachie. (The episode is in Roberts' article 'The Big Grey Man of Ben Macdhui & Other Mountain Panics'.)

Another encounter with the supernatural is given in Jack Stewart's memoir of his life in a travelling family, *Deeside Tinkers*. Around 1973 he and his father Joe were camping on the old road at Bennachie. Joe told him not to touch the rowan tree by the camp. After an evening of campfire ghost stories Jack could not sleep, so he set the fire going with the nearest wood available – the rowan. He heard a lowing in the distance, followed by a roar and galloping of hooves coming up the road. By the firelight he saw a shadow with the shape of a big black bull, stamping at the ground in a fury. Joe only managed to banish the demon by reading from the Bible and brandishing a crucifix. There is nothing in Stewart's tone to suggest this was anything other than a genuine experience, but given the tinkers' skill with storytelling, I have my doubts.

The summit of Oxen Craig (NJ66292259) is also known as Robbie Deson's Tap. The body of Robert Dawson, a mentally-limited pauper from Gooseknowe, near Ryehill, Oyne, was found here on 12 December 1856, the sixteenth day after he disappeared. No one had thought to search the summit because he had last been seen much lower down, and the weather had been terrible. The body, mutilated by crows, was buried at night in Oyne churchyard. A memorial was placed on the summit, but Dawson's mother broke it up because she received none of the money raised for its erection, and the inscription described her son as 'fatuous'. The rectangular-cut socket for the stone can still be seen on the south-east part of the summit, south of the cairn.

In the eighteenth century a man buried his wife in Keig churchyard but the next morning he found the body dumped outside his door – she had killed herself, and there was a horror of suicides being buried in consecrated ground. He next tried to bury her in Premnay, but the locals there were also having none of it. A midnight start was made for a secret burial in Oyne, but the coffin was too heavy, the mourners too few, and daylight came too soon. She was therefore buried where the funeral party stopped, on the top of Watch Craig (NJ652213), wrapped in a home-made plaid. In the mid-1840s peat workers found the grave. The moss had preserved both the wrap and the body, the latter described as 'quite plump and mulatto-coloured'. However, exposure to air caused rapid decomposition and the corpse was that evening buried in Oyne churchyard. The woman's name was Laing and her story had been known for a century before the discovery. About 1820 Jane Jack drowned herself in the Gadie near Harthill and was buried in unconsecrated ground not far from Hosie's Well. By now, however, attitudes to suicides had changed, and Jack's body was exhumed and reburied at Oyne Church.

In 'The Pursuit of Witches,' a 2002 article by Greg Dawson Allen in *Leopard* magazine, the story is given of a 'wise man' called Henderson, aka Skairy, who had a croft at the foot of Bennachie. In 1860 he was consulted about the death of cattle in neighbourhood farms, often associated with the sighting of a mysterious hare. The finger of suspicion pointed at two local beldames, Nannie Souter and Betty Berry. In return for his usual fee of £1 and a bottle of whisky, Skairy suggested the hare be shot with a crooked sixpence. However, the tenant farmer designated for the task was forbidden in his lease from shooting hares. It is not known if the problem was ever resolved.

OYNE

The place to visit here is Archaeolink Prehistory Park (open 10 a.m.–5 p.m. 1 April to 31 October, admission charge, mostly good wheelchair access). Educational and entertaining, it combines reconstructed sites and archaeological information with participative events, Stone Age skills workshops, historical re-enactments, storytelling – and the chance to get yourself painted blue like a Celtic warrior.

Among the permanent exhibits are several reconstructed sites – a Mesolithic hunter-gatherer encampment; a recumbent stone circle (used in 2003 for a pagan wedding); a henge (based on the one at WORMIE HILL); a Bronze Age metal smith's workshop; an Iron Age roundhouse and farmstead; and a Roman marching camp. There is also the ground plan of a Neolithic timber hall, based on the massive site excavated at Balbridie near BANCHORY. There are regular demonstrations at the exhibits, sometimes with explorations into folklore – for example, metalworking can include mention of the myths surrounding smiths, even bringing in King Arthur's Sword in the Stone. The Beltane celebration in early May typically involves fire juggling, storytelling and dancing in the stone circle before the culmination of the day when children, complete with animal masks, are driven between the Beltane fires – a reference, of course, to the time when herds passed between bonfires to protect them from evil for the following year.

Perhaps the highlight is the Wickerman event. The 40ft (12m) high willow and straw figure is built in June and burned on the last Sunday in October. The day includes a 'haunted house' tour of the Myths and Legends Gallery, fire-walking and other fire-orientated entertainment, and culminates with the burning of the Wickerman at dusk. Mark Keighley, Team Leader at the park, told me that even if there has been persistent rain in the weeks before the evening, the afternoon of the burning is always dry. If the structure is wet, the fire expels the moisture from the willow, causing it to 'scream'.

The Gowk Stone (NJ67652570), signposted just off the walk to the summit, is a large standing stone that was either chucked here by Jock o' Bennachie or is the perch for the first cuckoo of spring to return after spending winter in Africa ('Gowk' is a cuckoo). Up to the mid-nineteenth century the young men and women of the district visited the Hill Well west of Berry Hill on the first Sunday in May. Many arrived on Saturday night so they could be sure of drinking 'the cream of the well' at dawn. The crofter encouraged the idea that the well possessed medicinal virtues, as each year he claimed the coins that were left in the well as tokens.

In 1703 Robert Bainzie from Oyne was indicted for witchcraft but we have no further information.

Burning the Wickerman
at Archaeolink. (Photo:
Archaeolink Prehistory Park)

The *Scotsman* for 29 November 2001 reported that a number of official-looking signs had appeared outside Oyne stating 'Beware of haggis crossing' and directing motorists to 'Bob's Farm and Haggis Sanctuary'. The signposted route led merely to a country track which petered out within a mile. Elusive fellows, those haggi.

OLD RAYNE

Candle Hill (NJ67982798) RSC, once known as the Standing Stones of Rayne, is badly damaged, the main interest of the site being that in medieval times the stones had been rearranged into an open-air structure used by the District Head Courts. James Ritchie's 1926 article on the folklore of stone circles says that in 1349 a court was held here to settle a land ownership dispute between the Bishop of Aberdeen and William of St Michael. Two very good sculptured stones, one with Pictish symbols and the other with an Ogham inscription, stand just east of Newton House (NJ66232972). In one of the more unorthodox beliefs recorded in this book, the *Scotsman* for 1 December 2006 reported Stan Hall's claim that the double disc and Z-rod symbols on the Newton Stone represented the planet Jupiter breaking away from Saturn millions of years ago, a planetary catastrophe conveniently recorded by an advanced pre-human civilisation. Well, you never know.

KIRKTON OF CULSALMOND

A twelve-stone stone circle was demolished in 1791 so the church could be built on its site (NJ65053295). The kirk, now a shell, stands next to a large anti-bodysnatching morthouse. The damaged cairn of Mummer's Reive (NJ65723281) may have been named after a 'sham bishop' or mummer who conducted mock services here. The entrance to the former Cairnhill Quarry (NJ66973261) has a cross-incised stone. St Michael's Well (NJ64983170), now covered by a domed well-house, is on a road called Devil's Folly.

INSCH

A wonderful walk can be made from the car park on the B9002 west of Insch. First comes the Hill of Dunnideer (NJ61222817), topped with the gaunt remains of a medieval tower, itself built into the remains of a vitrified Iron Age fort. Vitrification occurs when stone is subjected to very high temperatures and melts. Vitrified forts are a phenomenon unique to Scotland and have long puzzled archaeologists. For generations the consensus was that the forts had been set on fire by enemies during a siege. However, experiments have shown that the only way to achieve the intense prolonged heat is if timbers are interlaced with the rocks (at Dunnideer a cavity can be seen where one of the timber posts was inserted into the matrix). In other words, the fort builders did this deliberately, presumably to strengthen the defences by forming sections of fused rock. Although Dunnideer is only a small hill, the gable of the castle, with its stark central window, is visible for miles around, and from a distance gives the impression of a prehistoric monument such as a trilithon from Stonehenge. It has a very 'sacred hill' vibe.

Dunnideer has a fine collection of legends. W. Douglas Simpson, in a piece for the Society of Antiquaries of Scotland in 1934, included a poem that appears in John Hardyng's diagrammatic map of Scotland of 1465: it is a list of places where King Arthur held his court, including Edinburgh, Stirling, Perth, Dunbarton and 'At Donydoure also'. From the sixteenth century onwards it was known as the 'golden mountain' because the sheep that grazed it had teeth covered with the gold they grazed from the soil. In an appendix to Simpson's article, James Ritchie explained that the yellow layer was just tooth plaque. The walk continues down the west slope to the huge recumbent and flankers of Aulton RSC (NJ60862844), and then along the road to a similar site at Stonehead (NJ60102869), both with excellent views of Dunnideer.

The ruined St Drostan's Church on Insch High Street (NJ63352814) has several good carved gravestones. Christ's Kirk of Rathmuriel (NJ60562680) at Christkirk Farm is comprehensively desolate; if you can find the single remaining gravestone it has the Grim Reaper holding a scythe and hour-glass. There is nothing to see of the fort on Hill of Christ's Kirk but there are several moving modern memorials on the top (NJ60362719). Dead Man's Howe lies to the east (NJ622275). The Picardy Stone is another fine carved Pictish monolith cared for by Historic Scotland (NJ60993026).

In March 1650 Margaret Ogg was accused of transferring her daughter's labour pains onto a servant, Isabella Robertson. Isabella's belly swelled, she vomited, and was sick for three days until the child was delivered.

A woman from Insch was attacked by a 'Labrador-sized' black cat on a croft near the Glens of Foundland on 11 January 2002. The animal clawed and bit her as she was leaving a steading where her horse was stabled. Her local MSP, Richard Lochhead, took the matter before the Scottish Parliament. Mark Fraser of Scottish Big Cats did not believe the woman was deliberately attacked – the cat might have been disturbed or felt cornered, and lashed out defensively. (*Daily Record* 15 January 2002; *News of the World* 20 January 2002; *Sun* 5 July 2002.) The *News of the World* (27 January 2002) also reported that a man saw a big cat on a lonely country road near Insch earlier in the month.

LESLIE

The RSC on Hawk Hill (NJ605243) has a terrific view of Dunnideer and Tap O' Noth, and the massive stranded recumbent (one of only two stones left) accidentally hints at the shape of a bull. Nearby on Mains of Leslie Farm a field called the Good Man's Fauld was marked on an estate map of 1797. The standing stone called the Ringing Stone (NJ57902517) is a puzzle because it does not ring. The name may be a corruption of Ringan or another similar word. The stone is said to be haunted but there are no details.

AUCHLEVEN (ALSO KNOWN AS PREMNAY)

McPherson's *Primitive Beliefs* states that a farmer who removed a stone circle near here paid the price when all his cattle died of disease. The site may have been the ravaged RSC by Druidstone Croft (NJ61532219), or the seven cairns that once stood about 100 paces west, or another lost site entirely.

KEIG

The damaged RSC at Old Keig (NJ59651939) has the largest known recumbent stone, weighing in at approximately fifty-three tons. The website www.ancient-wisdom.co.uk rates it as No. 40 in the Top 50 heaviest megaliths in the world. Cothiemuir Wood RSC (NJ61711981) has a magical, sylvan setting and strikingly tall flankers. Two natural hollows on the outer surface of the recumbent stone are known as the Devil's Hoofmarks. Nearby, but not intruding on the circle, is a natural burial site (for ashes only, no headstones). The roofless old parish church by the river (NJ61891891) has eighteenth-century gravestones. To the north-west is a place called Fairy Hillock (NJ603207) and within Priest's Wood there used to be Oberon's Well (NJ59342193). Oberon is the King of the Fairies, so the name is initially very suggestive of a fairy site; but the name is actually a corruption of 'Tobar', Gaelic for well. Another name for the site, St Tobran's Well, has the same derivation.

TULLYNESSLE

The church (NJ 55821964) has a few gravestones with symbols of mortality. The bellcote of its predecessor is set up in the kirkyard, looking like the doorway to a now vanished miniature mansion.

ALFORD

Haughton Country Park has a modern stone circle in its grounds (walk north-west from the edge of the caravan site, NJ580171). The path leading west from the entrance into Murray Park passes the Gordon Stane (NJ576166), a large boulder where the mortally wounded Lord George Gordon was laid after the 1645 Battle of Alford, a Civil War conflict in which a Royalist army under Montrose routed a Covenant force, killing more than 700. The story of the bloody defeat is told in a locally-available booklet by Bryan Hinton, *Alford 1645*. The Grampian Transport Museum has a 'Tardis' police box which is occasionally visited by a Dalek, and there are modern carvings of animals and humans on blocks outside the station of the narrow-gauge railway.

McPherson's *Primitive Beliefs* records several Alford folk in trouble in 1673 for consulting a deaf and mute person; such people were thought to have second sight and be able to see the future and locate thieves. In 1677 a mute woman's identification of an apparent thief caused 'great enmity amongst neighbours and scandal'. In *Exodus to Alford* (1988) Stanley Robertson recalls stories he heard among travelling people doing itinerant work around Alford in the

The modern stone circle at Haughton Country Park, Alford.

summer of 1946, with tales of the Devil, kelpies, and dancing trees. Robert Smith's *The Road to Drumnafunner* (2007) uncovered a very localised legend of an old woman named Meggie Stott who was stealing meal from a girnal in Asloun (west of Alford) when the head of the girnal came down and killed her. This may have been in the early nineteenth century. As she was a witch she had to be buried between the estates of two lairds and in sight of a mill and a kirk. The liminal spot chosen was on Reekie Brae above Reekie Farm (*c.* NJ533154). Everyone added a stone to the cairn as they passed – it was bad luck not to. However, the mound was pushed into the bank by a workman's vehicle when the road was improved, and is now just a small heap of stones on the track skirting the north of Craig Hill.

MILTON OF CUSHNIE

In an article for the journal *Folklore* in 1914, David Rorie recorded an old man's memories of events some sixty years earlier. A 'canny wifie' named Nannie protected a farmer's last calf from the disease that had killed his other beasts by passing the animal through the Muckle Wheel Ban', the band connecting the driving wheel of an old-fashioned spinning-wheel to the spindle. Nannie advised the man to offer bread soaked in milk to all his neighbours, and to contrive to spill milk on them at the serving; the one who refused the meal was the source of the curse. Presumably the refusal was based on the culprit's knowledge that the cows (and therefore the milk) had been bewitched.

An old woman, Mary D., was renowned as a witch and could transform into a hare. Merely meeting her on the road caused a man's new pig to choke to death (six months later!). Another crofter, primed by drink, burst in on Mary at night and verbally abused her, finishing with, 'Ye chokit Willie Tamson's pig last week; but jist try yersel wi' me, ye bitch!' Thoroughly cowed, the woman thereafter treated the man with respect and his enterprises thrived.

One old man never passed the Fairy Hillock somewhere in the Glen of Cushnie without holding his cap on, as he said the hillock always made his hair stand on end. From 1662–1672 seer Patrick McKomie was often in trouble with the Church. The minister of Leochel investigated five parishioners for consulting with him over stolen goods. The former St Bride's Church in Kirkton of Cushnie (NJ50641086) is 10 per cent stone, 90 per cent ivy and weeds.

CRAIGIEVAR CASTLE

(National Trust for Scotland. Closed during 2009 for conservation work, reopening 2010, check www.nts.org.uk for opening hours. Admission charge. Parkland grounds open all year, free.)

The pink-harled walls host a set of lion and unicorn panels, twelve grotesque human, animal and demonic heads, and seventeen false spouts, some with thistle and dragon motifs. In *Psychic Scotland* (2007) Tom Rannachan sensed the spirits of children, and a man jumping from a high window instead of facing an enemy with a sword. The *Daily Mirror* for 30 May 2005 reported that when Malcolm Forbes-Cable married Chloe Gardner he issued a formal invite to his dead ancestors. The card, addressed to 'Red Sir John and the other ghosts', was left on the mantelpiece in the Great Hall.

KIRKTON OF TOUGH

Although damaged, the Whitehills RSC (NJ64311350, signposted from the B993) has now been cleared of its surrounding conifers in Tillyfourie woods and is worth a visit. Up on the hills, Luath's Stone (NJ64041489) supposedly commemorates the death of Macbeth's stepson Lulach (who also has 'graves' at INVERURIE and TAP O' NOTH). More realistically the name is a corruption of the Gaelic word liath, 'grey', the stone itself being that colour. The King's Stone (NJ64111590) and Horseman's Stone (NJ64401574), both natural boulders, were vantage points for participants in a mythical medieval battle. The RSC at Old Kirk of Tough (NJ62500928) is now just a single stone; its interest lies largely in the name, indicating a recent belief that the circles were places of worship. The tenant, it is said, formed one of the stones into a field-roller; the first time he put it to use it broke, a clear indication that the powers-that-be were displeased with his sacrilege.

James Stewart, in *Deeside Tinkers*, related a story his Granny had told him about the old days. His father and two uncles, lost in the birch woods at Tillyfourie at night after a rabbit hunt, heard a horse and cart draw up. A man's voice said, 'I wonder if the laird up at Tilly's Farm has got any fresh bodies for us tonight as we are running low?' The boys realised they were 'burkers' – bodysnatchers. Their location spotted, the lads ran off and barricaded themselves in a fisherman's hut. The burkers attacked the hut with sticks and tried to break in through the roof, but finally gave up as dawn broke. Jack's sister Eliza told him another story about his Granny, Kate. She was fourteen years old and camping in an old quarry with her father and mother. On an errand with a friend, they were stopped by two men in a coach who grabbed Kate's companion and smashed her head in, putting the body in the boot of the vehicle then driving off. Stewart was born in 1954 so his Granny would have been fourteen probably sometime before the First World War, almost a century after the last of the bodysnatchers. The stories are all spurious, therefore, but their persistence shows the power the terrifying burkers had over the travellers' imaginations. Kirkton of Tough kirkyard (NJ61501298) has an iron and granite mortsafe.

MONYMUSK

The splendid church (NJ68491525) incorporates parts of a medieval Augustinian Priory and houses a Pictish cross-slab and two cross-incised stones. The old gravestones have been formed into arcs within the kirkyard. There is a tradition that the original building used stones from a stone circle at Tombeg, of which only a single upright now remains (NJ67931426). The stones were supposed to have been passed from hand to hand down the hill. The three stones at Deer Park (NJ68331564) are also known as 'The Druids'.

The highly recommended website www.monymusk.com gives several legends about the House of Monymusk (NJ689154, private). The castle was owned by the Forbes and then the Grants. According to the Grants the basement called Meg's Hole was named after a witch who was later burnt. The Forbes story is that she was the wife of a Forbes laird who, rather than submit to rape at the hands of raiders, impaled herself on a meat hook hanging from the ceiling. Several iron rings on the roof, set next to small stone seats, are supposed to have held prisoners in place while the crows did their work. In reality the rings were for workmen to tie themselves onto while they built the roof in the eighteenth century. A carving of an elephant was placed on the tower by a mason who had seen one on his travels. The most curious story concerns a pair of gargoyles. In the 1980s, when the house was being reharled, the owner Sir Archibald Grant ordered that the heads were not to be removed, as, 'he knew of another house where the owner had seen a huge beast lumbering through the grounds at twilight until their gargoyles were replaced'.

According to the website, the circle of beech trees by the curve of the river at Paradise Woods is a wishing-circle. For the wish to come true you should stand in the centre, look up at the sky – and ensure that you are not observed. You are rationed to one granted wish per year. The topiary hedge to Paradise Cottage garden is marvellously shaped into birds, animals and humans (NJ677177). Pitfichie Castle (NJ67761665, private) used to be haunted by a white apparition in a red nightcap, but, as Alex McConnochie puts it in *Bennachie*, it 'has somehow failed to make its appearance in these modern nights'.

The *Press and Journal* for 14 April 2004 reported that about 115 amphibians were found with their rear legs ripped off at a pond on the Monymusk Estate. Initially this was thought to be a case of animal torture, prompting fears of cultists or cruel children. After an investigation it turned out the culprits were probably otters, which cannot eat toad bodies (the skin is poisonous), but can take the legs for a tasty snack.

CLUNY

The old churchyard (NJ68481257) is dominated by the charming pepper-pot Fraser Mausoleum, with four anti-bodysnatching iron mortsafes spread on the ground before it. McConnochie states that the natural boulder called the Wolf Stone (NJ66131241) in Scare Wood was thrown by Mr Satan at Mrs Satan, but it fell short. The alternative legend, that a wolf had littered there and was killed by a woman throwing a girdle at it, is found at several places in Scotland. The stone may well have been the site of land-courts in the Middle Ages. On 14 January 1995 a 'small lioness' was seen in moonlight near the wood. McPherson's *Primitive Beliefs* gives the case of James Smith, reported to the Aberdeen Synod for 'casting knots at marriages for unlawful ends'. This would have been magical ill-will, intended to foment disharmony in the newly married couple, or prevent them having children

CASTLE FRASER

(National Trust for Scotland. Open 21 March–30 June, Wednesday–Sunday 11 a.m.–5 p.m.; 1 July–31 August, daily 11 a.m.–5 p.m.; 1 September–31 October, Wednesday–Sunday 12 noon–5 p.m. (last admission forty-five minutes before closing). Admission charge, guidebook, very limited wheelchair access. Gardens and grounds open all year, daily. NJ72281256.)

Exterior
Several heraldic panels, plus the *Arma Christi* stone, an angel carrying a shield bearing the five wounds of Christ, an explicitly Catholic piece of iconography that remained untouched after the Reformation.

The Great Hall
A groove indicates the 'Laird's Lug' or Ear, a small chamber secreted into the wall and only accessible from above via a trapdoor. The Romantic notion, largely promoted by Sir Walter Scott, is that it was used by the laird to eavesdrop on his guests as they congregated in the hall. More realistically it was a strongroom for valuables.

The Green Room
It's legend time. A princess was murdered here and her body dragged down the stairs (which princess? When? The children of royalty don't just disappear; someone would have noticed). Bloodstains on both hearth and stairs reappeared, no matter how much they were scrubbed away. The stains have now conveniently vanished. Despite reports of an apparition of a woman in a long black gown, and the sound of ghostly music and voices from the Great Hall, when medium Tom Rannachan visited he picked up no spectral presence.

Grounds
South-east of the castle, the Moses Wellhead has relief panels of the Old Testament prophet communing with Jehovah on Mount Sinai and bringing forth water by striking the rock. 220 yards (200m) north-west of the castle, in a small fenced enclosure is John Bell's Stone (NJ72121272). Long thought to have been erected in 1617 as a tribute to the castle's architect John Bell, it now appears only the small pyramidal stone placed on the top is seventeenth century; the main menhir is prehistoric.

John Michell's *The New View Over Atlantis* claims a ley-line, or at least an alignment, runs from the RSC west of the castle (NJ71501253) through the pair of standing stones close to the road (NJ71741250) and onwards east to the single menhir at Lauchintilly (NJ74971210). The first two monuments can only be visited if the field is not in crop. The massive 10ft 8ins (3.25m) high stone at Woodend of Cluny (NJ71061344) has a flat top, thus encouraging the game of throwing pebbles onto its upper surface.

MIDMAR

One of the more remarkable sights in Aberdeenshire, here a prehistoric stone circle sits in the centre of a landscaped Victorian graveyard next to a late eighteenth-century church (NJ69940649). The whole thing is very tidy, and very odd. The recumbent stone has nineteenth-century graffiti on its upper surface. The kirkyard contains a wonderfully sinuous Tree of Life with a spider, fish, mouse and lizard hiding among the brass and copper roots and branches. The moving and beautiful sculpture by Helen Denerley was set up in tribute to Anne Rochford (d.1991) by her husband Gerard Rochford. One-hundred-and-twenty paces through the woods north of the church brings you to Balblair Standing Stone (NJ69870661).

East along the B9119 is the ruined St Nidan's Kirk, with some good gravestones (NJ70210588). Opposite is Cunninghar motte, the site of a timbered castle (NJ70080596), abandoned by the end of the sixteenth century; traditionally it was built over a house afflicted by the Black Death. Another lovely RSC (NJ71590570) is signposted from Sunhoney Farm on the B9119.

James Stewart's *Deeside Tinkers* gives two sightings of the 'White Lady of Learnie'. On a moonlit night on 15 February 1978 he and his father, camping somewhere near Midmar, saw a strange white figure near a cottage, moving slowly along an old track road.

The recumbent stone and its canine-like flankers of Midmar Kirk RSC, in the centre of the churchyard.

Another view of Midmar Kirk Stone Circle, with gravestones and church.

The Tree of Life stone in memory of Anne Rochford, Midmar Kirk. The image also appears on the cover of Gerard Rochford's book of poetry *The Holy Family and other Poems.*

The tall and phallic Balblair standing stone, just north of the stone circle at Midmar Kirk.

The signpost to the delightful Sunhoney Stone Circle near Midmar.

Another time Jack saw a white-robed and hooded entity, with skeleton hands and face, floating down the road. Learney is north of Torphins (c. NJ6303), some distance from Midmar; it is not clear from the description exactly where the sightings took place.

ECHT

An example of just how dour Presbyterian thinking could be is given in *The Presbytery Book of Strathbogie*. On 4 February 1649 kirk officer James Arthour was punished for singing New Year songs at Hogmanay. He had to make repentance in front of the congregation and agree to refrain from all such 'old superstitious customes of that natour'. The churchyard (NJ73940564) contains an excellent war memorial in the form of a kilted infantryman, as well as the extraordinary monument to Viscount Cowdray (d. 1927).

DUNECHT

In 1881 Dunecht House, one of the grandest of Aberdeenshire's grand mansions, was the centre of an enduring mystery – the Earl's Stolen Body. James Lindsay, Earl of Crawford died at Florence. His body was embalmed and placed Pharaoh-like in three successively larger coffins (of soft wood, lead and polished oak respectively) and then deposited in a walnut shell, the entire contrivance weighing nearly half a ton. Transporting the sarcophagus over the Alps, then across the Channel, and finally to Aberdeen (in a snowstorm, with no hearse big enough to carry the load) was a considerable challenge. The triple coffin was interred in the new mausoleum at Dunecht, a minor fortress in stone. Several months later it was accidentally discovered that the tomb had been rifled and the body was missing. The press had a field day, accusing Florentine bandits, medical students and 'suspicious foreigners'. Alternatively, the earl's body had never left Italy. Two cryptic letters claiming knowledge of the crime were received before and after the discovery, the writer signing himself 'Nabob'.

Not the tomb of a Roman general, but the ostentatious memorial to Viscount Cowdray in Echt churchyard.

One of the gateposts of Dunecht House, topped with a magnificent griffon sitting on a sun. (Photo: Ségolène Dupuy)

After much hue and cry the body was found in a shallow grave a few hundred metres from the house, and a rat catcher and poacher, Charles Soutar, was eventually sentenced to five years' penal servitude for the deed. Soutar had admitted he had met the masked raiding party – two local men and a pair of 'gentlemen' – and had written the letters, but he did not commit the theft. Certainly he could not have broken into the tomb by himself. If the intention of the crime was to obtain a ransom, those involved were singularly inept at this task, with the theft not even being noticed for several months, and no attempt at communication. The whole bizarre episode is covered in William Roughead's *Twelve Scots Trials* (1913). A monument in the grounds is inscribed, 'This cross is erected as a mark of thanksgiving for the recovery of the body of her husband by Margaret Countess of Crawford. Under this spot the body of Alexander Earl of Crawford sacrilegiously stolen from the vault under the Dunecht chapel lay hidden during 14 months'. Dunecht House is private. The gateposts at the north entrance are crowned with magnificent griffons perched atop half-suns.

KIRKTON OF SKENE

The church (NJ80290764) has an iron and stone mortsafe and a few carved gravestones. McPherson's *Primitive Beliefs* relates that a man who had the Horseman's Word crossed the Loch of Skene with a carriage pulled by a pair of horses without sinking an inch in the water. This well-known local story usually describes the water-skimming individual as the Wizard Laird, Alexander Skene of Skene, supposedly deeply versed in the occult arts from studying in Italy, which probably simply meant he'd travelled and read a book or two.

GARLOGIE

Cullerlie Stone Circle, also known as the Standing Stones of Echt (NJ78500428) is cared for by Historic Scotland, with good interpretation on the eight burial cairns built within the oval of stones. The farm next door is called Standingstones.

3

FORMARTINE

ELLON – FYVIE – OLDMEDRUM – TURRIFF

BELHELVIE

The Belhelvie Kirk-Session did not have a good record when investigating charmers. On 3 June 1649 they could not decide if curing someone of the fever with an egg mixed with aqua vitae and pepper meant that Janet Ross had actually performed a charm. In 1676 Isobel Davidson confessed to knowing a person's past or future from their birth month and referring to 'the twelve signs', astrological knowledge she had learned from books. On 15 October, two weeks after her first appearance, it was reported that fear of the church courts had caused Isobel to drown herself. The cases are in *The Presbytery Book of Strathbogie*.

FOVERAN

In April 1597 at Aberdeen, Helen Fraser of Foveran was charged with eighteen points of witchcraft and found guilty on fourteen of them (the full case can be found in *Spalding*). The sentence, inevitably, was death. The range of charges is astonishing, from healing people and animals, casting disease from a horse onto a cow that then died, magically assisting fishermen to increase their catch, to killing cattle, transforming into a hare that sucked on a cow's teats causing it to give blood, and, most seriously, several cases of grievous bodily harm and magical murder. She kept company with the notorious witches Cowper Watson and his spouse Maly Skene, at least one of whom had already been executed, and attempted to recruit others for Satan. Her speciality seemed to be love magic, and there were several examples where men bewitched by Helen had 'unnaturally' fallen for hussies. The most intriguing charge concerned another witch, Janet Ingram, who died raving in great pain with Helen at her bedside. Helen and three of Janet's daughters, including Malye Finnie, another known witch, carried the body halfway to the church, at which point they were interrupted by the 'official' funeral party, and the women fled. What were they intending to do with the corpse?

Foveran church (NJ98492414) has the Turin Stone, a medieval slab incised with two armoured figures, possibly knights who fell at the BATTLE OF HARLAW.

NEWBURGH

There are many tank traps and 1940-era anti-invasion beach furniture on Foveran Links and the sands south. One concrete block, inscribed 'Hitler's Graveyard,' has Churchill looking on as Adolf is targeted by a bomb.

FORVIE

The Forvie National Nature Reserve has 4 miles of dunes. You'd swear you're in the Sahara (sun permitting). This is an elemental landscape, imaginatively powerful, the drifting sands suggesting the revealing of ancient secrets. And indeed Iron Age hut circles and several cairns can be seen (NK01042635, 01082628, 01172657). The tiny ruined Forvie Church (NK02042661) would be of little interest if it were not the sole remnant of a medieval community overblown by sands, possibly in 1413. Such catastrophes attract 'explanatory' stories. In 1570 a Protestant minister, with Scotland still in the struggles of the Reformation, suggested the event was God's wrath in action, punishing the villagers for being ignorant Papists. The more traditional tale is that three sisters were deprived of their inheritance by a ruthless relative, who set them adrift at sea. Their collective curse of revenge ensured the fertile estate would be lost forever.

LOGIE BUCHAN & DENHEAD

In 1596 Gilbert Fidlar of Auchmacoy was said to have put witchcraft into a pair of shoes he made for Lady Errol, causing her to fall sick and die. Lord Errol's kinfolk pursued and eventually imprisoned him in Slains. These events seem to have sparked some kind of inter-family dispute, with Fidlar, his mother-in-law Jonet Leask and Meriorie Mutche being taken to Aberdeen in November 1597 and charged with cursing, killing animals, causing impotency, harming humans by magic, and much more. The accusers were Patrick Cruickshank of Ardiffery and George Cruickshank, who appear not to have impressed the court, because all three accused were found Not Guilty by unanimous verdicts. At a time when witches were being frequently burned in Aberdeen this was an unusual verdict. Both the Cruickshanks and the three released 'witches' were then ordered to leave each other alone.

ELLON

Two UFO reports were logged for Ellon in 2009. The first, at 6.45 a.m. on 5 January, was of a distant object which appeared to be a satellite moving 'down' the sky to the south, except that it 'Turned 180 degrees in a large arc, and went back up'. It then turned again and faded out at the horizon. The anonymous report was on www.ufoinfo.com. The second sighting, on the night of 9 May and reported on STV News on 15 May, was a video of six drifting lights. The television station's weatherman concluded they were Chinese fire lanterns, an increasingly common cause of sightings as people release them at celebrations. The lanterns were seen later the same night at FRASERBURGH. Patrick Gordon's *A Short Abridgement of Britane's Distemper* gives another aerial phenomenon from 1644. Between midnight and 1 a.m. David Leich the preacher saw 'the sune to shine as if it had beene at midday'. He roused his beadle and neighbours, and all attested they had witnessed the phenomenon. Some thought it was a sign of God's displeasure at the Covenanters.

Both Margaret King and Ronald Hay were in trouble for using the sieve and scissors as a divination tool. Margaret absconded but Ronald made repentance in the jougs in sackcloth, barefooted and barelegged on three successive Sundays. Johnne Propter and William Young were arrested for witchcraft in 1626 but we have no further information. In June 1625 a couple asked Thomas Smith in Coldwells, a blacksmith and noted charmer, to heal their sick child. He told them to make a grave under the cradle, cut the cradle belt in nine pieces and bury them with a live cat in the grave. Another time he laid an epileptic child on the anvil and hammered three times around it chanting, 'Either pair [get worse] or mend, in the name of the Father, Son and Holy Ghost, in God's name.' All these cases are in McPherson's *Primitive Beliefs*. William Littlejohn, in *Stories of the Buchan Cottars*, tells of superstition-sceptical George

Milne, whose sister secretly hid a bannock below his pillow, along with a name written on paper. That night he dreamt of a good-looking woman shaking her head at him, and soon after he recognised her at church. They were married within the year; her name was the one on the paper. The Canmore website records that a collection sold in 1889 from Ellon had, 'Three naturally perforated flint pebbles, having been used as amulets'.

The Candle Stone (NJ921348) is a 10ft (3.1m) high menhir.

UDNY GREEN

In 1898 the *Journal of the Society for Psychical Research* had an account from Miss Henrietta Knight, who had been staying at Udny Castle. At 3.07 a.m. on 18 April 1897 she was woken by a gentle rocking, a shimmering light, and a sense of someone hovering over her. She realised she was being visited by a dying person; when she thought of her nurse, Med, there was a loud rap by the head of the bed. A little later there was a light all round her: 'It was a silvery radiance, and as it passed away flashes of gold and gold stars fell.' The whole experience was very positive. Thirty minutes later she awoke trying to remove insects from her head and neck, a dream phenomenon Med had always said indicated death. The next evening, after a day's travelling, she received a telegram at Lytham St Anne's, Lancashire, telling her that Med had died. When Miss Knight finally arrived at her home in Malvern Wells, she discovered that the nurse had spent the last day of her life constantly saying she wished to see Henrietta, to whom she had a great emotional attachment; she expired at seven minutes past three.

The parish church (NJ880262) has a unique circular morthouse. Coffins were placed on a revolving wooden carousel, the platform being turned each time a new arrival appeared. By the time the full circuit had been completed, so many days had passed the corpse was of no use to the bodysnatchers. It was then buried as normal.

TOLQUHON CASTLE

(Historic Scotland. Open 1 April–30 September, daily 9.30 a.m.–5.30 p.m. Winter, weekends only 9.30 a.m.–4.30 p.m. Admission charge, guidebook, some disabled access. NJ873286.)

Roofless, picturesque and decorated with the occasional figure and heraldic panel, Tolquhon has an agreeable atmosphere. However the *News of the World* (3 September 2000) reported it was haunted by a slim young woman in a long dress standing at the top of the stairs, who had apparently upset some visitors. Other phenomena included footsteps and the sound of humming. Custodian Lynn Laughton was quoted as saying that her on-site house also had strange occurrences, such as insistent banging at the kitchen window as if something was trying to come in. When a new custodian, Dawn Green, took up residence, the newspaper ran another story (16 March 2003) with suspiciously similar content. The 'grey lady,' footsteps and banging were all mentioned again, with the addition of bright lights seen on the inside of the living room window, and electrical devices switching on and off.

TARVES

The churchyard houses the Tolquhon Tomb under its protective Historic Scotland greenhouse (NJ86913118). Splendidly carved with a mixture of Gothic and Renaissance motifs, it sports boars, unicorns, foxes, symbols of mortality, and figures of William Forbes and his wife Elizabeth Gordon in sixteenth-century costume. Four gravestones stand nearby. From the car park east of the village you can walk south to the lovely South Ythsie Stone Circle (NJ88493039) and north to the Prop of Ythsie (NJ88433147), a monument to the 4th Earl of Aberdeen which looks like nothing less than a chess piece (a rook) plonked on the hill. Perhaps all the monuments on Aberdeenshire summits are simply the gods playing a landscape-spanning game of chess.

HADDO HOUSE

(National Trust for Scotland. House only open to pre-booked tours April–October. Call 0844 4932179 for times and booking. Admission charge. Good disabled access. Garden and country park open daily.)

More of an English stately home than a Scottish castle, this Adam house apparently has a resident ghost in the form of Lord Archibald Gordon (d. 1909), one of the first people in Britain to die in a car accident.

METHLICK

Several 'earth mysteries' websites have the unpublished work *Dowsing for Patterns of the Past – The Stone Circles of Aberdeenshire* by the Revd Angus H. Haddow, although it seems to come and go. In 1994 (or 1996 – the text varies) Haddow was asked to investigate poltergeist activity in a croft near Methlick. Phenomena included objects moving, a vague figure, the sense of a malign presence, bad atmospheres, and a point in the garden which generated fear. The occupants were in great distress. Haddow considered that part of the problem was psychological – there was a suicide in the recent history and evident tensions within the family. He counselled them, held prayer sessions, and blessed the 'bad' rooms. But there seemed to be an environmental factor as well. He and another dowser discovered a complex pattern of invisible grids and circles, with the centre of one circle being the poltergeist's favourite spot. There, unfortunately, the Methlick case breaks off, the rest of the work being concerned with dowsing various ancient sites.

The former Gight House Hotel is supposedly haunted by the Revd John Mennie (d. 1886 – the building was originally a manse). Reported phenomena include apparitions, footsteps and a door locked from the inside.

GIGHT

Ruined, romantic and risky to explore, Gight Castle (NJ82653920) was the ancestral home of the Gordons of Gight, a clutch of vipers and scorpions of abiding unpleasantness. After 300 years of Gordon occupation the last laird, Catherine, sold the castle to pay off the gambling debts of her wayward husband John Byron; their son was the poet Lord Byron. In *Buchan* (1858) John Pratt recorded three prophecies, all attributed, as such prophecies almost inevitably are, to Thomas the Rhymer:

> Twa men sat down on Ythan brae,
> The ane did to the ither say,
> An' what sic [such] men may the Gordons o' Gight hae been?

In other words, at some point in the future the once almighty tribe would be beyond remembering. The second runs:

> When the heron leaves the tree,
> The Laird o' Gight shall landless be.

This was said to be fulfilled when the inhabitants of a heronry in a tree close to the house quit the area on 12 May 1785, the date when Catharine Gordon the heiress married John Byron the asset-stripper; the estate had to be sold two years later. The third prophecy runs:

> At Gight three men a violent death shall dee,
> An' after that the land shall lie in lea.

The new owner, Lord Aberdeen, passed it to his son Lord Haddo, who fell off his horse and died in 1791, a fate shared later by a servant at the Mains or Home Farm. Prior to the arable land being turned into lea (meadow), one of the men demolishing the castle remarked that the prophecy had failed; within an hour a falling wall crushed him to death. Or so the story runs.

Pratt also records the tradition of a secret passage. Well, it wouldn't be a proper castle if it didn't have one of those. Even better, it has that standard of Scottish folklore, a piper who was sentenced to walk down it, his pipes being heard until he reached the burn of Stonehouse of Gight … and then, silence. The notion received a boost when a subterranean passage was uncovered in 1869 near Little Gight, 1,300 yards (1.2km) north-east (NJ839399). Sadly for the legend this turned out to be an Iron Age souterrain.

The easiest way to reach the castle is to walk south-west from the Forestry Commission car park on the B95005, through Badiebath Wood. If you carry on and branch left to the river you come to Hagberry Pot bridge. The pot or pool, supposedly bottomless (actually 12ft (3.6m) deep), is where the Gordons sunk the family plate and the great iron yet (gate) while the Covenanting army occupied the area. When the troubles had subsided a diver was sent down to recover the treasure (from a bottomless pool … errr …). He promptly surfaced saying he had seen the stash but, unfortunately, the Devil had nabbed it. Rewards and punishment were offered the diver, and eventually he returned to the depths. The watchers waited, only to recoil when what bobbed to the surface were the man's heart and lungs. The diabolic tale is in Gregor's *Notes on the Folk-Lore of the North-East of Scotland*. The slopes on the south side of the river rejoice in the names of Carlins' Craig (carlin being a name for a witch) and Craig Horror.

WOODHEAD

In *The Road to Drumnafunner* Robert Smith dug up 'The Grisly Ghost of Bairnsdale', an old ballad sent to *Scottish Notes and Queries* by Dr Nicol of Alford in December 1872. In it, the widow at Bairnsdale, between Woodhead and Fyvie, is much troubled by the ghost, so eventually a search party explores the Den of Dennilair and finds the shallow grave where a murdered man is buried. When he is interred in holy ground the hauntings cease. All Saints Episcopal Church in Woodhead (NJ790385) incorporates several bits and pieces from the Priory at FYVIE, including three crosses, a stone inscribed IHS (the monogram for Jesus Christ), and a carved quiver full of arrows.

FYVIE

Embedded in the east wall of St Peter's Church (NJ76853775) are three worn Pictish stones and a fragment of a cross shaft. Many visitors come to see the grave of 'Mill of Tifty's Annie'; Annie (Agnes Smith) features in a well-known eponymous ballad in which her father, the wealthy miller, forbids her to see her lover, a lowly trumpeter, with the usual fatal consequences incumbent on a tragic ballad. Much more interesting are a series of Victorian and Edwardian monuments featuring a phoenix, the Worm Ouroborus (the snake that bites its own tail, a symbol of eternity), a miniscule dragon and a superb set of military accoutrements. Somewhere

The winged Archangel Michael carrying a sword and the Banner of the Cross. The stained glass window was designed by L.C. Tiffany in memory of Percy Forbes-Leith, Fyvie church.

Percy Forbes-Leith's gravestone, Fyvie church. He died in the Boer War.

among the graves is buried (under an incorrect name) Francis Lathom (1774-1832), an eccentric and now-forgotten Gothic novelist whose works, such as *The Castle of Ollada* and *Astonishment!!!*, once shivered the spines of the novel-reading classes. *The Midnight Bell* is one of the novels mentioned in Jane Austen's famous satire on Gothic excesses, *Northanger Abbey*. So forgotten was Lathom that for years it was thought Austen had simply invented the book. Inside the church (which has very limited opening hours) is the astonishing stained-glass window by Louis Comfort Tiffany of the Archangel Michael. This is one of the great sights of Aberdeenshire. The Forbes loft has wooden carvings of winged souls, and there are stained glass windows of a saint killing a dragon and of a snake on a cross with the inscription, 'By Faith Moses lifted up the serpent in the wilderness'. On the south edge of the village is a nineteenth-century cross (NJ76493777) marking the site of the former medieval priory.

Jonet Wishert seems to have been an argumentative and unpleasant individual whose personality attracted many accusations of witchcraft. Typical is the case of the wife of David Hutcheon, a gardener working at Fyvie Wells. She called Jonet a witch, so Jonet cursed her, leading to her pregnancy being twenty days late. Only when she asked Jonet for forgiveness was the child delivered, but it was stillborn. Jonet reduced a man to beggary, spoiled a brew of ale, assisted in the death of one child, and poisoned a second one when her offer to wet nurse it was refused. Jonet was burnt at Aberdeen on 17 February 1597. A month later her husband John Leyis and daughters Elspet, Janet and Violet Leyis were all banished, and her son Thomas burnt. The details are in *Spalding*.

On 5 December 1650 Gavin Sinclair showed the Presbytery of Turriff a stone brought from Ireland which had 'an secret vertue in it to cure beasts of the quarter evil, and being layd in the fold gate, it would preserve such beasts as went over it … and being put thryse about the neck of the beast infected it would cure it'. The quarter evil is also called black leg or blackquarter, a fatal condition of cattle. In 1651 a Fyvie farmer looking to cure his herd of the disease buried an ox alive. All these cases are in McPherson's *Primitive Beliefs*.

In the 1720s, servant Donald McQueen procured 'the tempting cheese o' Fyvie', a love charm so powerful it enchanted his mistress, Lizzie Menzie, the Lady of Fyvie, into falling in love with him. The past truly is a foreign country if people once found love through a bit of old cheese.

FYVIE CASTLE

(National Trust for Scotland. Castle: 21 March-30 June and 1 September-31 October, Saturday-Wednesday 12 noon-5 p.m.; 1 July-31 August, daily 11 a.m.-5 p.m. Admission charge, guidebook, poor wheelchair access. Garden: all year, daily 9 a.m.-sunset. Grounds: all year, daily.)

The chief attractions of Fyvie Castle are archaeological, historical, legendary and romantic …
The Times 5 February 1885, quoted in the Guidebook.

Exterior
The towers are topped with finials in the shape of huntsmen, musicians, bowls players, and bears.

Entrance Hall
Fireplace with foliaceous dragons, cherubs, lion heads, and a relief marble carving of a medieval battle. Monstrous heads on the curtain rails.

Great Stair
Statue of 'Sir' Geoffrey Hudson, Queen Henrietta Maria's dwarf, with arquebus, armour and a helmet topped by a sphinx.

Fyvie Castle.

The musician on the east tower of Fyvie Castle supposedly represents the laird's trumpeter, Andrew Lammie, forever blowing towards the Mill of Tifty, home of his doomed lady-love Annie.

Among the vast number of heraldic
panels, crescent moons, inscriptions
and crowns that adorn Fyvie Castle is
this eroded enigmatic figure apparently
hiding its face. It is probably a fragment
of a large sculpture.

The skirl of the bagpipes. A finial figure at Fyvie.

Morning Room
The carved plaster ceiling of 1683 has six bewigged and two bald heads spewing vegetation,
and two winged souls.

Library
Five phrenological heads made in Edinburgh in 1824, all cast from death. Flanked by 'Boy,'
'Girl,' 'Lady' and 'Gentleman' is John Pallet, hanged in Colchester in December 1823 for the
murder of James Mumford. If you look closely you can see the rope mark. Phrenology was a
pseudo-scientific fad that sought to establish a person's personality and intellect from the shape
of their head. A report on Pallet's head in the *Phrenological Journal* states: 'a moment's inspection
of the cast now before us will satisfy even the most incredulous as to the striking resemblance
which it bears to the worst specimens of that class of criminals to which he belongs.'

The Charter Room
Suitably panelled with grotesque wooden figures of St Michael trouncing Satan, this is the
heart of the castle's legendary lore. Beneath the floor is a cursed secret room; opening it will
cause the death of the laird and the blindness of his wife. Two lairds, it is said, explored it, both
died, and their respective spouses suffered eye problems, one going blind. In a basin is the
Weeping Stone, physical 'proof' of a curse pronounced by Thomas the Rhymer. When the seer
arrived at Fyvie a great storm slammed the gates in his face, although no wind disturbed the
grass where he stood. Two versions survive of what he said next. Robert Chambers' *Popular
Rhymes of Scotland* (1841) has:

Fyvie, Fyvie, thou'se never thrive,
As lang's there's in thee stanes three:

There's ane intill the highest tower,
There's ane intill the ladye's bower,
There's ane aneath the water-yett.
And thir three stanes ye'se never get.

John Pratt's *Buchan* has a slightly different version:

Fyvyn's riggs and towers,
Hapless shall your Mesdames be,
When ye shall hae within your methes [boundaries],
From harryit kirk's land, stanes three –
Ane in Preston's tower;
Ane in my lady's bower;
And ane below the water-yett,
And it ye shall never get.

The standard interpretation is that the three stones were church boundary markers removed by a laird so he could annex 'kirk's land'. One is supposedly in the fabric of the oldest tower, one is 'below the water-yett' or gate, and hence unreachable, and the third, once in 'my lady's bower', is the crumbling specimen in the Charter Room. Apparently it has 'wept' periodically, filling the basin with water, thus accounting for its current resemblance to a cake made of dust. The Rhymer's curse is supposed to prevent Fyvie being passed from father to eldest son, which it has singularly failed to do.

Drummond Room
Time for a ghost story. In 1601 Dame Lilias Drummond, first wife of Alexander Seton, died from a) an illness, b) a broken heart;, or c) being starved to death by her husband for not producing a male heir (guess which option is preferred in the story?). The laird quickly married attractive young Grizel Leslie. On their wedding night Alexander and his trophy wife heard mournful sighing outside their second floor chamber window. In the morning they found words carved upside down on the outside sill: D LILIES DRUMMOND. As the guidebook gently puts it, 'this story will not bear scrutiny from either an architectural historian or a genealogist'. The original inscription has long since faded, but in the spirit of, if not the manufacture of tradition, then at least the maintenance of it, a replacement sits in its place. Dame Lilias, aka the Green Lady, allegedly haunts the castle to this day. Sue Coburn's *Fyvie Castle Unexplained* (2006) musters an impressive casebook of eye-witness accounts, mostly from staff and visitors before the castle was open to the public, of phenomena throughout the castle, including: apparitions of several different female figures; sounds of a baby crying, footsteps, and voices, including a man and woman arguing; interference with electrical items and lights, and power drains on batteries; doors locking themselves; dogs being scared by something invisible to the human eye (possibly the ghost cat reported from several quarters); strange luminescence at night; objects going missing or being rearranged; small items flying into the air and smashing; phone calls from unoccupied rooms; and the fragrance of Attar of Roses, long associated with the Green Lady.

Gordon Bedroom
Engraving of Queen Maria with her dwarf, 'Sir' Geoffrey Hudson, whose statue is on the Great Stair.

Dunfermline Passage
Tapestry of Samson battling the Philistines, filled with remarkably bloody eye-gouging mayhem.

Top of Great Stair
A circlet of edged weapons supported on boars' tusks.

Douglas Room
Also known as the Murder Room. A.M.W. Stirling's formidable *Fyvie Castle, Its Lairds and their Times* (1928) mentions the tradition that here a laird's wife (possibly 'one of the ladies Dunfermline') was starved to death; when her kinsmen attempted a rescue they were killed in front of her and dumped out of the window. In July 2004 a reality television show, *I'm Famous and Frightened*, placed several celebrities in this and other rooms and attempted to 'make contact' with the Other Side.

Gallery
Leaf table decorated with sea monsters, birds, and horned satyr heads spewing vegetation. Fireplace carved with foliaceous humans, winged heads, griffons, sea monsters and human-dolphin hybrids. Strange and impressive firedogs with grotesque faces supported on tortoises.

TOWIE

Pratt's *Buchan* gives the legend of Towie Barclay Castle (NJ74434394, private). Through nefarious practices the Barclays acquired and pillaged a nunnery, causing Thomas the Rhymer (yes, him again) to proclaim: 'Towie Barclay of the Glen/Happy to the maids/But never to the men.' This was taken as a curse on the male line, with the heir not surviving his father. This belief was so strong that in 1753 it prompted the Barclays to sell off the estate to the Earl of Findlater, who passed it on to his second son. Just as the boy came of age he died, a further verification of the curse. Thereafter whenever Lord Findlater passed through the estate he closed the blinds of his carriage.

A copy of the winged lion of St Mark, on the south wall of the Playhouse at Fyvie Castle. The book reads PAX TIBI MARCE EVANGELISTA MEUS ('Peace to you, Mark my Evangelist'). The message was supposedly given to Mark by an angel.

Other antique marble fragments on the Playhouse include flying heads, animals, birds and, here, a pair of dragons.

TURRIFF

The roofless St Congan's Church (NJ72234983) off Castle Street, has, among the usual heraldry and symbols of mortality, a face on a sunburst, a fragment of religious carving with a bishop(?) presiding over an arc of nine heads, and the double graves of John Westwood Hay of DELGATIE CASTLE ('Soldier Farmer Engineer and Scottish Patriot') and his wife Everild, both carved with a profusion of modern symbols reflecting their interests and occupations.

In 1647 Andrew Hogs confessed that, with five other men, 'on the Lord's Day he had drunken the Devil's good health at the Cross of Turriff'. This may have been an early 'Hellfire Club', where rebellious young men of good families got drunk and mocked religious conventions. (Source: Peter Anson's *Fisher Folk-Lore*.) In *A United Parish* (2001) Margaret and Bill McKay claim that at Marnonwells on the A947 north of Turriff (NJ739521) the sick were cured by drinking the water in which the skull of St Marnan or Marnoch was washed every Sunday. This story of Marnoch's head or skull relic is attached to several sites in Banffshire and Moray. Another well-travelled tale is attached to the Eigre's or Ogre's Howe or Grave somewhere between Turriff and Towie Barclay. The tradition, as given in Pratt's *Buchan*, is that a boundary dispute arose in the seventeenth century. The oldest tenant of the district, known as the Eigre, was asked to adjudicate on oath. Clearly bribed by one laird, he put earth from each estate into his shoes, encroached deep into one property and swore he had a foot on each of the lairds' lands. The other laird promptly ran him through with a sword, saying, 'Then let you and your master, the foul fiend, be the wardens of your march till doomsday'.

DELGATIE CASTLE

(Open daily all year, 10 a.m.–5 p.m., except Christmas and New Year period. Admission charge. Poor disabled access. NJ755506.)

Is this the most enjoyable castle in Aberdeenshire? If it is, it is largely due to the lingering presence of Captain John Hay (1906-1997), a permanently kilted and highly vital individual

Remembering death at St Congan's Church, Turriff.

who combined practicality with a distinct eccentricity. This was his home and everywhere he has left notes for the visitor – deeply politically-incorrect jottings filled with antiquarian ramblings, legendary lore, personal reminiscences, clan prejudices, old-school colonial attitudes (for example, to big game hunting), and jokes. Lots of jokes.

A good example of the captain's style is the story of the castle's ghost. In 1594 Protestant forces loyal to James VI besieged the castle, which was ably defended by a 6ft nineteen-year-old redhead called Rohaise (pronounced 'Rohaisha'). After six weeks the cannon fire finally demolished the west wall and the invaders poured in, only to find Rohaise and the Catholic garrison had escaped along a secret tunnel to CRAIGSTON CASTLE – 3 miles (5km) away! – from where they skipped to France. Rohaise now haunts the castle, although she only appears to male guests. The siege was real, and the Hays did go into exile in France, but I detect the good captain's hand in much of the rest. With little supporting documentation this story has been extensively recycled in print and online, partly because I suspect many men find the idea of a strapping 6ft redheaded Amazon quite fetching.

Exterior
Captain Hay had eclectic antiquarian tastes and the courtyard is a stramash of curiosities in stone – leopards, unicorns (rescued from the roof of the *Scotsman* building in Edinburgh), cannonballs, heraldic plaques, grotesque faces, dolphins, dogs, gravestones, religious structures and a dovecot. There are cannons at the gate and gargoyles on the parapet. The cobbles in the courtyard tell their own personal story, being filled with designs instigated by 'Jock' and his English wife Eve (their names are in the concrete). Among the symbols are a thistle, the Rose of England, the Lion Rampant of Scotland, a heart, and a multi-pointed Masonic star.

Front hall
Three replicas of ox-yokes. The Hays' entirely mythical founding legend is that they were granted their lands when their ancestor defeated a Viking army at the Battle of Luncarty in Perthshire, armed with just an ox-yoke.

The Mannie Stone, a dwarfish
caricatured human figure, one of the
many sculptures at Delgatie Castle.

'Best Foot Forward' – a giant foot
pointing towards the gate in the
cobbles at Delgatie Castle.

The multi-pointed star, symbol of Freemasonry, set into the cobbles at Delgatie Castle.

Chapel
Stone figure of a bishop in a niche and a female saint standing on a human-headed serpent.

Stair
Just before the first floor, a mischievous smiling face carved by the captain.

Solar
Two carved male heads, a female winged head, and a mason's apprentice carrying a stone, presumably a Masonic reference. Over the fireplace is the inscription, '1570 My Hope is in Ye Lord'.

Ballroom
Pair of excellent brass griffons on the fire fender.

Tulip Room
This is the first of three rooms with painted ceilings. Here the decoration consists of wise saws from a book of Scottish proverbs, such as 'Put hoipe in god & for no wraike take feir, For rwit of all evill is gredines of geir [money]'.

Second painted ceiling room
This is 'Rohaise's Room'. Here the ceiling decoration is astonishingly florid – human-headed foliaceous monsters, grotesque faces, female sphinxes with sagging breasts, dragon-headed snakes, dogs, elephants (probably a pun on the Oliphant family name), a triple-headed figure (possibly the three Wise Men), a cartoon-like stag, and a merman playing a stringed instrument. Some of the faces may have been contemporary portraits. The proverbs on the ceiling beams are taken from *The Treatise of Moral Philosophie Contayning the Sayings of the Wyse* by Thomas Paulfreyman (1547).

Marie's Bower
This room, where Mary Queen of Scots once stayed, has text painted on the ceiling from a poem by James Hogg called 'Kilmeny'. This is part of *The Queen's Wake* (1813), the conceit of

which is that all the poets and bards of Scotland supposedly assemble at Holyrood Palace to hold a competition (a 'wake') to celebrate the return of Mary from France in 1561. Each of the poems has an individual topic and 'voice', allowing Hogg to demonstrate his ability to write in various styles. 'Kilmeny' is the tale of the eponymous innocent girl who is transported to fairyland, where she sees episodes from the history of Scotland, including an allegorical vision of Mary. In the version that follows, the lines in italics are missing from the beams at Delgatie – or perhaps they have faded or been painted over:

> She saw a lady sit on a throne,
> The fairest that ever the sun shone on!
> A lion lick'd her hand of milk,
> And she held him in a leish of silk;
> *And a leifu' maiden stood at her knee,*
> *With a silver wand and melting e'e;*
> *Her sovereign shield till love stole in,*
> *And poison'd all the fount within.*
>
> Then a gruff untoward bedesman came,
> And hundit the lion on his dame;
> *And the guardian maid wi' the dauntless e'e,*
> *She dropp'd a tear, and left her knee;*
> *And she saw till the queen frae the lion fled,*
> Till the bonniest flower of the world lay dead.

The 'leifu' maiden' and 'guardian maid' appear to be Mary's guardian angel. The lion is Scotland. The 'love' who 'poison'd all the fount within' is Darnley. The 'gruff untoward bedesman' is John Knox.

Attock Fort

An attic room named after Captain Hay's last command in Afghanistan. Hay carved the strange corbels himself; their subjects include an elephant with shell tusks, a demon with fangs and horns of shell, and a devil holding a kneeling naked woman.

Library

In the early part of the twentieth century the castle was owned by the Ainslie Grant-Duff family, who in just one generation managed to produce individuals with the surnames Ainslie, Grant-Duff, Ainslie-Grant-Duff and Grant-Duff-Ainslie. Rachel Ainslie Grant-Duff dreamed of something hidden behind the wall of an alcove in this room. When it was opened up a body was found, which crumbled to dust, apparently leaving just a shinbone chained to the wall. The belief was this was Father Joseph (or Andrew) Hay, a Catholic priest secretly retained by the family after 1597 (when they had promised to be good Protestants). The surmise was that when the monk died he was walled up in the closet to prevent his discovery. Once the body had been discovered Father Hay became something of a nuisance, so eventually the Episcopal minister from St Luke's in Cuminestown was brought in to exorcise the spirit. The place where the discovery was made is probably the alcove within the wall to the right of the door. It was always thought Rachel undertook the excavation with permission but in 2008 Joan Johnson, the custodian of the trust that runs the castle, was told by a distant descendant that Rachel had waited until her parents were at church and then got a workman to depoint the wall. An artist of the 'Celtic Twilight' school, Rachel painted the illustrations for Winifred Parker's *Gaelic Fairy Tales* (1907) and J.F. Campbell's *The Celtic Dragon Myth* (1911), and copied the main Delgatie ceiling for A.W. Lyons when he contributed an article to the *Society of Antiquaries of Scotland* in 1910. In the article Lyons

Female andro-form sphinxes on the painted ceiling in 'Rohaise's room', Delgatie Castle.
(Photo reproduced with permission of Trustees of Delgatie Castle)

Delgatie Castle: two of the many grotesque figures painted on the ceiling in 'Rohaise's
room'. (Photo reproduced with permission of Trustees of Delgatie Castle)

mentioned a tradition that a 'mad woman' had burned the castle records, and that ten years
previously a quantity of charred parchments had been found in a turret.

KIRK OF AUCHTERLESS

A parish of human superlatives. The *NSA* recorded that farmer Peter Garden died in *c.* 1780
aged 132. Lucid to the last, he married his second wife when he was 120 and she was a mere 80,
and 'he danced with great glee on that occasion'. He lived under ten sovereigns from Charles

I to George III. On 29 October 2003 the *Daily Record* reported that of the sixty-six pupils at the primary school, twelve were twins. The six sets of twins were a record for a Scottish school.

In the seventeenth-century 'superstitious' health pilgrimages were being undertaken to St Mary's (or Chapel) Well at Chapel of Seggat (NJ71374159) so the church took action. In 1649 the Presbytery of Turriff filled the holy well with stones. The following morning the stones had been removed. The process was repeated several times until finally in 1653 the authorities simply gave up. The well continued to be venerated: in 1842 the *NSA* recorded that the old people remembered drinking the water after Palm Sunday and leaving money and other items behind. The well is currently dry, a stone-lined cavity hidden in vegetation below the farm.

When the farmer took the stones of the Mains of Hatton RSC (NJ69934254) and used them for gateposts, the horses would not pass through the gate. Accidents also took place. Eventually the stones were replaced – the task only requiring one horse uphill, while removing them down the slope had needed two horses. The stones of Corrydown RSC (NJ70684446), earmarked for building materials, proved harder to work than anticipated and the mason hurt his fingers. After reconsideration it was agreed to let well alone and the search for alternative, non-sacrilegious, stones proceeded without further difficulties. This is all in McPherson's *Primitive Beliefs*.

CROSS OF JACKSON

In 1738 John Alan of Speymouth in Moray came here to consult William Angus about the theft of goods to the value of £16 10s. Angus was well known as a 'wise man' whose supposed occult skills helped solve such problems around Fyvie (largely through having a network of local gossip and knowledge). Not surprisingly he was unable to help Alan, whose home was beyond his information horizon.

Mackinlay's *Folklore of Scottish Lochs and Springs* (1893) describes how mothers of sickly children would pass them under the Shargar Stone, apparently a remnant of an old church raised off the ground by two other blocks.

DAVIOT

The excellent Loanhead of Daviot RSC (NJ74772885) is cared for by Historic Scotland, so has easy access and good interpretation. Popular with dowsers.

OLDMELDRUM

> Capt: 'I wish some one would go for that ould wizard, Adam Donald, prophet of Bethelnie … He can make the stars whirl round as easily as a child would do his whirly-gig, by a nod of his head or a tramp of his foot, and make the sun and the moon hide their heads in darkness.'
>
> Will: 'Then shall I go on this midnight errand. I long to see a man that can keep the waves of the ocean in awe, and make the wind blow as he listeth. [Aside.] Poor deluded mortal, thy superstition is unconquerable.'
>
> Peter Buchan,
> *The Peterhead Smugglers of the Last Century* (1834)

The famous healer and seer Adam Donald was supposed to be a fairy changeling who obtained his occult knowledge from conversing with the dead in an old churchyard (presumably the overgrown Auldkirk, NJ78653127, the site of the parish church until 1684). Born in

1703, he was lucky to have lived in a time when most witch persecutions had ceased, and he happily plied his trade as cow doctor, fortune-teller and manufacturer of charms to heal broken limbs and broken hearts. His standard fee was sixpence and his fame widespread. In 1737 Robert Innes from Speymouth undertook the long journey to Oldmeldrum to consult with Donald about some stolen goods (Innes was investigated by his Kirk-Session). The first printed account of Donald appeared in *The Bee* in 1791, ten years after his death. The author, James Anderson, claimed Donald had told him most of his powers were an act, enhanced by owning an impressive library of books in several languages, none of which he could read (more importantly, his credulous neighbours could not read them either). Anderson concluded that Donald's numerous physical infirmities, by denying him the possibility of undertaking agricultural labour, had caused him to seek an alternative way of earning a living. His natural cunning, ability to listen closely and his word-of-mouth reputation did the rest. Donald's posthumous reputation also soared in the retelling, so by the time Peter Buchan came to write his play in 1834 the 'Prophet of Bethelnie' was the local equivalent of Merlin or Prospero.

The *Sunday Post* for 7 May 1978 reported that Madge Hislop and her family moved out of their house after only nine months residence partly because of the ghostly footsteps, violin music, and faces at the window, but mostly because once when Madge was sleeping alone the room went cold, there was a smell of roses, a voice called 'Marjory' three times … and something started to choke her. When she put the light on there were red marks on her neck.

A portrait of 'Doctor'
Adam Donald, the
'Prophet of Bethelnie'.
From *The Bee*, 1791.

Meldrum House Hotel is supposedly haunted by the White Lady, possibly Isabella Douglas, whose portrait hangs above the fireplace in the reception area, although, as always with hotels that make something of their ghosts, it is hard to decide what is authentic.

'Satan gran's coven is a cauldron of sin' screamed the headline in the *News of the World* for 27 October 1996. The report was an old-fashioned sex-and-sorcery exposé, a long-standing speciality of the paper. 'Devil worshippers … vile rituals … black magic … weird ceremonies … mind-blowing orgies at which devotees call up underworld spirits.' Undercover reporters had 'infiltrated' a witch coven in Oldmeldrum run by a respectable grandmother and found … people performing harmless pagan rituals with their clothes off. Oh, the horror.

The Oldmeldrum Golf Club website carries the following warning: 'Look out on the 14th fairway for the Groaner or Groaning Stone … If struck by a wayward shot, it can cost strokes by deflecting a speeding ball straight into oblivion.' The hazard, also known as the Grenago or Girnigoe Stone (NJ822276) is probably a glacial erratic. In one of the stupidest derivations for a place name ever, it is said that after John Comyn, Earl of Buchan, was defeated by Robert the Bruce at the Battle of Barra in 1307, he was so disheartened he lay beside the stone crying and groaning. The site of the battle, north of North Mains of Barra, is still called the Bruce Field (NJ79712673). A signposted path runs from near here to the Iron Age hillfort of Hill of Barra (NJ80252570). The huge boulder on the summit is 'Wallace's Putting Stone,' thrown by William Wallace from Bennachie. (The 'giants' of Scottish history – Bruce, Wallace, Macbeth – occasionally turn up in folklore as, well, Giants.)

KIRKTON OF BOURTIE

The Hill of Barra footpath continues down to this hamlet, where the church (NJ80452485) has a Pictish stone on the south wall and a simple incised cross in the kirkyard wall. The nearby Piper's Stone (NJ80552495) is a glacial erratic on which stood the piper at weddings, and the Bell Stone is where the church hand-bell was kept. The RSC to the west (NJ80092488) has an enormous recumbent.

COTHALL

The roofless St Meddan's Church (NJ87191556) has a crucifixion scene and several excellent medieval gravestones with equal-armed crosses, swords, shears, an enigmatic rectangle divided into six squares, and two very strange cross-marked circles with four 'handles'. A lovely and puzzling site.

4

BUCHAN

KIRKTOWN OF SLAINS AND COLLIESTON

Slains was one of the first places to stoke the witchcraft fires of 1597, with investigations and executions starting in January. Ellen (or Helene) Gray was found guilty on six points, including: spoiling or stealing milk from several people; reducing Johne Hay to poverty by cursing; appearing in William Chalmers' house in the likeness of a dog; transforming into a dog in the company of another witch, Mergie, who became a cat; conversing with Satan, who appeared in the form of a bearded man in a white gown when she was imprisoned in Slains; and giving Thomas Reddell a permanent erection, which caused his death. She was executed in Aberdeen on 27 April, two weeks after another witch, Nellie Pennie, had been burned at Slains.

In 1649 the church identified a field on the farm of Brogan 'dedicated to Satane'. The reprimanded farmer promised to plough the 'Goodman's land.' In 1658 Janet Edmond, accused of charming, started to repeat the words she had used to cure John Symson: 'The Lord God spake it with his own mouth, and commanded me in his own name to oration for the head fevers and the heart fevers, for the livers and the light fevers.' At this point she noticed the clerk was writing down what she said, and promptly shut up. (Maxwell-Stuart, *An Abundance of Witches*.)

CRUDEN BAY

> … And then, *mirabile dictu*, between the piers, leaping from wave to wave as it rushed at headlong speed, swept the strange schooner before the blast, with all sail set, and gained the safety of the harbour. The searchlight followed her, and a shudder ran through all who saw her, for lashed to the helm was a corpse, with drooping head, which swung horribly to and fro at each motion of the ship.
>
> Bram Stoker,
> *Dracula* (1897)

This is how the doomed ship carrying the world's most infamous vampire arrives at Whitby. But in the early drafts of the novel the count touched British soil for the first time at Cruden Bay. Stoker, holidaying in the area for several years, found his imagination stimulated by the dramatic cliff top location of Slains Castle (NK102361). *Schloss Dracula* was born. When Stoker saw Slains it was a grand, sprawling mansion. These days it is a grand, sprawling ruin, a medley of smashed corridors, roofless rooms and gaping holes that open onto precipitous rock faces, next stop the raging waves below. Explore, as they say, at your peril. The most direct way is via a rough track that leaves from the end of Castle Road; there is also an equally rugged route from the car park on the A975 further east (NK10213700). There are plans, current since at least 2007, to convert the castle into holiday homes.

Writing in the *Transactions of the Buchan Field Club* in 1979 B. Henderson noted a tradition of a secret passage from the castle to a nearby farm, built as a precaution against a siege when Slains was first constructed in 1597. The passage was said to connect with a 'Smuggler's Cave' in the Long Haven sea-cleft below the castle. The key word here is *tradition*.

In his book *Psychic Scotland*, medium Tom Rannachan recorded reports that apparitions of marching soldiers and a horse and carriage had been seen near the castle. He himself made contact with a young girl from the seventeenth century and two men from the Victorian era.

In 1994 Stuart Nicol was murdered at his home in Ellon. One of the accused, Jason Simpson, suggested Nicol's wife, Nawal, had planned the murder, one of her ideas being to push her husband off the cliffs here after she saw Slains Castle in a television documentary on vampires. Simpson and Muir Middler were jailed for life for murder while on the second day of Nawal Nicol's trial all charges against her were dropped.

Stoker set more fiction in the Cruden Bay area. The short story 'Crooken Sands' is a weird tale of dreams, doppelgangers and deadly coincidences. In *The Mystery of the Sea* (1902), one of Stoker's major works, an English tourist discovers he has the power of second sight and is beset by distressing visions of phantom funerals and the ghosts of drowned seamen, but he can do nothing to save those prefigured for death. He finds a coded manuscript, the deciphering of which leads him and his lady-love – who is on the run from bandits and a sinister secret agent – to a treasure buried by the Spanish Armada. With its mix of adventure, romance and the supernatural, it would make a fine television drama. Like Stoker on his holidays, the hero stays at the Kilmarnock Arms in Cruden Bay. The hotel seems to make little of the Stoker connection these days.

'St Olave's Well, low by the sea / Where peat nor plague shall never be.' The now-enclosed St Olave's Well on the golf course (NK08263534) is a reminder of the other major story associated with Cruden Bay, that of a great battle in 1012 between the Scots led by Malcolm II and the Danes under Prince (later King) Canute. The fighting took place on the low plain skirting the bay. The Scots were victorious and as part of the truce both leaders ordered a memorial chapel and graveyard to be built on the spot. Several decades later Olaf, King of Norway (killed in 1030 by Canute) was canonised as a saint and the church and well were both dedicated to him. The church was overwhelmed by the sands, as was a later version, and the

Schloss Dracula … Slains Castle.

Slains Castle before being Gothicised. From Charles Cordiner's *Remarkable Ruins and Romantic Prospects of North Britain*, 1788.

present St Olaf's Church is a mile (1.6km) inland at NK071366 (not to be confused with the Episcopal Church of St James on Chapel Hill, which has a spire). St Olaf's walls were fashioned from a single granite boulder called the Grey Stone of Ardendraught which had been so prominent it was used for both the lighting of 'Hallow Fires' and as a landmark for fishermen at sea. A large un-inscribed marble slab in the graveyard is said by, yes, tradition, to have been sent over from Denmark to mark the grave of a high-born Dane killed in the battle. Tradition may be erroneous in this case. Another story is that a Danish military chest was hidden during the battle, and has never been found.

The Revd James Rust, minister of Slains, wrote a fascinating antiquarian book, *Druidism Exhumed*, in 1871. In it he stated he knew Mary Findlay, who died at a great age. She was the last child laid on the Lykar Cairn overnight for being a fairy changeling. The relatives left an offering such as bread, dairy products, eggs, fish or a chicken, said some unknown words and then kept watch from a distance through the night. If the offering disappeared by morning the fairies had restored the human child. The cairn was 800 yards (730m) north–north–east of the church and when dismantled in 1826 made 100 yards (91m) of road. The senior workman reported finding many rags in which the food offerings had been left. Local people predicted 'evils innumerable' would befall him for his sacrilegious conduct, but in the end there was no supernatural comeback.

And he's rode by the wells of Slane, Where washing was a bonny maid.
'Wash on, wash on, my bonny maid, That wash sue clean ye're sark [shirt] of silk;'
'And well fa you, fair gentleman, Your body's whiter than the milk.'
Then loud, loud cried the Clerk Colvill, 'O my head it pains me sair;'
'Then take, then take,' the maiden said. 'And frae my sark you'll cut a gare [cloth].'
Then she's gien him a little bane-knife, And frae his sark has cut a share;
She's ty'd it round his whey-white face, But aye his head it aked mair.

Then louder cried the Clerk Colvill, 'O sairer, sairer, akes my head;'
'And sairer, sairer, ever will,' The maiden cries, 'till you be dead.'
Out then he drew his shining blade, Thinking to stick her where she stood:
But she was vanish'd to a fish, And swam far aff' a fair Mermaid.

Peter Buchan,
'Clerk Colvill; or, the Mermaid'

This cautionary tale of how an idle flirtation turned into an encounter with a murderous mermaid is in Buchan's *Annals of Peterhead* (1819, see PETERHEAD). He claimed the ballad was much older, and also noted: 'in the recollection of some old men, it is said of a Mermaid, that she pitched upon the bowsprit of a small vessel belonging to Peterhead, which was driven among the rocks near Slains castle, and that all hands perished save one man, who bore the tidings to land.' In *Past and Present* (1870) Sir Hugh G. Reid wrote there still lived 'a man who had seen and conversed with the mermaid under a great cliff off the Bullers of Buchan.' Unfortunately we have no more details. The Bullers are spectacular natural arches and cliff stacks north of Cruden Bay (NK110381, visitable from the car park on the A975). During one terrible storm seven vessels were wrecked here, all the crews being lost.

On 27 October 2006 the *Daily Mail* reported that the shredded remains of a ram had been found at Nether Broadmuir Farm. There was little left other than the bones, and the attack was blamed on a big cat. The 'Beast of Buchan' was spotted by a couple near a wood by Cruden Bay (*Evening Express*, 8 August 2007) and on the A975 on 18 October 2008 (*Press and Journal* 20 October). The latter witness described it as rusty brown in colour with black spots. To confuse matters, a headless corpse of an alleged native wild cat was found by the roadside in Boddam (*Daily Mirror* 2 May 2002). The creature was 3.5ft (1m) long, very large for a wild cat; the British Big Cat Society thought it might have been a hoax.

A Romantic view of the Bullers of Buchan, from Cordiner's *Remarkable Ruins and Romantic Prospects of North Britain*.

HATTON

A deep pool in the Water of Cruden is called Witches' Pot (NK061374). Just to the east is Fairy Hillock.

BODDAM

Several ports around the country – Greenock, Mevagissey and Hartlepool – have a legend that their inhabitants hanged a ship's monkey. And usually their neighbours don't let them forget it. Hartlepool, where the locals supposedly mistook the creature for a French spy during the Napoleonic Wars, has embraced the story, with their football team nicknamed the Monkey Hangers and their mascot called H'Angus the Monkey. Boddam also shares the legend, only here the poor animal was lynched because it was the only survivor of a ship deliberately lured onto rocks by wreckers, and salvage rights could only be claimed if all the crew had died. Folklore researcher Fiona Jane Brown identified the first appearance of the tale in an anonymous ballad of around 1772 called 'The Boddamers Hanged the Monkey, O'. This pre-dates later versions associated with Hartlepool and elsewhere in North-East England, and the suggestion is that the Boddam ballad is the *ur*-text, with the song being transposed and adapted by music-hall performers around the country. (*Hartlepool Mail* 12 January 2009, *Press and Journal* and *Buchan Observer* 13 January.) As to whether the Boddamers ever did hang a monkey, O, that remains unknown. There is a grotesque element in the last verse:

> Noo a' the folk fae Peterhead
> Cam' oot expectin' t' get a feed
> So they made it int' pottithead
> Fin [when] the Boddamers hanged the monkey, o'!

'Pottithead', potted head, is a dish made from a cow's head. Does this mean monkey brains were on the menu?

PETERHEAD

Local writer Peter Buchan made several curious additions to the lore of the strange and supernatural. In 1823 he published *Witchcraft Detected and Prevented; Or, the School of Black Art Newly Opened*, containing 'the most approved Charms in Magic; Receipts in Medicine, Natural Philosophy, and Chemistry, etc. By a Member of the School of Black Art, Italy'. Rather than being about witchcraft *per se* it was a collection of recipes, medicines and supposed magical secrets. It went through three editions. In 1824 he printed *Scriptural and Philosophical Arguments; or Cogent Proofs from Reason and Revelation that Brutes have Souls*, which claimed that most of the higher animals are on a spiritual par with humans. His masterpiece was *Annals of Peterhead, from its Foundation to the Present Time*, published in 1819. As well as the CRUDEN BAY Mermaid, it had much on Peterhead's magical history. He mentioned Sandy Hay, a blacksmith burned at the Stonyhillock for being a warlock (this was Alexander Hay of Kinmudie, put on trial in April 1629, along with Helen Knight of Grange, Peterhead, about whom we know very little.) Sandy Strachan, the 'cripple smith,' had a reputation for magically fixing tools. When he died the mother of all storms arose, causing the citizens to petition the clergy for a speedy burial. As soon as Strachan was laid to rest, the tempest ceased. In an otherwise ploughed field a few hundred yards from the manse was a patch of untouched ground, wherein were buried two duellists who had killed each other in the distant past, 'say in the time of the Picts or Romans'.

Buchan personally visited two magical practitioners somewhere in the vicinity of Peterhead, although he does not give their exact locations. They could 'cure all diseases, reveal the most hidden secret, and verily make the dead forsake their graves'. One was a respected middle-aged man who had inherited his gifts from his father. The other was a woman who had apparently learned her skill from Adam Donald (see BETHELNIE). Buchan's description of her makes great play of the standard, even clichéd, iconography of the witch – she was a wizened crone, living in an isolated, self-sufficient cottage with eccentric furnishings. And had a cat, of course.

On 8 September 1630 five Margarets – Buchan, Ritchie and Small from Boddam, and Fisher and Whyte from Peterhead – along with Mathow Will's wife from Peterhead, were all accused by the witch Marion Hardie from Elgin of congregating at the mouth of the River Dee in Aberdeen and throwing stones into the water when a boat was coming in. The action was intended to destroy the vessel and drown its crew. No more details of the trial are recorded.

'Spae-wives' were still casting weather spells with knotted cords in the nineteenth century. McPherson's *Primitive Beliefs* records how counter-magic was worked against the last spae-wife, Ann Silver:

> Ann Silver says we'll a' be nip'd
> And wont get out the morn,
> But we'll nail the horse-shoe to the mast
> And let her blow her horn.

Buchan also described the ravages of the bubonic plague in 1645. A servant of Robert Walker in Chapel Street received a trunk and clothes as a legacy from a recently deceased aunt in Leith. The articles were infected, the maid died, and the disease spread, partly through the insistence of people attending wakes in the houses of the dead. A cordon sanitaire was set up around the town, with the inhabitants forbidden by the neighbouring parishes to pass beyond the Kirkburn. One man named Scott breached the boundary and was hunted into the hills, where he survived alone and shunned until the epidemic was spent. A child was baptised by being held up on the (clean) side of the burn while the minister stood on the unclean side. A cauldron was set up to boil the coins coming from the infected area. Pent up in the town, perhaps 300-350 died, some in specially-constructed isolation huts which were pulled down and burned around them, while others were interred in mass graves. Buchan thought a number of victims may have been buried alive. The plague huts and burial pits survived on the 'pest ground' untouched and feared for decades, only finally being developed in 1774. On 17 November 2008 the *Press and Journal* reported that the sites of these graves had been 'rediscovered' on a map showing them to be under Ives Road, Gadle Braes and Harbour Street in Buchanhaven, on the north side of the town. One inhabitant, Mabel Green of Ives Road, thought the revelation might explain some minor poltergeist-type activity in her house: 'Almost every night we have to get up to turn off the taps in either the bathroom or the bedroom.'

Pratt (1858) states that the junction of the Collie Burn and the River Ugie (between Waterside and Blackhouse) is haunted, but he gives no details. The booklet *Peterhead Stories & Legends* states that the Chain House, next to the Bayview Hotel on St Peter Street is haunted by a young girl who fell down the stairwell and died, and that there is allegedly a secret tunnel between the Town House and Arbuthnott House. On 17 June 2001 'Moira' from Peterhead wrote to the *News of the World*'s psychic, Ruth, about night-time experiences in her home that included invisible entities that sat on her bed and pinned her down, and a vision of a burning cross on the bedroom wall. Ignoring the clues that in each case Moira had been asleep before the incident, and that therefore the phenomena could have been entirely hypnopompic dream imagery experienced in a semi-awake state, Ruth stated that Moira was being visited by two deceased relatives.

Frank Podmore's *Apparitions and Thought-Transference: An Examination of the Evidence for Telepathy* (1894) had a case reported in the *Aberdeen Herald* on 8 and 18 May 1850. On 22 April, a Mr Reid of Peterhead hypnotised 22-year-old John Park in front of 'twelve respectable inhabitants of this town' and sent him on a 'remote viewing' voyage. Park first made contact with *Erebus* and *Terror*, the two missing ships on Sir John Franklin's expedition to find the North-West Passage. The fate of the vessels was of consuming interest at the time, but later all of Park's information was shown to be incorrect. His second hit, however, was with the *Hamilton Ross*, a Peterhead whale ship stationed in Old Greenland. Park mentally explored the ship, and saw the second mate, David Cardno, getting his hand bandaged by the doctor in the cabin, while the captain stated they had upwards of 100 tons of whale-oil. The following night Park went astral travelling again and found Captain Gray of the *Eclipse* conversing with the captain of the *Hamilton Ross* about the seal fishing. When *Hamilton Ross* arrived in Peterhead in May it was carrying 159 tons of oil, Cardno was found to be wearing a sling because of an injured hand, and the two captains had indeed been in conversation on 23 April. Park had known Cardno but had no personal relationship with the Franklin explorers. Could this have been a factor? Podmore finishes with an insightful comment: 'As generally in visions of the kind, the false was mingled with the true … the percipient appears quite unable to distinguish between pictures which are obviously the work of his own imagination, and those which are apparently due to inspiration from without.'

In 1642 there was a supernatural visitation. On the night of 5 November, in a seaman's house, drums, trumpets, pipes and bells played, 'to the astoneishment of the heireris.' It was regarded as an ill omen, and the report concluded accurately: 'Trubles follouit.' The reference is in Groome's *Ordnance Gazetteer of Scotland* (1882-1885).

The Arbuthnot Museum on St Peter Street (open Monday-Tuesday and Thursday-Saturday 11 a.m.-1 p.m. and 2 p.m.-4.30 p.m., Wednesday 11 a.m.-1 p.m., free, no wheelchair access) has maritime and Arctic exhibits, including several Inuit items: a charm necklace with carved ivory pieces representing animals, weapons and possibly spirits; two bracelets of animal bones or teeth, the number of which indicated how old a woman was; and a pair of 'yakky dolls' made from sealskin, one bearing a truly creepy expression. St Peter's on the Links on South Road retains only an arch and a tower from the old church, but the spacious, attractive cemetery contains a goodly number of stones bearing the usual symbols of mortality and immortality, some of which are built into the north wall.

In January 1982 a very bright 'round crimson object' was seen for six minutes moving south to south-west along an old muddy deer track near Peterhead. The police investigation produced nothing. (*Scotsman* 14 May 2008.)

The *News of the World* (7 January 2001) reported that a couple living near Peterhead had released a leopard into the wild, although the initial tip-off may have been a hoax. On 27 October 2006 the *Daily Mail* noted a sighting of a big cat near a McDonald's on the outskirts of Peterhead.

Fishermen on the *Sharon Louise* were puzzled by the weight of the net they were heaving in 200 miles east of Peterhead. When it came to the surface the reason became clear: they had hauled up, from the depths of the ocean floor, a large heavy goods vehicle. They held it long enough to read the registration number before cutting the net and Skipper Simpson sent a report to the Scottish Fishermen's Federation. (*Fishing News* 3 July 1987.)

> On the coast of this country a great piece of amber was driven on shore by the force of the sea, as big … as a horse. I shall add nothing to the story, because 'tis hard to give credit to it …
> Daniel Defoe,
> *A Tour Thro' the Whole Island of Great Britain.*

'Five breaths belong to this burial ground.' An example of a gravestone inscribed with the dimensions of its associated burial plot. 'Breaths' should read 'breadths'. One of several such inscriptions at St Peter's on the Links, Peterhead.

INVERUGIE

Ruined Inverugie Castle (NK 10224830) has attracted two pronouncements of doom attributed to Thomas the Rhymer. The prophetic one stood on a stone and declaimed:

Inverugie, by the sea,
Lordless shall thy lands be;
And underneath thy hearth stane
The tod [fox] shall bring her birds hame.

This is in Robert Chambers' *Popular Rhymes Of Scotland*, quoting the manuscript *A View of the Diocese of Aberdeen*, written about 1732. By this time the castle's owners, the Earls Marischal or Keiths, had lost their estate for participating in the Jacobite rebellion of 1715.

Pratt, meanwhile, has another prophecy:

As lang's this stane stands on this craft,
The name o' Keith shall be alaft;
But when this stane begins to fa',
The name o' Keith shall wear awa'

The stone on which the seer sat was removed to build the St Fergus Church in 1763, around about the time the last of the family of the Earls Marischal died. The fun thing about alleged ancient prophecies is that, given the violent and changeable nature of politics, you can always find some event that seems to 'prove' the prophecy.

Gregor's 'Kelpie Stories' tells of an Inverugie man who captured a kelpie (in its guise as a big black horse) using a magical bridle, and made it carry the stones to build the bridge over the Ugie. When it was finally set free the kelpie complained:

Sehr back an sehr behns
Cairryt a' the Brig o' Innerugie's stehns.

Versions of this story, and of the rhyme, are found all over Scotland.

ST FERGUS

From here the dunes march up the coast in a great procession as far as Fraserburgh. The fragmentary but delightful St Fergus's Church close to the sands (NK11575075) has a small anti-Resurrectionist watch-house, iron rings of various heights in the wall (to tether horses great and small) and a very good collection of carved gravestones. One has the inscription *Vive Memor Lethi Fugit Hora*, a quotation from the first century AD Roman poet Persius: 'Live mindful of death. The hour is fleeing.'

Alex McAldowie's 1896 article 'Personal Experiences in Witchcraft' details the beliefs he had encountered in the parish during his boyhood. His uncle's farm had a fairy hollow; a well at its entrance required a 'witch-water-stone' to prevent the fairies from poisoning the water. Prehistoric arrowheads were used as charms to cure humans and animals. The ploughing up of a cairn prompted some people to gather on a neighbouring hill 'expecting to see the earth open and swallow up both horses and ploughman.' Up to the 1870s the Bridge of Savock was thought to be guarded by witches, and was avoided at night.

McAldowie knew one of the local witches, Lizzie Davidson, who had a spinning-wheel and kept a frog in a milk jug. She could charm her neighbours' cream into her own pan. After her death the spinning-wheel was acquired by Bell Adam, another witch, possibly as an object of power (nothing is said about the frog). Both McAldowie and William Littlejohn (*Stories of the Buchan Cottars*) have described the technique employed by the witchdoctor 'Auld Sautie' or 'Foreman'. If you visited him with a problem he was never in. His daughter or wife would, as part of polite conversation while you were waiting, question you closely. The crofter was listening through a hole from the next room, so when he appeared at the door he appeared to know everything about your problem without you saying a word. Having seen his power at first hand, you would be happy to pay the asking price for a nostrum or charm.

A strange atmospheric phenomenon was witnessed by a clergyman on 10 November 1766. A light appeared in the sky. 'The rays gradually became more vivid and stationary, seeming like a gleam of fire, extending about a quarter of a mile from E. to W. It continued for several hours, and then disappeared.' The report is in the *OSA*.

CRIMOND

The clock on the spire of the parish church has sixty-one minutes. The charming old church north of the village (NK05225758) has armorial panels and gravestones inserted willy-nilly into the ruins and gateposts, and a reasonable selection of skulls-and-bones. St Mary's Chapel way out east (NK08515753) has fewer carvings but a great location overlooking the Loch of Strathbeg. The loch used to be connected to the sea but in 1720 a great storm sanded over the channel, trapping a ship within the now inland waters. The church was once at the heart of the burgh of Rattray but is now surrounded by a great welter of nothing. Hidden within trees, Netherton of Logie RSC (NK0434572) still retains its recumbent stone and flankers and is worth a visit, as is the RSC at Berrybrae (NK02765716). Janet Currie and Margaret Rid of Crimond were accused of witchcraft on 21 January 1630 but other than their names we know nothing more about them.

'The (sixty-one-minute) Hour is Coming.' The clock on Crimond Parish Church. The extra minute is between '11' and '12'.

RATHEN

In 'First-Footing in Aberdeenshire' (1893) James Crombie describes a cat-related belief in Rathen. Whenever anyone died in a house the cat was immediately shut up. If it jumped over the corpse and then got out, the first person who met it would be struck blind.

Pratt gives an episode related to the fugitive Jacobite Lord Pitsligo (see ROSEHEARTY), who was hiding in the House of Auchiries (NJ97746068) in March 1756. One night Mrs Sophia Donaldson had a recurrent dream that the house was surrounded by soldiers. Rising before dawn to clear her head, she saw that the redcoats had indeed arrived surreptitiously. Pitsligo was quickly hidden in a small recess concealed by a bed, into which Miss Gordon of Towie was hurriedly bundled. She remained in the bed while the troops searched the room, and had to simulate a coughing fit to disguise the old man's asthma. The ruse worked and Pitsligo went undetected, all apparently thanks to a premonitory dream.

Patrick Gordon's *A Short Abridgement of Britane's Distemper* is a history of the Covenanting years, filled with omens, visions and signs from God. One of these supernatural visitations took place at Rathen in 1644, when for several days music of great beauty was heard in the church in the morning. The preacher entered the building in search of the 'woces, organes, and other instruementes' but as he did so the music ceased with a long note. Its source seemed to be an upper loft, but nothing was visible.

MEMSIE

The Cairn of Memsie (NJ97666205, Historic Scotland, free) is one of three huge cairns that used to stand here in a straight line, a linear prehistoric cemetery. The tradition is that the mounds marked the graves of three Viking nobles killed during one of the several Scots *v*. Danes clashes in the area. Intriguingly, there may be something to the notion. The cairns were dismantled in the eighteenth century. Most of the reported finds were probably prehistoric, but there was also a medieval urn containing bones, and a short brass-handled iron sword in a wooden scabbard. It is possible that the impressive cairns received secondary burials during the Middle Ages. To the north-east is Witch-hill, but there appears to be no associated tradition.

LONMAY

Cairness House, currently undergoing restoration, is a neoclassical mansion suffused with subtle Masonic symbolism and architectural conceits; it appears to have been intended as both a dwelling and a Masonic Temple. The gatehouses, known as The Inkwells, are each topped with a female sphinx. The front is a fairly standard Georgian block with wings, while the rear is a great granite semicircle of offices, the ground plan thus forming a 'CH' (either for Cairnness House or Charles Gordon, the man for whom it was built). The two pavilions at either end of the semicircle have arched recesses each containing a platform supported by two columns: the Royal Arch enclosing the Masonic altar. A pair of stunted columns either side of the porch are Masonic, as is the design on the pediment scroll. The centre of the courtyard is dominated by a round ice house modelled on a classical temple, at once a practical item and a folly.

Inside, there are temples within temples, the Drawing Room being modelled as the Temple of Apollo, the Dining Room as the Temple of Bacchus, and the Library as the Etruscan Room, all with appropriate statues, vases and busts. The Egyptian Room, the earliest of its type in Britain, has firedogs in the shape of sphinxes and is decorated with a hieroglyphic frieze. As this was installed before Egyptian hieroglyphs were translated, the symbols are simply decoration and not writing; unless, of course, there is a covert message encrypted within the glyphs. Cairness' website suggests the room was used for the Egyptian Rite of Freemasonry.

Cairness has limited opening, currently Wednesdays and Sundays 1 p.m.-5 p.m., July and August only. Admission charge. See the website or call 01346 582078 for up-to-date details. Disabled access is limited.

ST COMBS

David Buchan's *St Combs My Buchan* has two curious snippets. When someone died most children came to see the corpse and Buchan remembers being lifted up to see the body of a distant male relative who had a penny over one eye, as the eye had not closed. Buchan also notes St Combs was made up of two parts, the boundary being the Millburn. The southern section was in the parish of Lonmay, and the northern part, Charlestown, was in Rathen parish and was nicknamed Sodom – with the inevitable result that the people there were known as Sodomites.

The Gallow Hill to the south on the edge of the dunes (NK060619) has a vague reputation for having been the execution place for witches, and there is a Fairy Hillock to the west near Cairness Wood (NK035622).

FRASERBURGH

The Museum of Scottish Lighthouses (typically open 10 a.m.-5 p.m. Monday-Saturday, 12 noon-5 p.m. Sunday, all year, admission charge, no disabled access for the lighthouse) is a splendid place, featuring the sixteenth-century Kinnaird Head Castle which was converted into Scotland's first lighthouse in 1787. Graeme Milne's *The Haunted North* records staff and visitors experiencing temperature drops, a sense of being watched, footsteps in empty corridors, strange atmospheres, objects being moved and, on one occasion, seeing a fisher-wife. Milne himself encountered a positive female energy in the kitchen of one of the old keepers' cottages, and got the impression that 'she' was very surprised to be receiving visitors. The almost adjacent Wine Tower, an enigmatic three-storey structure that has no clear function (defence? chapel? wine cellar?) is supposedly haunted by thwarted lovers (the laird accidentally drowned his daughter's lover in a cave below the tower, and she threw herself off the tower). The tower is currently closed; someone who worked there when it was open to the public told Milne he sometimes had a sense of being watched.

Kinnaird Castle within
the Museum of Scottish
Lighthouses, Fraserburgh.

On 19 July 1998 the *News of the World* reported that 20-year-old Elaine Garden had twice
seen an apparition of her dead grandfather in broad daylight, once in a cemetery and again
while shopping in Fraserburgh.

Janet Castell from Fraserburgh was arraigned for witchcraft in 1649, but we have no further
information. The Kirk-Session heard several cases of charming. Agnes Duff sold charms to fisher
folk and cured sick children by melting lead and pouring it through scissors into cold water in
a vessel placed on the head. Constantine Kennedy healed a child by transferring its fever into
the hearth fire. Alexander Fraser confessed to writing the names of all the Kinbog people on
paper and throwing the pieces on water; the one that sank was the thief who stole John Philip's
sark. In 1844 the son of a noted smuggler found his cow dead. Cutting it open he found a hole
in the heart, proof positive that the animal had been killed by elf-shot (fairy arrows). All are
in McPherson's *Primitive Beliefs*. Walter Gregor (*Notes*) describes how at Hallowe'en young
women took a straw of thatch to a wise woman in Fraserburgh, who, marvellous to behold,
broke it and drew forth a hair of the same colour as the girl's husband-to-be.

In 1864, to drive away the evil forces that had reduced the fishing, a fisherman was chosen
as the 'burryman'. He was dressed in old clothes and every part of him, including his hair
and beard, were stuck all over with burrs gathered from the countryside. Red herrings were
suspended head down from his hat alongside a paper reading, 'Plenty o' herring an' nae dogs /
Honest men an' nae rogues'. He was then mounted on a horse, or carried on the shoulders of
another man, and paraded through the town in procession with a piper. (McPherson, *Primitive*

Beliefs and Gregor, 'Some Folk-Lore of the Sea'.) Burrymen are uniquely Scottish examples of communal attempts to placate the forces of nature; folklorists continue to argue about what they actually mean. South Queensferry still has its Burryman.

A Broadsea fisherman met a club-footed man from Pitullie whom he suspected had counted his herring nets – a double dose of ill-luck. The only way to negate the spell was to draw blood, so he smacked the Pitullie man hard on the forehead and blood flowed (Anson, *Fisher Folk-Lore*).

Next to the old parish church in Saltoun Square is the Fraser/Saltoun Mausoleum of 1623, a truly odd structure, a kind of stepped pyramid topped by an undersized obelisk supporting an egg. The four closed-up walls are inset with eroded heraldic panels. To its front is a Victorian fountain rejoicing in a quartet of fierce blue griffons. Close by, the Town House has heads of cows on its Corinthian columns. The elaborate wrought-iron fountain on Saltoun Place is a riot of griffons, birds, lions and geometric patterns. A wrought-iron sunflower stands proud above the corner of Cross Street and Saltoun Place. South of 'The Broch' can be found place names such as Nine Maidens' Hill (NJ966647), Witch-hill (NJ983631) and Hippy Hillock (NK002636).

ROSEHEARTY

Pitsligo Castle (NJ93736694, free) is not only an impressive ruin, it was also the home of one of the great characters of Scottish history, Alexander Forbes, twelfth laird and the 4th Lord Pitsligo. Having already been exiled for six years for participating in the Jacobite Rebellion of 1715, the highly-respected asthmatic 67-year-old found himself back in the saddle when Bonnie Prince

One of the blue griffons of the Jubilee Fountain. In the background is the stepped pyramid of the Fraser/Saltoun Mausoleum, Fraserburgh.

Charlie turned up in 1745. After the rout at Culloden he was a hunted man and spent three years hiding out in caves and barns on his estate (his wife and maid sewed a beggar's costume for him). More than once in his disguise he was employed by the redcoats to guide them to the hiding place of the 'fugitive laird', although strangely their target had just managed to elude them. Kind and generous as a laird, his tenants repaid him by never betraying him to the Government troops.

Forbes's spiritual life was just as interesting. After an early education in France he returned to Scotland in 1700 and founded a 'school' of mystical Christianity at Pitsligo. More of a club in which ideas were exchanged than an institution, it had a profound effect on several intellectuals whose correspondence was later catalogued in G.D. Henderson's *Mystics of the North-East*. The major trend was towards Quietism, a kind of Zen-like contemplative acceptance of the world. In 1710 the Church, scenting something beyond the confines of Presbyterianism, caused the school to close. During his exile in Europe after 1715 Forbes travelled with Baron Wolf von Metternich, a well-known German mystic. From 1720 onwards he was at Rosehearty studying and writing. In church in Fraserburgh one day his face seemed to shine with an inner radiance, an experience which had a powerful effect on the congregation. Despite being aged and in poor health he weathered his post-'45 troubles with great equanimity, apparently spending much of his cave-dwelling time meditating; his earlier spiritual convictions and experiences seem to have stood him in good stead. A good introduction to his adventures is James and Liz Taylor's *The Vanishing Laird*.

Just beyond an arch in the south wall of the castle is a concrete-covered structure that now hides the Nine Maidens' Well (NJ93726688). Not that long ago this was a circular building with a conical roof and a door that gave access to the water.

PEATHILL

The old ruined church (NJ93386623) is of abiding interest, with many excellently carved tombstones, including one dated 1724 of a crowned but armless Christ standing atop a

Seventeenth-century grave panel on the old church at Peathill.

More *Memento Mori* at Peathill.

skull-and-bones and flanked by two angels wearing kilts, another with a winged soul exhaling vegetation or breath, and a tomb-end decorated with the Masonic symbols of the sun, moon, set square and compass. The adjacent replacement church, now closed, houses the magnificently carved wooden Forbes Loft of 1634, with several grotesque heads. Information on how to get inside is displayed on the kirk door.

The new church was built in 1890 when the minister was Dr Walter Gregor, the great folklorist. Ironically he found himself a participant within a piece of living folklore when, after a 13-year-long dispute about the funding of the new building, he was burned in effigy on The Links. Not surprisingly, Gregor collected many stories from the Rosehearty and Peathill area. Here are just a few, told to Gregor in person, often by the witnesses or their relatives:

John Chalmers threshed his straw during the day while the fairies did the night shift. A man incurred his mother's wrath when, instead of placing a Bible under his wife's pillow shortly after she gave birth, he substituted a peat: the lack of divine protection had made her vulnerable to fairy abduction. A farmer whose cows were bewitched removed the spell by going to the culprit, a neighbouring farmer, knocking him down and cutting a cross on his forehead ('above the breath'). (All from 'Stories of Fairies from Scotland'.) Salt, silver coins and the hair of a cow's tail kept witches away from the beasts and products of the dairy. A local woman, still living, had the power of the evil eye and could prevent butter from churning. On one occasion she had worked her woe and so 'Auld Sautie' (see ST FERGUS) was sent for. His counter-magic involved some unknown ceremonies involving a half-crown, water from the local well, and mixing the cow's milk with a little milk from a neighbouring farm. Heating pins over a fire in a pot of milk from a bewitched cow caused the witch so much pain they would have to rush to the house and remove the pot, thus identifying themselves. (All from 'The Witch'.)

To the south-west is the Hanging Stone on Gallows Hill (NJ92126553, ask permission at Craigiefold Farm). The 7.5ft (2.3m) high stone is within the junction of three walls and is wrapped about with barbed wire. It is not clear when it was set up, or whether it was somehow

The Hanging Stone on Gallows Hill,
near Rosehearty.

used in the hangings, or erected as a memorial, or a marker. A little to the east was The Pit, a
pond where apparently lesser crimes were punished. This has now vanished.

On 26 August 2008 the *Press and Journal* reported that a black big cat had been seen at
Pitullie, Tyrie Castle and Peathill over the previous days.

TYRIE

Inside St Andrew's Church (NJ93006311) is the Raven Stone, with Pictish carvings of a raptor
(not a corvid), recently blacked in. Access is a bit *ad hoc*. For those who enjoy spooky abandoned
military sites, there is an evocative set of Second World War bunkers and other buildings off the
minor road at NJ942616, and in the fields to the north. A torch and due caution are required.

NEW ABERDOUR

If an entry in *The Book of Deer* (see DEER ABBEY) is accurate, Aberdour Bay may be one of the
earliest Christian settlements in North-East Scotland. St Drostan, a disciple of St Columba, is
said to have landed here in the sixth century. According to Barrett's *A Calendar of Scottish Saints*,
Drostan, having evangelised the area, was buried at Aberdour 'where miracles were wrought
at his tomb'. The present ruined medieval church (NJ883645) is an utter delight, with carved
grave slabs built into the wall-tops of what remains of the structure, a dovecot fashioned from
the fabric, and a great many symbols of mortality and immortality. One tomb-end has Masonic
symbols, another has the trade emblem of the hammermen and, as at PETERHEAD, some of the
stones are inscribed along their edges with the dimensions of the burial lair: 'One bredths [*sic*]
on this side ... two bredths [*sic*] on this side.'

A short walk east of the beach car park brings you to St Drostan's Well (NJ88686456), a strikingly whitewashed open-air structure with extensive seating, a well-head carved with a scallop shell motif, a second outlet down the slope, and an overall air of genteel Victorian optimism. This was long held to be the well blessed by Drostan when he landed on the beach, and hence thought to have curative properties. Further east, past the caves and rock arches, and reachable by the cliff top footpath, is Dundarg Castle (NJ89516491), a dramatic promontory defence, now comprehensively ruined and requiring care to explore. It started as an Iron Age fort and it has been suggested that this was where Drostan founded his primitive Celtic monastery, although as yet there is no convincing evidence for this. Ask permission from the private house in front of the castle.

The *NSA* records a tradition associated with 'Brodie's Cairn' which once stood at NJ86376460. The body of a murdered woman was brought to the gate of the Aberdour churchyard and everyone in the parish had to place their hand on the naked corpse. This was the 'ordeal of blood'; the belief that if a murderer touched his victim the body would bleed. The woman's son, Brodie, kept back. He was about to be forced to touch the corpse, but confessed before it could happen. His fate, apparently, was to be drawn and quartered, with his four parts buried on the sides of four roads leading to the church.

In 1654 George McGrigor and George Cowie were condemned for using a sieve and shears to divine the identity of a thief. They came to the attention of the Church because they had wrongly accused an innocent man, who complained to the authorities. In 1702 George Michie and Helen Lamb in Quarryburn were found guilty of using a charm to discover the nature of their child's sickness. They had heated stones named for the head, heart and body. The stones were dropped into water and the loudest sound indicated the location of the disease. Unfortunately one of the hot stones had set their house on fire – which is how the Church found out about their sin. (McPherson, *Primitive Beliefs*.)

PENNAN

Famed for being the fictional village in *Local Hero*, with the red phone box at the film's heart being listed as an historical monument. In the eighteenth century visitors in search of the Sublime in Nature flocked to Hell's Lum to see waves erupting through the narrow chasm. Cullykhan (NJ83736621, easy walk from car park) is an evocative site, a promontory that has remains from

The twin outlets of the Victorianised St Drostan's holy well, Aberdour beach.

Dundarg Castle near Aberdour, one of several spectacular (and ruined) promontory fortresses on this coastline.

the Bronze Age, Iron Age, Pictish period, Middle Ages, nineteenth century (anti-Napoleon) and twentieth century (anti-Hitler). It's mostly lumps and bumps, but the cliff top setting is dramatic.

McPherson recorded that up until the late nineteenth century a well at Glenquithle (NJ843645) had living in it a trout that was so deeply venerated no one would dare try to catch it. Anson described how if a cradle was borrowed at Pennan, a live peat was thrown into it for a few minutes before it was used, and a flaming brand was sometimes whirled three times round the head of a mother and child. In both cases the fire purged evil. Gregor notes widespread belief in fairies at Pennan. As well as stealing healthy children and replacing them with sickly changelings they were often seen fishing in little boats on summer mornings and evenings, wearing their usual green clothes and red caps.

NEW BYTH

When the turnpike from Peterhead to Banff was being built the money run out, and the road stopped abruptly at Auchnagorth, 2 miles (3.2km) north of New Byth. Surrounded by huge desolate moorlands, this 'road to nowhere', the raw transition from civilisation to wilderness, was regarded as 'an eerie, uncanny place'. As well it would. (Source: Robert Smith's *Buchan – Land of Plenty*.)

On 20 January 2009 the *Press and Journal* reported that a big cat had been seen the previous night somewhere on the B9170 or B9027.

CUMINESTOWN

Monquhitter churchyard (NJ802505) has a monument bearing a horizontal skeleton and other symbols of mortality. Somewhere to the south was Charlie's Houff, the troglodyte dwelling of a notorious robber in the sixteenth or seventeenth century. Pratt's *Buchan* says the tradition is that when he was caught 'he was summarily condemned by the public voice, torn asunder by a couple of oxen, and his mangled remains thrown into his own Houff, and buried under its ruins'. A Forestry Commission plantation at NJ803464 commemorates the site in his name.

FEDDERATE

Katherine Gerard bewitched the Mill of Fedderate, then had Christen Reid approach Walter Innes the miller and offer to un-witch it for a fee. This he agreed to and Christen, on Katherine's instruction, cast a little sand on the west part of the north door 'in the name of God and Chrystisonday' and the mill resumed working. Katherine and Christen seemed to be working this con quite frequently. Both were burned in Aberdeen in 1597 (*Spalding*).

Charles Tibbets' *Folk-Lore and Legends* tells the story of Mains (or Mauns) Crawford of Fedderate, the biggest, baddest, meanest laird on the block. He was tricked into a boulder-lifting contest with a stranger; only when the strain had broken his bones and burst his eyeballs did he find out that his stronger rival was the Devil himself. He was the last of the family, which is why Fedderate Castle is a ruin, obviously. In fact, the tower (NJ89694984) owes its fragmentary state to the very first Jacobite Rebellion, when it was one of the last places to hold out for the deposed James VII, and in consequence was blasted with gunpowder by the forces of William III in 1690. Pratt's *Buchan* has the tale that the castle supposedly could not be taken until 'the wood of Fyvie' came to the siege. When King William's soldiers arrived at Fedderate, they had with them siege timbers from Fyvie, scene of a previous victory over the Stuart supporters. Hence the unlikely legend was fulfilled, even if it had been borrowed wholesale from Shakespeare's *Macbeth*.

NEW DEER

A tenant was forced off his farm in the eighteenth century so he drove the twelve-oxen plough, carrying all the earth it could hold, off the land and onto the Goodman's Fauld on a neighbouring property. The fertility of the first farm was thus transferred to the untouched, untouchable patch. (Source: Banks and Banks, *Folklore* 1939.) Dillyverge the witch was brought to heel by a counter-charm involving a bottle of urine from the cow she had bewitched. (Gregor, 'Stories of Fairies from Scotland'.) Mary Gillan of Whitehill (d.1901), the daughter of a famous witch, used her reputation to live off the bounty of her neighbours. She had a habit of cursing people, and they had a habit of breaking whatever she had cursed – fingers, legs, etc. Hence when she asked a farmer for a cartload of peats, he immediately ceased his harvesting and brought them to her. Better safe than sorry. (McPherson, *Primitive Beliefs*.) Around 1801 James Murdoch and William Smith had places adjoining each other at Bushel Greens. James was lazy and stole his neighbour's peats, so William bored a hole in a peat and filled it with gunpowder. The next morning the fire exploded, making the inhabitants believe the Devil was amongst them. (William Littlejohn, *Stories of the Buchan Cottars*.)

St Kane's Well at Mains of Auchreddie made the transition from miracle-working medieval holy well to health-giving 'medicinal' spring for Georgian visitors taking the waters, and a weaver who lived opposite supplemented his income by selling ginger beer and gingerbread. The local minister, however, closed the well because the visits smacked of 'Popish pilgrimages' and now nothing remains. (Sandy Ritchie, *Stories from New Deer and St Kane's*.)

MAUD

In February 2004, two years after his death, the ashes of firearms expert James Booth were mixed with shot powder, loaded into 275 12-bore cartridges, blessed by the Revd Alistair

Donald of St Kane's, and handed out to his wife and twenty friends, who proceeded to 'bag' seventy partridges, twenty-three pheasants, seven ducks and a fox. The unusual tribute took place on Brucklay estate, owned by a family friend of the Booths. Mrs Booth said: 'It's difficult to say what I was feeling as the first shot sounded. I guess my main feeling was, 'I wish James was here. He would love this.' (Source: *Daily Mail*, 17 February 2004.)

STRICHEN

Strichen RSC (NJ93675448) has had a rum time recently, having been demolished in the 1830s by a tenant farmer, rebuilt incorrectly, bulldozed in 1965 and finally re-erected, with all the stones in their original positions, in 1981. There is a signposted footpath from the Newmill road, off the Formartine and Buchan Way. A visit can be combined with a saunter to the nearby dovecot and, down the slope to the south, to the rent asunder but very atmospheric mansion ruins of Strichen House (NJ936543). The circle gives a good view of the White Horse on the south slope of Mormand Hill (NJ962566). One of the original myths of the horse is that it was cut in 1773 to record the visit of Johnson and Boswell (they also went to the stone circle; neither were impressed). The more accepted version is that its

Staircases to nowhere: the shattered remains of Strichen House.

Gravestone at Strichen old Parish Kirk: skull, femurs, coffin, the Book of Life, death-bell, and a rare winged hourglass ('time flies').

creator was Captain Fraser (who obviously didn't build it himself – he left that to the tenants of his estate) in memory of a sergeant who saved his life at a battle in the Napoleonic Wars. Fraser had been unhorsed, the sergeant gave him his own white mount – and was promptly shot dead.

As Buchan has no chalk hills, *à la* southern England, the 164ft (50m) long beastie is constructed from white quartz which needs cleaning periodically (the cleaning is apparently a jovial, masculine and ultimately drunken affair). Hazel Weeks from Aberdeenshire Museums told me a local anecdote (or legend, she found it hard to tell) that perhaps sometime in the 1980s some of the men got hold of agricultural strips of black plastic, and temporarily transformed the horse into a zebra. A less obvious white stag, dating from 1870, can be seen on the east side of the hill from the A952, below the radio towers. The old church in the cemetery east of the village (NJ940548) has another very good collection of carved gravestones.

Gregor's 'Kelpie Stories from the North of Scotland' identifies a deep pool in the Burn of Strichen, near Braco Farm, as the home of a murderous kelpie that could appear as a horse or an old man.

The *New Statesman* (3 March 1995) reported that in August 1994 thieves stole 75,000 gallons (340,000 litres) of manure from the storage tank of Kindrought Farm. Owner John Mundie estimated that the blag would have required fifty tankers to transport the load, a logistically mind-boggling operation.

FETTERANGUS

John Gray's *A Baronry and a Realm* has a tale in a chapter entitled 'a tale from the Cheyne twilight'. In 1348, year of the Black Death, the vicar of Fetterangus, chanting a prayer of protection, crawled round the parish boundary on his knees – a marathon task which included crossing the great bog at the border with Cortiecram. With the supernatural cordon complete, he was resting when he saw a monk approach. This cowardly individual had fled Arbroath

An Angel of the Resurrection wearing a kilt. *Fugit hora* is Latin for 'the hour flies'. Fetterangus old parish church.

Louden Hill RSC, in Drimmie Wood near Fetterangus.

Abbey, leaving his colleagues behind to tend the sick. But he had brought the plague with him, and died within the Fetterangus boundary. Not just the people, but the ravens, fled in fear, leaving the priest to bury the impious monk where he fell. For years no grass would grow on the grave. The foundations of old Fetterangus Church (NJ9815506) have only a few carved gravestones but they are good ones. The symbols on the Pictish stone to the right of the gate are no longer visible.

Footpaths from the Forestry Commission car park lead through Drinnie's Wood to the Observatory (NJ973454987), a folly designed not to view the heavens but the action on a huge racecourse that once spanned the area. A plethora of information panels lie within. A bit of agile map-reading along the forest tracks running west will bring you to Loudon Wood RSC (NJ960497), a real pleasure in a glade within the dark conifers, and, further north, White Cow Cairn (NJ947519). Pitfour Estate is now private so it is not possible to visit the Temple of Theseus, a Greek-styled folly in the top of which, so the story goes, 'Mad' Admiral Ferguson kept his alligators. Although that might be a real crock.

DEER ABBEY

(NJ96864811. Historic Scotland, open most times, free.) Although important in the religious and economic history of Buchan, what remains of Deer Abbey today is, compared to many ruined abbeys, quite dull. This can be put down to the 'Mad' Admiral, who in 1854 practically demolished the buildings to make way for a mausoleum, which has itself now vanished. There are a few examples of badly eroded sculptured heads, a stone coffin, and a modern plaque commemorating St Mary and St Drostan. Drostan, if the early records are true, landed at ABERDOUR and founded a monastery at OLD DEER. That Celtic foundation was replaced in 1219 by this Cistercian Abbey, 2 miles (3km) west of the original site. The original monastery may have been the place where the tenth-century *Book of Deer* was kept. Now in the Cambridge University Library, the work gives the founding legend of the monastery and among other things has twelfth-century notes in Gaelic, the earliest written record of the language. For more information on and analysis of this important manuscript, see the very detailed website of the Friends of the Book of Deer Project.

Deer Abbey was dismantled at the Reformation and eventually came into the hands of the Keiths, the Earls Marischal of Scotland. Patrick Gordon's *A Short Abridgement of Britane's Distemper*, full of visions and portents of God's ire, shows how this sacrilegious annexing of sacred buildings rebounded on the great family. The wife of Earl George dreamed of a procession of monks proceeding from the abbey to the Keiths' main home, DUNNOTTAR CASTLE, which they demolished armed only with penknives. Within seventy years of Gordon recording this, the Keiths were history. Charles Tibbets' *Folk-Lore and Legends* (1894) has an alternative explanation, furnished by a local man supposedly interviewed by Tibbets in a tavern. The abbey was not a religious building, it was a castle owned by the Comyns. During a great siege the garrison survived by taking their horses to water along a secret tunnel through Saplinbrae hill, and when the castle was finally taken the Comyns' last act was to hide their gold in a well. Only one man tried to find this treasure, and he did so by summoning up Satan within the ruins. This, as you might imagine, did not go well, and the would-be magician ended up a) treasure-less and b) dead.

Immediately west of the abbey is one of the strangest bridges in the country. The Fergusons of Pitfour had a falling out with the Russells of Aden, and the bridge marks the boundary between the two estates. The Fergusons widened their side to allow carriages to pass. But the Russells refused to conform, and so to this day the miniscule Abbey Bridge narrows from two lanes to one in the middle of the river. Fortunately it is only a minor road.

Abbey Bridge, Deer Abbey: two lanes into one lane in mid-stream, the legacy of an aristocratic spat.

OLD DEER

Many churches find their foundation determined by supernatural intervention. Several works (such as Robert Chambers' *Popular Rhymes of Scotland*) tell how when the church of Deer was being built a Voice was heard:

> It is not here, it is not here,
> That ye shall build the church of Deer,
> But on Taptillery,
> Where many a corpse shall lie.

The church was accordingly moved to the site used today. The ruins of the former church stand behind the present edifice, and there is a wealth of heraldic and other carved stones. One marble monument has a fierce Angel of Judgement holding a cross and the scales on which souls are weighed, while below a skull and bones swing in a hammock. Two hundred paces south along the road to Stuartfield is St Drostan's Well, now recast in an 'English wishing well' format.

Folk magic is often brutal. To prevent cattle disease, James Crowden beheaded a live cow and buried the head and body in separate pieces of land. Thomas Forbes did the same at 'the threshold of a door, over which the living and the dead had gone,' a liminal act, and then buried the head in another man's land, thus sneakily transferring the disease to his neighbour. The Presbytery of Deer pursued them for over a year, and they eventually did penance late in 1659, although both clearly thought they had done nothing wrong. In the records you can sense the resentment of practical men against the Satan-obsessed ministers, who, the farmers thought, clearly had no idea how to deal with potentially ruinous cattle disease. The case is in Maxwell-Stuart's *An Abundance of Witches*.

Aikey Brae RSC (NJ95884709, signposted from the minor road near Parkhouse Farm) has a numinous quality, partly because you arrive at its bright open vistas after walking through densely-packed dark trees. Robert Chambers' *Popular Rhymes of Scotland*, quoting *A View of*

The lovely Aikey Brae Recumbent Stone Circle.

the Diocese of Aberdeen, written about 1732, states the stones were called Cummin's Craig. The story given was that one of the Cummins (Comyns), the Earls of Buchan, had insulted Thomas the Rhymer by calling him Thomas the Lyar, so Tam replied with a prophetic curse:

> Tho' Thomas the Lyar thou call'st me,
> A sooth tale I shall tell to thee:
> By Aikyside
> Thy horse shall ride,
> He shall stumble, and thou shatt fa',
> Thy neck-bane shall break in twa,
> And dogs shall thy banes gnaw,
> And, maugre all thy kin and thee,
> Thy own belt thy bier shall be.

And the disrespectful earl duly fell off his horse at Aikey Brae and dashed his brains out.

STUARTFIELD

Cecilia Penny's book *Stuartfield, Our Place* has two intriguing stories. Tommies returning from the trenches of the First World War typically brought back a German bayonet or rifle. General Sir John Burnett-Stuart, however, decided to return with a large field-gun, a logistically impressive feat in itself. He installed it in the Square at Crichie, where its presence rankled with those who had lost loved ones in the war. So one Saturday night the gun was tipped over the bridge into the Ugie at Aden. The general recovered it. The following weekend the removal and recovery was repeated. A week later the gun was kidnapped for the third time and deposited into a quarry at Middlethird, and there it remains to this day.

Sometime in the early nineteenth century an unusual folly was constructed somewhere in the area of Hill of Dens (NJ953455). 'The Walls of Troy' was a labyrinth cut into the turf, its path low-edged with sods and stones (and so similar to the modern labyrinth at BROOMHILL). It was designed and cut by John Cumming, a tenant farmer from King's Crown, Crichie. Follies are usually the domain of the upper echelons of society; labyrinths, however, seem to have had a powerful appeal to people of all classes: the first British stone labyrinth (1726) was built by a lighthouse keeper on the Scilly Isles, and more than 200 turf labyrinths have been identified around the country, many built by the local community on village greens or common land. A number of these turf structures were called 'Troy Town'. The illustration for the Stuartfield labyrinth shows it to have been a simple four-circuit design of the 'classical' type that has been known since antiquity. Sadly Cumming's creation, its genesis and inspiration unknown, was destroyed by 1869.

MINTLAW

Set in a striking circular courtyard in Aden Country Park, the excellent Aberdeenshire Farming Museum (open May–September 11 a.m.–4.30 p.m. daily, April and October 12 noon–4 p.m. weekends and school holidays, free. Wheelchair access to main exhibition) is the best place to learn about the agricultural practices that underlie so much of the region's folklore. Among the exhibits is the original weathervane from the top of the high dovecot tower, complete with a bullet hole as a reminder that the Gordon Highlanders trained at Aden in the First World War.

The exhibition also tells the story of the Russells of Aden. *Phantasms of the Living*, a book by Edmund Gurney, Frederic Myers and Frank Podmore of the Society for Psychical Research, contains a contribution by J.G.F. Russell. Sometime after midnight on 2 December 1885 he was woken at his London home by hearing his name called from outside his bedroom door. The next morning he asked a relative staying with them if she had called him, but she had not. It transpired, however, that on the night in question her sister, living many miles away, had disturbed dreams about Mr Russell, and found herself sitting up in bed, having been woken up by calling his name loudly. A member of the museum staff told me that a woman whose father used to work on the estate came in one day and related how the daughter of the last laird (Sydney Russell) kept seeing the apparition of a young woman in her first-floor bedroom.

The roofless mansion at Aden Country Park, Mintlaw. The removal of the floors seems to have thwarted the once resident ghost.

The figure, which ran from a door and through a window, was so persistent the laird had a partition built to screen off the section. The mansion concerned is now an attractive shell, one of a series of remains of the once grand estate, including the gasworks, icehouse, neoclassical entrance lodge, and a large mineral well. The museum's courtyard also houses the Friends of the Book of Deer, a resource on the medieval Celtic manuscript (see DEER ABBEY) which is open on weekend afternoons in the summer.

Also highly recommended is Aberdeenshire Heritage Museum Store in Mintlaw Station (open the second Saturday of each month 9 a.m.–1 p.m., telephone 0771 622807 to arrange a free tour). This is a modern depot holding the items that are not on display in Aberdeenshire Museums, or are still being conserved. This means that what can be seen will vary depending on when you visit, but my saunter through this treasure trove of wonders included fossils, ethnographic and archaeological items, giant moa bones, walrus tusks, a tiger skull, a walrus baculum (penis bone), a coffin board, swords, coprolites (ancient dung) and a Chinese repeating crossbow. Special mention goes to a pair of bezoars (cow hairballs once thought to have magical anti-poison attributes); a whaling log which contains the entry, 'plenty of unicorns going westward' (this would be a reference to narwhals, but it is fascinating to find a sea captain calling them unicorns); and 'Gonzo' the vulture, whose semi-skilled taxidermy job has left him looking like the eponymous Muppet.

Graeme Milne's *The Haunted North* describes a series of poltergeist events at the store, and staff confirmed to me episodes of lights being turned off, waste bins upended and strange noises and atmospheres. One member of staff refuses to go into the upstairs store. There have been reports of apparitions and odd smells. On one occasion in 2006 the person sitting at reception heard two large crashes from the staff room. When the canteen's lights were switched on the wall clock was found on the other side of the room, as were all the papers from the notice board, although the pins were still in the board.

LONGSIDE

McPherson's *Primitive Beliefs* describes a sustained poltergeist attack at Broodie Brae, one of the crofts in Braehead of Auchtydonald. Every night for six months in 1825 the respected tenant, James Wylie, was assaulted. On one occasion neighbours sat with him and at midnight a pail came down the stairs and emptied its contents over a woman, blankets rose of their own accord, crockery jumped about on the plate rack and chairs and tables danced. One man was hit on the cheek by the potato chopper and two others were knocked down, one by a peat, the other by a pail from under the table. Only when dawn came did the manifestations cease. Later witnesses included more neighbours, and doctors and ministers. The assaults finally stopped when Wylie left the croft, and he died soon after.

On 24 April 1597 Agnes Wobster from Ludquharn was burned for witchcraft. The trial details, given in *Spalding*, are quite detailed. She had first met the Devil sixteen years earlier, when he appeared to her as a lamb or a calf. She visited a stone called the Curstane three times at sunrise in May, found fire in a stone wall when snow was all around, caused a cow to dry up after she was refused milk, made a boy ill, killed a lamb by cursing it, made a 'devilische potage' which would have killed a woman had she eaten it, and, in company with Catarein Gib, bewitched Charles Elrik to death. Most astonishingly, she 'did vomeit and spew out fyrie brunndes out off thy mouthe.' This is the only example I know of where a witch breathes fire.

5

BANFFSHIRE

PORTSOY – BANFF – MACDUFF – ABERCHIRDER

SANDEND

Findlater Castle (NJ54186720) is one of the great sights of Aberdeenshire, a ruined medieval fortress built on – and into – a peninsula joined to the mainland by the narrowest of necks. Some of the cellars, now partly open to the sky, are carved out of the rock. It makes DUNNOTTAR look easily accessible by comparison. Such a spectacular site cannot avoid legends, and they are summarised in James Spence's *Ruined Castles* (1873). Findlater was the first place in Scotland to be roofed with slates, so when the slater was finished, the laird, not wishing the knowledge to be gained by others, pushed him off the roof into the sea (this is a migratory legend: lairds throughout Scotland are claimed to have pushed builders, architects and skilled craftsmen off battlements, usually to avoid paying a bill). In a variant of the story, the slater survived the plunge and swam to a nearby rock (called Slater's Rock), only to be picked off by musket fire. The other legend is that the family nurse accidentally dropped the lord's infant son over the cliffs and died in the attempt to rescue him; the baron left the castle never to return (thus accounting for the ruinous state of the site). Could it be, I hear you ask, that, on dark and stormy nights, people claim to have heard the crying of a ghostly baby? Yes it could. The two stories spring from Findlater's vertiginous position: both the approach and the ruins are very precipitous and slippery and should not be attempted in bad weather or after rain. The castle can be reached via the coastal path from Cullen or Sandend, or there is a signposted car park; the rough track leading from it passes a restored sixteenth-century dovecot (NJ53996674).

FORDYCE

The quiet country churchyard of the ruined medieval St Talorgan's Church (NJ556639) is a smorgasbord of delights. Several fine symbols of mortality and immortality lurk on the gravestones. An arched recess holds a full-figure armoured chap with his iron-clad feet resting on a pet dog. This combination seems to have inspired a story that as he was attempting to leave to visit the House of FRENDRAUGHT the dog prevented him from so doing by barking and blocking the horse. That night Frendraught was burnt down and all perished; so the faithful, psychically-gifted hound had saved his master from certain death. Delightful though the story is, it does not stand up to scrutiny: the effigy is dated to around 1509, and Frendraught took afire in 1630. A second tomb arch has the incised outline of a second knight.

The bell tower has a been augmented by a seventeenth-century loft which now houses a small heritage centre (free); not only are the information boards full of fascinating information on local antiquities, this is a good opportunity to see what a typical Session House looked like. Here in this sparse, cramped space the Kirk-Session met and pontificated on the fate

Winged (and wigged) soul, Fordyce church.

of parishioners who had broken the rules. In 1646 it was noted many parishioners went on 'superstitious' pilgrimages to the well of Spey. In 1650 William Grant was declared 'a fugitive warlock' but there are no more details. In 1655 John Young accused Isobel Ogilvie of taking away a cow's milk by witchcraft and 'a quarter of a cow also', whatever that means. In 1690 Margaret Denoon was convicted of cursing her enemies and praying that God might cause them to be 'turned seven years upon a tedder' (a device used to turn hay). In 1729 Bessi Chisholm was fined twenty shillings for wishing that some persons might fall and 'tumble nineteen times in the falling ill'. These examples are all in McPherson's *Primitive Beliefs*.

Christine Urquhart's *Mither o' the Meal Kist: A Pictorial History of Fordyce* describes yet another secret tunnel, this time a smugglers' passage stretching from Fordyce Castle next to the church to a cave under FINDLATER CASTLE, a mere 2.5 miles (4km) as the mole burrows. Urquhart notes that Bob Gray lived in the castle for almost fifty years and never found the tunnel, and that it is more likely that the illicit goods were offloaded at Findlater, transported overland by horse and cart, and then stored in Fordyce cellar.

Writing in the journal *Folklore* in 1923, David Rorie described the ceremony of the Fordyce Mortar Stone, a kind of debased fertility ritual. On Hogmanay the youths of the village would congregate noisily and deposit the stone at the door of the young woman whom, it was decided, should marry in the next year; if she did not have a beau, the stone would provide one. Given the public nature of the ceremony and the year-long visible presence of the stone it is not surprising some women found the whole thing humiliating or intrusive, and someone broke the original stone, so a substitute had to be found. Urquhart adds more details: the stone originally belonged to Maggie Wilson, whose success in marrying off four ugly daughters obviously meant she possessed luck – which was thought to reside in the mortar stone at her door. Some lads left it at the door of a spinster to assist her with her matrimonial prospects, and she was married within a year. Hence the tradition was born, and the (second) stone was still bringing couples to the altar in the 1930s.

PORTSOY

On 28 May 2007 a black and white moggie was catnapped from the outskirts of Portsoy. What made this case unusual was that the victim could be easily identified because a) he was blue and b) his eyes glowed red when he was plugged into the mains. The abduction of the concrete and steel model of Pilchard, the cat from the children's television series *Bob the Builder*, was a mystery, but equally mysterious was his return: on 31 October the critter was found very early in the morning, with a helium Hallowe'en balloon tied to his tail, and a guiser's mask on his face. (*Banffshire Journal* 27 June and 31 October 2007.)

The cemetery on St Comb's Road is home to a wonderfully Victorianised holy well. St Colm's Well (NJ59226599) has a tunnel-type entrance built into a large earth mound. Within the darkened interior, a circular seat surrounds the well, where the water still flows weakly. The well is claimed to date from the seventh century and be contiguous with a chapel dedicated to St Columba; the building disappeared about 200 years ago and the dedication was more likely to St Colm, an obscure saint active in the area who is frequently confused with the more celebrated Columba. Some have thought the mound was a prehistoric burial structure, but James Slater's local history, *Bonnie Portsoy*, suggests it was built to screen the chapel from French privateers. Slater also mentions Langie's Brae to the east, where Satan stood and claimed Portsoy as his own, only to be thwarted by the town preferring Christianity. Andro Man, one of those accused of witchcraft in 1597, recanted and turned witchfinder. He confronted Jonet Leask in William Bain's house, accusing her of being a witch for thirty years and having under her left breast the Devil's mark, which was visible. Likewise, William May confronted Meriorie Mutche in a Portsoy house and pointed out the Devil's mark under her left ear, 'and a pin being inserted therein by the Laird of Esslemont, she could not feel the same'. Both cases are in *Spalding*. McPherson's *Primitive Beliefs* describes how at an unnamed date James, Earl of Fife, was in his carriage near Banff when the horses became restive and then refused to move. The diagnosis was that they had been arrested by witchcraft. Lily Grant, the local wise woman from Whitehills, was brought into the carriage beside his Lordship; after some prognostications the horses were freed from the power and the journey continued.

It was common for fishermen to keep back a skate, dry it in the sun, cut their name on it and take it home. The item brought luck, usually related to fertility or prosperity. In 1960 an aged fisherman in Portsoy told Peter Anson that he had kept a dried skate in his house for twenty years, and then presented it to a newly married couple, convinced it would give them a large family.

The *Press and Journal* for 11 August 2004 reported that at 9.30 a.m. on 9 August a female motorist had seen a 'naked, yeti-like man' on the B9022 at Brodiesord, about 3 miles (4.8km) south of Portsoy. The description implies that the individual was human rather than anthropoid, as he was said to be tall, well-built and in his late forties, with extensive body hair. He twice walked in front of her car and then calmly strolled into the trees. Forestry workers and police investigations both drew a blank.

BOYNDIE

A sanguinary prophecy of Thomas the Rhymer is associated with St Brandon's Stanes (NJ60756105, two stones of the RSC remain):

> At two full times, and three half times,
> Or threescore years and ten,
> The ravens shall sit on the Stanes o' St Brandon,
> And drink o' the blood o' the slain!

Like most such prophecies it flaunts its ambiguity. One 'explanation' is that this was the site of a battle between the Scots and the Danes. Which of course would have happened long before True Thomas was spouting prophecies. (Source: Robert Chambers' *Popular Rhymes of Scotland*.)

WHITEHILLS

The Red Well on the shore (NJ661653) currently resides within a beehive-shaped building. This chalybeate spring was thought to have healing properties, and at one time farm workers were given time off to visit it for their health. There is no record of it having been regarded as a holy well. Norman Adams' *Haunted Scotland* has a dramatic account of an encounter with a terrifying spectre on Red Well Road at 7.15 p.m. on New Year's Day 1990. An old woman in black appeared before 16-year-old Christopher Christie and repeatedly passed through his body, even as he was running in fear back home. The phantom was less than 5ft (1.5m) tall, with a pale face and sagging cheeks and walked with her hands clasped in front of her. Christie never again set foot on Red Well Road; a short time after the encounter, he woke in his bedroom unable to breathe, and saw a dark cloud drifting towards the window; it seemed the 'thing' had followed him home.

The *Herald* on 19 March 2001 and the *Daily Mail* (23 March) reported on a mysterious hum that was ruining the lives of a Whitehills couple. After nine months of sonic attack Adele and Douglas Farquharson were forced out of their house to take refuge in hotels, relatives' homes and even their car. The effect was so severe that Mrs Farquharson said 'I felt like my head had been in a spin dryer all night – like my brain had been vibrating in my skull'. Several such hums are reported from around the world, with the nearest example being the long-running 'Largs Hum' in Ayrshire. In all cases the cause is unknown, although the assumption is that some nearby industrial or technological process, such as pipelines, radar or radio waves, is emitting infrasound that can only be picked up by a small number of people sensitive to the low frequency.

INVERBOYNDIE

Phantasms of the Living (1886), a collection of first-hand accounts of doppelgangers and apparitions of those still alive or very recently dead, includes a letter from Mrs Gardiner of 30 Skene Street, Macduff. Around 1843 her father was the tenant of Mill of Boyndie Farm. Three men left the service of the farm one morning. That night Mrs Gardiner's sister, who managed the household, was woken by a servant asking for the key of the kitchen door. When asked why, she said she had seen two of the lads looking in at her bedroom window. She had asked them what they wanted, but they made no reply, only moving slowly from the back of the house where the servant saw them meet up with the third man. The premises were searched, but the men were nowhere to be found. The following morning they learned the trio had got drunk, pushed a boat out, and drowned in the night.

The badly ruined St Brandon's Church (NJ666645) has a worthwhile collection of carved skulls, winged souls and trade emblems, as well as a pair of angels carrying a basket of corn. In 1649 the church authorities condemned a piece of unlaboured ground called 'the halie man's ley' which was 'dedicated to superstitious uses'.

BANFF

The densely-packed graveyard of St Mary's Kirk on Carmelite Street has possibly the finest collection of funerary sculpture in Aberdeenshire. Happy hours can be spent pottering about the many dozens of symbols of mortality and immortality, heraldry, trade emblems and Masonic symbols. The highlights include: two stones where the loin-clothed Angels of the Resurrection flank the deceased, lying in a four-poster bed balanced on a skull; an Egyptian-style winged disc; an arched recess with the full figure of George Baird (d.1636) in archaic knightly armour, his feet resting on his faithful hound; tomb-ends inscribed 'Life how short' and 'Eternity how long'; a pair of grotesque heads holding a hammock containing a skull and bones; and a stone

St Mary's graveyard, Banff, Aberdeenshire's greatest collection of funerary monuments: Death extends its welcoming arms.

The Grim Reaper, St Mary's graveyard, Banff.

A skull and bones swing in a hammock supported by a pair of grotesque heads. St Mary's graveyard, Banff.

Life how Short ... St Mary's graveyard, Banff.

Angels of the Resurrection blow their trumpets above the compass, set square and other symbols of Freemasonry within a Masonic altar. St Mary's graveyard, Banff.

A distinctly Asian looking boar on a tomb, St Mary's graveyard, Banff.

'Time Flyeth, Death Persueth.' More cheerful thoughts from St Mary's graveyard, Banff.

from 1827 carved with a delicate butterfly. If there is one monument that sums up the delights of this graveyard it is the Renaissance-styled Sharp memorial from 1698, a riot of skulls, bones, gravedigger's tools, winged souls above Corinthian columns, angels with trumpets and books, and a lovingly-detailed horizontal skeleton lying in its grave. Visit this place and indulge your inner Goth.

Banff can provide a satisfying walking tour full of incidental, curious and bizarre architectural and anecdotal details. Starting from the graveyard:

High Shore
The Market Arms: a sinister moustachioed face on a stone dated 1585 (go through the pend arch). The garden next door has a sculpture of a sunflower and spider's web (with spider). The Forbes House at No. 3 has a grotesque lion mask over the door. The sign of The Ship Inn has a sailing ship menaced by a sea serpent and other marine monsters, naively-painted versions of aquatic horrors that first appeared in Olaus Magnus' famous map of Scandinavia in 1539, *Carta Marina*. The public bar was the location for the filming of the interiors of the 'Macaskill Arms' in the film *Local Hero*.

Low Street

The Mercat Cross is a replica of the original, a brightly-painted rare pre-Reformation survival of Catholic iconography, with Jesus on the Cross flanked by the two Marys, and a golden Virgin and Child. Two more Virgin Marys, one very eroded, are on the wall next to the clock tower, beside the painted coat of arms of 1634. The neo-Gothic Biggar fountain has bulldog waterspouts and heraldic panels. This area, the Plainstones, was the site of the hanging of the notorious freebooter James McPherson in 1700, an event shrouded in what might be called 'execution mythology' because of its popularity in song and verse (with famous contributions by Robert Burns and Sir Walter Scott). In his book *Hangman's Brae* Norman Adams effectively demolished the legends. Myth: the Banff clock was put forward an hour to thwart a messenger approaching over Banff Bridge with a pardon. Reality: the execution took place between 2 and 3 p.m. on market day, as ordained, and Banff Bridge did not exist in 1700. Myth: on the way to the scaffold McPherson played a tune on his fiddle later called 'McPherson's Rant'. He then offered the instrument to any member of his clan who would play over his body at his wake. There were no takers, so he smashed the fiddle over the executioner's head and hanged himself. (In another version he broke the fiddle so no one else could ever play it.) Reality: McPherson was a high-risk prisoner – his hands would have been bound at all times, so there was no possibility of him striking up a tune.

High Street

Banff Museum (open June-September, Monday-Saturday, 2 p.m.-4.30 p.m., free) has a copy of the Deskford Carnyx, a stupendous Celtic war trumpet from the first century AD. The original is in the National Museum of Scotland in Edinburgh. The Royal Bank of Scotland at the junction with Strait Path has several seventeenth-century heraldic panels high on its walls, as well as a more modern coat of arms supported by splendid griffons. Somewhere under the road surface near here lies the Grey Stone, the last remnant of a stone circle. The former Town Hall, now a carpet warehouse, has a bearded head over the archway and a full set of crowned female capitals, all different.

Castle Street

In October 2008 Castlegate Newsagents was criticised by the group Banff Churches Together, which branded the shop's 'morbid' and 'distasteful' Hallowe'en window display as disrespectful to Christianity and promoting an unhealthy interest in the occult. The somewhat baffled owner William Gatt stood his ground and refused to remove the mock skulls, gravestones, black cats and spiders. A week later the shop window was smashed. (The story is in the *Banffshire Journal* 21 October 2008 and the *Daily Mirror* 30 October.)

Quayside

A modern plaque of Neptune and his trident on a wall on the west side on the road.

Stuart Street

No. 14. The most unlikely carving in the town, a panel of three nude figures, two female and one male, taken from an erotic temple sculpture in India.

Car park by Tourist Information Office

Seatree sculpture, a modern star-topped column carved with Pegasus, a mermaid, fish, shells, whales, sea monsters, ships and abstract geometric shapes.

   John Philp is Banff's most famous witch, largely because his trial records have survived in such detail. He was clearly a folk healer of many years experience and a wide geographical range. Equally clearly, he refused to give up his profession and, having been condemned and banished by the Kirk-Sessions of, among others, Fintray, Ellon, Aberchirder and Auchterless, he paid the ultimate price at Banff, when he was strangled and burned in 1631. He washed and

Who is this sinister mustachioed man? The Market Arms, Banff.

Hindu erotic sculpture, high on a wall in Stuart Street, Banff. (Photo: Ségolène Dupuy)

charmed people who were ill through witchcraft, including Andro Clerk in Fintray, whose sickness he cast onto an ox, which died. In another case the curing water was thrown outside, and a cat that ran across it went mad and attacked a man. He washed Alexander Gifford in Alvah in a manner he had learned from the Devil. He cured Gilbert Leslie in Fintray by putting him through a hasp of yarn, and did the same for Thomas Byth's oxen. He charmed a cow with a belt that had been put around the waist of a dead child. He taught George Fraser and his wife how to charm their oat seed in the barn so the crop would be more productive. He had dealings with the Queen of Fairy, and used potions and orisons (formal speech, or ritual language). His downfall may have come because one of his patients, George Brebner in Cullen, got worse rather than better.

We know substantially less about other witches. In 1615 Margaret Davidson was accused by Andrew Aitkenhead of injuring his health and causing his cat and dog to run 'wode', wodnes being an animal insanity caused by witchcraft. Jonet Jack, Margaret Livie and Margaret Nicol were brought to trial in 1637 but there is no further information. In 1671 Elspeth Thomson from Fortrie, Inverkeithny, was also charged but the details are scant. In 1674 two lairds and a bailie in Banff attempted to prosecute Margaret Clerk of Seatown, Cullen for witchcraft, but she went to the High Court in Edinburgh and successfully had the case dismissed on the grounds that the men had not followed legal procedure and were insufficiently educated to hear the case. The most interesting of these cases is the last one in the records. On 1 June 1674 Margaret Spence was convicted of throwing five stones into the waves, and casting water seven times out of the sea towards Banff. She protested 'on her soul's salvation' that the action was designed to prevent the spread of an epidemic of fever. Presumably the stones represented the fever; but what was the throwing of the seawater for? (These cases are taken from the Survey of Scottish Witchcraft, McPherson's *Primitive Beliefs* and Anson's *Fisher Folk-Lore*.)

Anson gathered many examples of fisher beliefs on the Banffshire coast. On New Year's Day in the mid-nineteenth century fisher folk assured good luck for the year by sprinkling seawater over the fire and placing a certain kind of seaweed above the doors and corners of the home. Death omens were common. In 1958 Anson and the son of a fisherman were asleep in adjoining rooms in a house beside the harbour of a Banffshire port when both were awakened by a loud and eerie rapping inside the house. The next day a letter came, stating that at the exact time of the noises a dear friend had died 500 miles away. Anson's host said similar omens had happened in his family. Walter Gregor's 'Some Folk-Lore of the Sea' has the tale of a Banff fisherman who gave some free fish to a woman when he was in Invergordon. In return she presented him with a bottle with strict orders not to uncork it until the boat reached his home harbour. Curiosity got the better of him and he opened the bottle at sea, with the consequence that a wind overtook the boat, making landfall very difficult. The same article also described a cure for rickets in Banff. The child was taken before dawn to a smithy in which worked three men of the same name. The child was washed and placed on the anvil where the blacksmith's tools were passed over it. Gregor's *Notes on the Folk-Lore of the North-East of Scotland* noted that a boy in Banff had been born feet first, an omen that he would die by hanging. Although he gave no hint of a criminal career, his mother was always worried, and when he died of a natural illness she felt greatly relieved.

Michael Barrett's *A Calendar of Scottish Saints* tells how a wooden image of St Fumac survived the Reformation at Botriphnie, and its aged female custodian would wash it in St Fumac's Well every 3 May (presumably as a form of rain-charm). In 1847, or thereabouts, the statue was swept away by the Isla in flood, and stranded in Banff, where it was recovered – and promptly burnt by the Protestant minister as a relic of superstition.

In July 1973 Mrs Taylor and her children found a UFO-type object on the beach at Banff Links. On the side was a message from outer space: 'High Altitude Weather Sensor. Not Dangerous. Reward for Return. Mail to A.I.R. Inc, 1830 S Flatiron Ct, Boulder, Co, USA.' The polystyrene device had been detached from its parent balloon. (Source: *Banffshire Journal*, 15 July 2008.)

DUFF HOUSE

(Historic Scotland. Open April–October daily 11a.m.–5 p.m.; November–March, Thursday-
Sunday 11 a.m.–4 p.m. Admission charge, good wheelchair access.) This eighteenth-century
Baroque mansion now houses part of the collection of the National Gallery of Scotland.
The exhibits are well-labelled; here is a guide to the quirkier elements.

Grotesque heads on exterior of Duff House, Banff.

One of several elaborately (and monstrously) carved urns on the parapet of Duff
House. (Photo: Ségolène Dupuy)

Exterior
The gods Mars, Apollo, Minerva, Bacchus, Mercury and Diana look down upon us from on high. Grotesque faces hold swags between their teeth. Magnification shows that some of the urns on the roofline are finely carved with human, animal and demonic heads, many of them foliaceous. One monster's very eyes are composed of leaves.

Room 1, The Vestibule
Portrait of Elizabeth Gunning, 1734-98, a famous beauty of her day. She died from lead poisoning – her make-up was the culprit.

Room 2, The Great Staircase Lobby
Two of the original 1740 lead statues from the roof (the ones up there at present are modern copies). Axe-wielding Mars sports a griffon on his helmet and a lion on his chest while spear-bearing Minerva has the snake-haired Gorgon's face on her shield. Both gods have lion heads as shoulder-pads. A font with a giant lion's paw pedestal is in part a first-century AD Roman fragment. The backs of four wooden chairs are carved with fierce angels holding coats of arms, a curvilinear grotesque head, and two cross-eyed Green Men.

Room 5, The Dining Room
A pair of corner candle-holders spring from bearded heads and support large grinning serpents. The mirrors are decorated with ho-ho birds, mythical Oriental creatures equivalent to the phoenix. Griffons on a piece of brass tableware, a satyr's head spewing vegetation on a jar, and a fat mustachioed face on a furniture edge.

Room 7, The Oriental Closet
Cobra inkstand, wall sconces with phoenixes in flames, and a large green and pink famille rose Chinese frog with bulging eyes, bridging the gap between curio and kitsch.

Room 9, Countess Agnes' Boudoir
El Greco's gaunt, unnerving painting of St Jerome, with a skull and hourglass, symbols of mortality so familiar from the old graveyards hereabout. More ho-ho birds on the mirror over the fireplace.

Room 12, The Antiquarian Closet
A seventeenth-century German brass plate with gravedigger's tools and the Angel of Death on a tomb beside a church. A pair of large animal vertebrae painted to represent preaching clergymen, easily the weirdest objects in the entire house.

Room 15, The North Drawing Room
Griffons galore on the pediment and the chair armrests, with one chair sporting foliaceous monsters.

Room 16, The Great Drawing Room
More griffon chairs, joined here by a sofa with sphinxes, a central table with solar heads, candlesticks with Egyptian motifs and winged maidens supporting dragons, and a wonderful armchair decorated with rams' heads, cornucopia, serpents and winged lions. The neoclassical fireplace has a Roman charioteer with lions in harness, protected by a flying female Victory. The superb firedogs have winged sphinxes, goats' heads and female masks.

An easy walk south through the park passes the Victorian Dogs' Headstone commemorating Bevis, Tip and Barkis; a rough monolith that is a former boundary stone (and which may be a prehistoric standing stone); an ice house; and eventually reaches the slightly creepy Mausoleum (NJ68046283). At the rear of the rectangular Georgian building is a medieval arched tomb housing the effigy of a medieval knight and decorated with a skull and other symbols. Surely for this high-born fellow to be placed here he must be an ancestor of that noble family the Duffs, former eponymous owners of this great estate? Well, no: this is a gigantic con. The Earl of Fife had no famous ancestors because the Duffs had only recently been elevated to the peerage, so the tomb and effigy were purloined from St Mary's kirkyard and installed here. To complete the fraud, an inscribed slab from Cullen Kirk was added, with the original name (Innes) removed and the name Duff added, along with a false date of 1404. *Voilà!* – instant medieval ancestors. The Cullen slab has been returned, and the chap in the tomb has now been identified as Provost Douglas of Banff, who died in 1663 – which means that even his medieval armour is a fake.

On 29 February 2004 David Clark took some photographs of what appeared to be the paw marks of a big cat in the snow at Duff House Royal golf course. In a pleasing coincidence, they were published in the long-running *Leopard* magazine (April 2004). There had previously been similar prints in the sand of one of the bunkers, and about 1.15 a.m. one night on the road from Alvah to Banff, Clark had caught what he thought was a big cat in his headlights. Then in 2007 the 'Beast of Banff' became a media star. All following references are to the *Banffshire Journal*. The black panther-like animal was seen above Banff Links on 1 January (reported 17 January, along with two earlier undated sightings); on the road to Whitehills (28 January) and at Inverboyndie (29 January), both reported 7 February; and at Boyndie in summer 2004 and in Tannery Street, Banff, in 1999 (both reported 14 March 2007). On 28 March 2007 the paper's website had a video of the cat from the Cornhill area, date-stamped 26 June 2006. Public and expert opinion was split as to whether it showed an actual big cat, or just a large but ordinary moggy. Perhaps sulking at the insult, the cat apparently disappeared from view, only to resurface in November 2008 near Whitehills, and in the Montcoffer area outside Banff on 28 January 2009 (reported 3 February). On 7 February the *Press and Journal* reported the Beast (or perhaps a beast) had been captured in a makeshift trap at Crudie – and it was a native Scottish wildcat. The animal was released back into the wild.

KIRKTOWN OF ALVAH

Norman Allan's *The Kirk at Alvah* tells the story of the 1865 Dunlugas Case. The son-in-law of Hans Leslie, the Laird of Dunlugas, underwent a long legal battle to exhume the body because he claimed it was interred with documents that would change the will in his favour. Nine years after the funeral he finally won a ruling from the Court of Session in Edinburgh. The coffin was duly opened in Alvah kirkyard, a packet of papers was found beside the corpse … and they turned out to be entirely irrelevant to the will. The Bridge of Alvah has a room incorporated into the structure for the toll collector. The partly-restored Inchdrewer Castle (NJ65596071) is supposedly haunted by a white dog and/or the spirit of Lord Banff, apparently murdered by his servants when he found them stealing the castle valuables.

MACDUFF

Towering over the town from its elevated site, the parish church on Church Street has within its graveyard the Bodie Enclosure. Walford Bodie (1869-1939), the 'Electrical Wizard of the North', stage magician, hypnotist and controversial showman famous for dramatic exhibitions of electrical manipulation on stage, passed 30,000 volts (of harmless static electricity) through his body and illuminated sixteen incandescent bulbs and two arc lamps with his bare hands. Other props included an electric chair. MacDuff was his home, and the various monuments here commemorate Bodie himself, his wife Jeannie (stage name

Macduff parish church. The last resting place of the 'Electrical Wizard of the North,' Walford Bodie. The image is of his sister-in-law Isabella ('La Belle Electra').

'Princess Rubie') and her sisters Mary ('Mystic Marie') and Isabella ('La Belle Electra'). Isabella's likeness is carved on a pillow stone and the main monument is topped by a marble angel.

In October 1956 traffic and pedestrians were brought to a halt in Skene Street by a weasel trying to climb up a lamp-post. Eventually, the beast threw in the towel – slippery metal not being ideal for musteline ascent – and ran into a hole in a wall. (*Banffshire Journal* 10 October 2006.)

Tarlair Road leads east to one of the area's eeriest and most atmospheric sites, an abandoned 1930s Art Deco outdoor swimming pool. Sitting isolated in a bowl of hills and slowly decaying, Tarlair feels like something out of one of J.G. Ballard's 1960s 'urban desuetude' science fiction stories. When visiting on a damp and grey but warm May evening, I found my breath clouding as if it was a chilly February morning, but I did not feel cold. Outside Tarlair my breath was unclouded.

The eerie abandoned Art Deco Tarlair swimming pool, Macduff.

An eighteenth-century well-house sits above a once-popular but now long-forgotten chalybeate spring just east of the pool; between the two a 'Crazy Frog' face has been painted on a natural rock outcrop.

GARDENSTOWN

On 6 December 1957, at 4.30 p.m., just before dusk, several people saw a slow-moving aerial object above Gardenstown moving in the direction of Turriff. It was described as 'cigar-shaped with a round bulge at the point' and was so bright it could be seen through heavy clouds. After fifteen minutes it disappeared in 'a shower of coloured sparks' only to reappear some minutes later several miles further south, now moving at high speed. (*Banffshire Journal* 12 December 2007.)

The roofless cliff top St John's Church, Gamrie (NJ791644) was once known as 'The Kirk of Skulls'. The story goes that after defeating a Danish force in 1004 the victorious Scots decapitated three of the Viking leaders and installed their skulls as trophies in the walls. In some versions this was done because the invaders had sacrilegiously polluted the church. A possible location for 'the Battle of the Bloody Pits (or Pots)' is Bloodymire (NJ726635) south-east of Macduff; another is a spot a few hundred paces west of the church. The skulls certainly existed. They were mentioned in the *OSA* in the 1790s (when only two remained) and given a lurid description in the *NSA* in the 1840s: 'I have seen their skulls, grinning horrid and hollow, in the wall where they had been fixed, inside the church, directly east of the pulpit, and where they have remained in their prison house 800 years!' The *NSA* does not say where this report came from but John Parker Lawson's *Historical Tales of the Wars of Scotland* states it was written by the schoolmaster Alexander Whyte for the *Aberdeen* Magazine in 1832. In the 1830s a more central new church was built and as the old kirk decayed visitors started pilfering parts of the skulls. The *NSA* states that one was placed in Banff Museum. Aberdeenshire Museums have been unable to locate it. There are several niches in the ruined church walls that could have housed the relics, and the graveyard has a good set of stones carved with symbols of mortality. One is inscribed 'though after my skin worms destroy this body yet in my flesh shall I see God Job 19th 25 26.'

CROVIE

In 'Some Folk-Lore of the Sea' Walter Gregor has many beliefs among the fishermen of Crovie. The appearance on a boat of the electrical phenomenon known as St Elmo's Fire ('Fiery Cock' in Crovie) foretold a disaster or a death. Crews would not go to sea in a boat on which a man had been drowned. J. Watt had his run of poor fishing reversed when his landlady at Gardenstown threw a broom after him. Cats, rats, hares and salmon all brought bad luck. A collie dog prevented his master going to sea, pulling at the men when they were putting the lines into the boats. The fishing was abandoned and minutes later a great storm broke that swamped boats from other villages. On another occasion the same dog, a keen sailor, refused to enter the boat and had to be taken on it by force. The boat was driven ashore by a storm at Stonehaven, two of the crew perished, and the third was only saved by the dog bringing a rescue party from the town.

CLOCHFORBIE

Writing in the *Proceedings of the Society of Antiquaries of Scotland* in 1926 James Ritchie gave the tradition of a bull's hide filled with gold at the Gray Stone, also known as the Muckle Stane o' Clochforbie (NJ79685863). Treasure-seekers sought to move the stone but desisted when they heard a voice command from beneath the ground, 'Let be!' The chthonic-protected item is the recumbent stone of an otherwise vanished circle.

CRAIGSTON CASTLE

The front parapet of this splendid tower-house is wonderfully carved with monster-headed gargoyle spouts, King David with his sling (presumably about to take out Goliath), three knights and a piper who look as if they belong in the illustrations to *Alice's Adventures in Wonderland*. Several of the rooms have wooden panels featuring the Virtues, the Evangelists and the Nine Worthies (see CRATHES CASTLE), along with grotesque faces, winged souls, and phoenixes. The closet of the north-east room on the second floor has a secret room in the floor. There are carved faces on the steading and office court.

   The Urquhart family have lived in Craigston for several hundred years. In 1652 Sir Thomas Urquhart of Cromarty wrote the *True Pedigree and Lineal Descent of the most Ancient and Honourable Family of Urquhart, in the House of Cromarty, from the Creation of the World until the Year of God 1652*. In it he traced the family tree back from historically-attested Urquharts to King Arthur's daughter, Charlemagne's godson, fictional Scots and Picts of the Dark Ages, and then onto the Queen of Sheba, Pharaohs, and the Queen of the Amazons, back to the year dot. He himself was 143rd in direct descent from Adam and Eve.

   After a period of being occasionally open, Craigston now seems to be closed to visitors. Check with the local tourist office to see if the situation has changed.

KING EDWARD

The *OSA* notes that local resistance had only recently been overcome to ploughing a piece of land at Strathairy Farm called the Given Ground. 'It is now a corn field, nor has any interruption been given by the ancient proprietors [the spirits]. This is mentioned as one instance, among many, of the decline of superstition.'

James Spence's *Ruined Castles* has a tale that the widowed mother of a wayward and difficult lad asked the laird of Eden Castle to threaten him with punishment if he did not mend his ways. The laird, however, drowned the boy, so the woman knelt down on her bare knees and uttered a curse:

Cauld blaw the win'
Aboot the Hoose o' Edin!

This explains why the castle is a ruin (NJ69795878), and why it is always windy there.

MOUNTBLAIRY

A cottage on the B9121 near Hill of Mountblairy (around NJ679540) is decorated with thousands of garden ornaments including cats, dogs, skunks, butterflies, ducks, fairies and gnomes. The owners have spent thirty years putting the collection together.

ABERCHIRDER

On 24 January 1993 the *Sunday Post* reported that about three days earlier a 'dark gingery' big cat had been seen. It was estimated to be 4ft (1.2m) from nose to tail.

MARNOCH

The graveyard on the B9117 (NJ59494993) is supposedly the burial place of the seventh-century St Marnan, whose relics were venerated by pilgrims here until the Reformation. The church and the saint's holy well are gone, but the site does have two elaborately-decorated monuments. The lesser has symbols of mortality, a skull in the round and a coat of arms. The second has a structure almost unique in my experience. An oval cavity houses a self-satisfied and well-upholstered bearded gent wearing a cloak and ruff and holding what may be a purse. Grotesque faces loom out of the ornamentation along the oval's rim and the coffin, hourglass and death-bell circle round. A skull, two sets of bones and the Grim Reaper's scythe are linked by the thread of Life and Death. Two Corinthian columns support a pediment with a coat of arms flanked by two Angels of the Resurrection lustily blowing trumpets. Winged souls, flaming pillars and crossed sexton's spades and flaming torches complete the imagery. At the very bottom a skeleton lies horizontal in its grave. Two other recumbent gravestones have similar, if less flamboyant, decoration. The basement of the house-like building on site was an anti-bodysnatching vault, while the upper storey was used as a schoolroom. 'If you don't behave, young Farquhar, you'll have to stand in the cellar with the corpses.'

The present church just to the north-east (NJ5971520) is next to a substantial standing stone called St Marnan's Chair, probably the lone survivor of a massacred circle. Further north-east is the White Stone or White Cow, a large block of striking white quartz now fenced off in a field (NJ60125110). It does not appear to be a standing stone, and is scheduled as a medieval land boundary. In 1926 James Ritchie related its folklore: some treasure-seekers tried to move the stone to uncover the gold hidden below. They knocked off for the night with their work unfinished; the next morning all the diggings had been filled in by unseen forces and the stone was back in its place. The adventure was wisely abandoned.

At once a meditation on the inevitability of death, and a massive ego-trip declaring the individual's wealth and status. Marnoch graveyard.

A skilfully-carved skeleton in its grave, Marnoch. Even the folds of the winding-sheet have been included.

Tree and Thorax Stone Circle.

FINNYGAUD

With its substantial cairn platform, central tree, elevated site and wonderful views, the small six-stone Thorax Stone Circle is a real treat (NJ58225495). One of the stones is extensively cup-marked. Ask permission at Thorax Farm.

GORDONSTOWN AND ORDIQUHILL

On 15 June 1657 Agnes Bayne of Ordiquhill was charged with laying on and taking off illness, and refusing to treat someone. George Henderson from FORDYCE wanted Agnes to heal his wife because she was a doctrix. The term implies not a physician but a schoolteacher, so perhaps Agnes laid claim to specialist knowledge she could pass on to others. Agnes asked to lie in his wife's bed so she could cure her. This was refused – not for sexual prudery, because strangers often slept in the same bed, but for another reason that is not recorded. Agnes took the huff and left, and refused to return despite three entreaties by George. Shortly after, his wife died. The case is in Maxwell-Stuart's *An Abundance of Witches*. McPherson's *Primitive Beliefs* tells of an Ordiquhill man who sometime before 1870 watched an old woman milking a berry bush to transfer the goodness of a neighbour's milk to her own cows.

St Mary's Well (NJ57215554), now just a fenced-off concrete cover, was once much visited by health-seekers. This was the big well, able to cure illnesses that the local holy wells in several neighbouring parishes could not deal with. J.M. McPherson related that in 1632 the minister of Ordiquhill interfered with some visitors to the well, hoping to identify them so they could be censured by the Kirk-Session. That night his manse was attacked and he was assaulted and disfigured.

6

STRATHBOGIE

HUNTLY – GLASS – RHYNIE – LUMSDEN

HUNTLY

Huntly Castle (Historic Scotland, open 1 April–30 September 9.30 a.m.–5.30 p.m. daily; October–March 9.30 a.m.–4.30 p.m. Saturday to Wednesday; admission charge, guidebook, limited wheelchair access) was the seat of the powerful Clan Gordon, Earls of Huntly, and the focus of Catholic resistance to the Reformation in the North-East. The Gordons were not shy at proclaiming their own magnificence; an entire exterior wall is covered with an immense inscription announcing a dynastic marriage, and the elongated vertical heraldic panel above the chief doorway would not be out of place on a royal palace; the second panel is flanked by a unicorn and a sinuous fire-breathing wyvern, each topped by a four-legged dragon. There are more heraldic beasts on the carved fireplaces within the ruin.

Walking west along the south bank of the Deveron will bring you to the Devil's Stone or Chair. The hollows in the stone are interpreted either as the imprint of His Infernal Majesty's cloven hoof, or as the place where he would park his Satanic posterior at midnight and smoke a pipe (the tobacco was stored in the second hollow).

The Brander Museum (The Square, open all year, Tuesday–Saturday, 2 p.m.–4.30 p.m., free, good wheelchair access) has a display on Huntly-born writer George MacDonald, whose major fantasy works *Phantastes* and *Lilith* are acknowledged influences on C.S. Lewis and J.R.R. Tolkien. With its themes of vampirism and morbid dream-imagery, *Lilith* in particular has considerable appeal for fans of contemporary Goth-fiction: the male protagonist is guided by a shape-shifting raven/librarian into the other-world of the dead and attempts to waken the eponymous Lilith, only to find she is secretly drinking his blood. MacDonald's fantasy books for children, including *The Princess and the Goblin* and *At the Back of the North Wind* are more wholesome but still brushed with the uncanny and the touch of death. One of MacDonald's key motifs is his use of mundane objects – such as a mirror in a dusty attic – as magical portals into trans-dimensional other-worlds. A leaflet is available containing a self-guided tour around MacDonald sites in Huntly.

'The Standing Stones of Strathbogie,' two low stones at the rear of the statue of the Duke of Richmond in The Square, are all that remain of a six-stone circle with a diameter of around 50ft (15.25m). The circle was clearly once a well-known landmark, as a court was held here in 1557, and in 1594 it was the rendezvous for the Earls of Argyll, Huntly and Errol before the Battle of Glenlivet. One stone once bore a Pictish 'horseshoe' symbol but this has now faded away. The fountain, decorated with owls, is supposedly above a secret tunnel that leads to the castle; this is possibly a memory of the old well that once stood nearby. In recent years the highlight of the local Hallowe'en celebrations, known as the Huntly Hairst, has been the parade in the square by the Huntly and District Pipe Band, with all the musicians wearing grotesque masks made by Cath Whippey. Think a Venetian masked ball in kilts.

Huntly is home to Deveron Arts, a 'dispersed art' organisation whose motto is 'The Town is the Venue'. Instead of filling an exhibition space, they percolate through the ordinary life of the town, so that artworks can be found in hotels, bars, businesses and leisure centres. Several pieces have a pleasing congruence with the subject matter of this book. Bob Pegg devised *A Storywalk through Huntly*, with fantasy stories jointly inspired by the works of George MacDonald and the architecture of Huntly. Raeburn Butchers on Bogie Street has a stuffed lamb, one of several that did not survive the lambing season and formed part of David Blyth's *Knockturne*, a meditation on life and death and ritual in collaboration with local farmers. Another of Blyth's taxidermy projects, *Pheasant Bomb*, is in the Brander. In 2000 two temporary projects by Paul Carter saw the world's cheapest spaceship installed in the garden behind the Brander, and the installation of stained glass and the playing of the musical notes from *Close Encounters of the Third Kind* transform a Second World War pillbox near Gartly into a place of extraterrestrial communication. Bonkers, but in a good way. See www.deveron-arts.com.

In 1843 historian John Stuart published *Extracts from the Presbytery Book of Strathbogie 1631-1654*, which contained *verbatim* reports from the Huntly area church records, mostly concerned with breaches of the social order, from the occasional (murder and assault) to the frequent (drinking, fornicating and non-attendance at church). The Presbyterian authorities were also much concerned with attempting to suppress folk magic; they had their hands full with this, as people from all social classes – including church elders – insisted on consulting 'charmers' on health issues. At the Synod of Moray in 1637 the representatives of the Strathbogie Presbytery noted there were a great many charmers in their area and asked for advice on how to deal with them. Again at the Synod in 1672 Strathbogie charmers were described as 'using spells and other heathenish superstitions, expressions and practices over sick persons for their recovery.' An interesting point is that none of the punishments handed down were severe: no 'witches' were tortured or executed in Strathbogie.

In 1631 four witnesses testified that Issobell Trayl of Grange had got down on her knees, cursed the minister Robert Watsone, his wife and his children, and uttered a malediction on 'all them that called her a witch'. Kneeling while cursing was regarded as a means of giving the malison greater power. Issobell confessed to obtaining charms from John Philp (see BANFF) and seeking advice from the witch called Walker for something that would make her ale a sure-seller. Walker (who might have been male or female – the record does not say) told Issobell to take mould from a grave and place it twice under her gate; Issobell denied she actually performed the ghoulish deed. There is no indication what her punishment was. In *Notes on the Folk-Lore of the North-East of Scotland* Walter Gregor added that churchyard mould or 'meels' was a common material in sorcery – if thrown on a mill-wheel the machinery would immediately stop. Anything to do with burials seemed to possess the potential for a magical re-use: 'arresting' involved removing a coffin-screw from a grave at midnight while repeating the Lord's Prayer backwards, then inserting the screw into a footprint from left to right, again with the repetition of the blasphemous prayer. If this was done the human or animal so 'arrested' would be unable to move any further.

In September 1636 Margaret Fraser, suspected of witchcraft in Aberdeen, was said to be on the run near Inverkeithny. Margaret next turned up in the Strathbogie records fourteen years later, in January 1650, when she was again described as a fugitive, this time from the Presbytery at Turriff. A month later the minister at Grange noted Margaret had died. In October 1643 George Seifvright of Acharn was rebuked for consulting Janat Maconachie about his sick wife. George denied he knew Janat was suspected of witchcraft and claimed no knowledge of any charms.

One charmer who turns up several times in the records is Issobell Malcolme from Botarie. On 12 April 1637 she confessed to having been in the charming business for twenty years, curing a child's sore eye at Bade in Ruthven, and applying fertility charms to two gentlewomen, Jeane Rudderfuird, wife of James Gordoune in Torrisoyle, and [Unnamed]

Innes, spouse to Johne Ogilvye of Miltoune. Perhaps she thought that by naming the toffs she would be treated more leniently; this may have worked, as apart from being censured there is no further record of a punishment. In January 1640 Christane Rind and Thomas Duff were summoned for consulting Issobell. Reading between the lines, it seems that Issobell conducted a physical examination on Thomas and diagnosed his impotency as due to magical ill-will from someone in the house of Alexander Spense; she advised the couple to go to the house and confront the inhabitants. Other than an order for Issobell to appear at a future meeting of the Presbytery, there is no more mention of the case. Brief inconclusive mentions of Issobell are made in February and August 1644, but after that she slips away from recorded history.

A truly intriguing episode with poltergeist overtones was heard on 28 February 1644; unfortunately, as is so often the case, the recorded details are sparse and difficult to interpret. The central character was Patrik Malcolme, who appeared to have an unpleasant reputation. Refused milk by the wife of John Maltman in Botarie, he promised revenge, and the cow died a short time later. He asked Alexander Gray for a shirt in exchange for returning the goodness of Gray's corn (presumably Malcolme had diverted the goodness in the first place). But the core of the evidence concerned the house of Alexander Chrystie in Grange, where Malcolme was lodging. Chrystie's servant Margaret Barbour declined to, as the report says, 'committ filthiness' with Malcolme. He then asked for her left shoe, saying this would cause her to follow him. She refused, at which point he told her that she would not prosper that year and revealed the contents of a closed cupboard (presumably both statements were meant to show his psychic powers). Then, as both Chrystie and his neighbour Walter Brabner testified, a fearful 'clodding' began. 'Clodding' in other cases (see CRATHES) usually means the house was subjected to a mysterious assault of stones and clods of earth, as well as other objects apparently moved by occult means (or covert human agency). Sadly here no details are given other than that the disturbances lasted for twenty days and only ceased when Margaret Barbour was removed from the house. This frustrating case has hints of the sexual power over women later attributed to the Horseman's Word, a ritual object (the left shoe), malevolent magic (or hoaxing), and poltergeist activity, but we know nothing more. The Presbytery deferred the case for a month, and no more is heard thereafter.

The Presbytery also found themselves continuing to punish former Catholic practices such as visiting holy wells for healing. On 28 March 1633 Jonet Abercrombi from the mill of Botarie and Agnes Jerret in Aucharn were summoned for 'going in pilgrimage, setting on of bonfyres, and for other superstitious rites and ceremonies'. On 14 September 1636 Peter Wat and Agnes Jack of Inverkeithny repented for going on pilgrimage to the chapel 'beyond the water of Spey.' Agnes confessed that she accompanied 'ane diseased woman' to the chapel but 'gave her great oath that she used no kynd of superstitious worship.' And on 26 July 1643 James Watt of Bucharne managed to avoid turning up for the third time to face charges of going on pilgrimage to wells and chapels (and for being an adulterer).

Perhaps the strangest – and saddest – case in the records concerns Jean Symson, a young woman from Rothiemay made pregnant by the fourteen-year-old John Wat. Symson apparently genuinely believed that she was not carrying a child – but a bellyful of cats. (There was a belief at the time that if a male cat jumped over food it might emit semen; hence any woman who then consumed the food would have kittens.) In December 1653 Symson applied to the minister for a certificate attesting she was gravid with cats, so she could receive appropriate medical attention from a doctor in Aberdeen. The minister refused and reported the case to the Presbytery. Examination of the witnesses the following March showed that Symson had tried to get a potion to kill 'the cats in her bellie' first from an older woman, then from a second minister, and finally from Annas Bain, a suspected witch. Bain gave her a hot drink with something like garlic or onions in it, but the pregnancy was not affected. Symson's mother, Issobell Chrichtoun, also stated under oath she believed her daughter was carrying cats. The investigation continued with the Presbytery failing to prove their suspicions that the real progenitor of Symson's swelling belly was Alexander Wat, John's father, who had encouraged his son to sleep with the girl so as to deflect the punishment from himself onto a boy below the age of legal responsibility. If this was true, Symson's fixation on her feline pregnancy, and its subsequent round of seeking abortion advice, may have scuppered his plans. However, at this point the records cease, and we know no more of what happened to all concerned.

The ruined churches at Dunbennan (NJ5042408) and Kinnoir (NJ54434321) have eighteenth-century carved gravestones. The latter is claimed as another burial site of the seventh-century St Marnan. Only one upright, called Cummer's Stone, remains from Roddentree Stone Circle (NJ52404214). Writing in *Antiquity* in 1929, H.O. Forbes describes a dolmen that formerly stood on Battle Hill (NJ542401): three massive pillars supported a large horizontal capstone. The site, now long gone, had generated several legends: it was the tomb of a mighty warrior; a druid's altar; or had been accidentally dropped by the Devil while practicing low-altitude flying on his way to deposit the cloven-stone on Knock Hill. St Mungo's Well on the Hill of Mungo (NJ55074270) was 'Of no medicinal quality but what arises from superstitious quality' (*OSA*). Cold Well, by a track on Hill of Drumfergue (NJ46843357) was also said to have healing properties. West of it is Carlin Hill. Place names in the vicinity of Gallow Hill (NJ503363) include The Watchman and Cutbeard Hill.

GLASS

The pleasant but undistinguished graveyard on the site of the former Walla' Kirk next to the River Deveron (NJ42673724) is the locus for a clutch of strangeness. The first known church on this site was probably built in the twelfth century, and St Wallach's Fair was held at Haugh of Glass for several hundred years thereafter. The waters around the church became the focus of pilgrimages for healing, and in 1648 the Presbytery of Strathbogie ordered all such superstitions at the site to be suppressed. In fact, they seem to have continued in one form or another for at least another two centuries, with reports in 1725 and the mid-nineteenth century. Offerings of pins were left in a twin-holed stone in exchange for healing afflictions of the eyes at the now-lost St Walloch's Well, below the church. In his book *Glass, Aberdeenshire* James Godsman states the last recorded example of a child being thus treated was in 1812, and in the early twentieth century fathers were still collecting the water for use in baptisms. At the riverside is a pool called Walla' Pot, with another cavity, St Walloch's Bath, about 440 yards (400m) upstream. Both were used for bathing, and rags and pieces of clothing were left as offerings on the trees or cast on the water. The pools were mostly visited in May, and the water was especially potent in curing sick children. Writing in the *Proceedings of the Society of Antiquaries of Scotland* Arthur Mitchell noted that in 1874 an invalid was brought from the seaside to bathe in the pool, a remarkably late example of such a practice, and an indication of the extent to which the healing powers of these waters were locally regarded.

In 1998 the magazine *Folklore Frontiers* published a piece by Alexander Fenton and David Heppell called 'The Earth Hound – a Living Banffshire Belief'. It described a longstanding local belief in a creature called a 'yird pig', 'yird swine' or 'earth hund', a ferret-sized rat-like burrowing mammal with a dog-like head and a bushy tail. The animals were thought to live in graveyards and feast on the dead. This unusual addition to the cryptozoological files was first mentioned by Walter Gregor in *Notes*:

> When a graveyard on the east coast of Aberdeenshire had to be in a great measure closed, nothing would induce the inhabitants of one of the villages of the parish to bury their dead in the new one. What was to be done? A shoemaker, whose shop was the meeting-place of many of the people of the village, was equal to the difficulty. One night, when a few of the villagers were in the shop, the shoemaker announced that there were 'yird swine' in the old graveyard.

... A water rat was produced. 'An' that's a yird swine, is't, the creatir it eats the dead bodies?' said the men, standing at a distance, and looking in horror on the abhorred beast ... The news spread like fire through the village, and many visited the shop to convince themselves of the dreadful truth. The fate of the old graveyard was sealed in that village.

Although in this case the creature was obviously a ruse, the canny shoemaker was clearly playing on an existing belief. Fenton and Heppell dug up two eye-witness accounts of earth-hounds, one from the 1870s (somewhere on the banks of the Deveron, near a churchyard which was eventually abandoned because it was believed to be infested with the corpse-chewing critters), the other from around 1915 (at Warthill, near Inverurie). In both cases the labourers had killed the animals. Then in April 1990 Fenton visited a friend in Keith, who described the coffin-burrowing beasts as a cross between a rat and a rabbit, and knew where they could be found – Walla' Kirk. Sadly an expedition to the graveyard produced no evidence of their existence, despite the man's insistent searching for scrape marks or nests. Almost certainly the creatures are just rats, given a new identity from the frisson of horror that comes from finding voracious rodent omnivores in or near graveyards. But the idea of an unknown corpse-eating creature has a certain Gothic as well as folkloric appeal, and there may well be further sightings of the earth-hound to come.

On 25 November 1646 William Seifwright and George Stronach of Glass were 'accused of sorcerie in allotting and giving over some land to the old goodman (as they call it)'. They were censured by the church and promised to work the field they had previously put aside for the Devil. In 1996 the *Evening Express* reported a different kind of magic, when Sandy Stephen of Douls Farm discovered a surprise crop of giant puffballs on an undisturbed dung heap. One was more than 6ft (1.8m) in circumference, while one of the twelve monster fungi produced the previous year may have been even larger.

In the village of Haugh of Glass the Barons of Edinglassie used to hang Highland thieves at the bridge. The dool or dule (grief or sorrow) tree is claimed to be the strange-shaped tree by the side of the road; marks on the branches are said to be from ropes. The hills north and south of the A920 are replete with various cairns, a small fraction of the once far larger number in the neighbourhood. There are fairy hillocks north of Upper Hillside (NJ42454338) and on Muckle Long Hill (NJ45493649), while the Giant's Stone sits above the Deveron on the track to Little Gouls at NJ41788354. A holy well dedicated to St Ann at NJ45194025 near the north bank of the Deveron east of the village was much visited by those seeking health. The restored Beldorney Castle (NJ42263698, private) has a gargoyle in the angle between the main roof and the Dog Tower (which is topped by a canine figure); the hill visible to the west is Gallows Hill. Another grotesque face pokes out from the date stone (1678) on Davidston House (NJ41954515).

CAIRNIE

The walled burial enclosure in the churchyard of St Martin's Church (NJ48994454) contains a sixteenth-century male effigy and a possibly pre-Reformation image of St Martin. Trekking through the forestry plantation on The Bin will bring you to New Found Aisle, a fissure opening out into a cave (NJ497434), and the Gallon of Water, a natural pool at the foot of an outcrop on the summit (NJ50344382) whose spring-fed waters were once believed to be medicinal; small offerings such as pins, nails and buttons were left behind after drinking. At 55in x 39in x 7in deep (1.4m x 1m x 18cm) the pool could hold 54 gallons (245 litres). No longer extant is the Elf House, a cavern at NJ499433 which was walled up in the nineteenth century to prevent loss of cattle. The associated legend has a cow, a little girl, and her piper father, all disappearing one after the other into the cave, the only evidence of their existence being the respective sounds of lowing, crying and piping heard from beneath Dunbennan Hill on the opposite side of the River. This is a variant on the 'piper in the tunnel' motif found in folktales right across Scotland.

RUTHVEN

The fragmentary old parish church (NJ50614690), dedicated to St Carol (or perhaps Caral or Cyril), has an effigy in full knight's armour. The north side of the churchyard wall incorporates a cist cover found in 1860. Auchanachie Castle (NJ49864692, private) has inscribed over the door FROM OVR ENEMIES DEFENDEVS O CHRIST 1594.

ROTHIEMAY

This is a good area for those seeking prehistoric rock art. There are cup-marks on several boulders around Avochie (at NJ53984684, NJ54174655, NJ54034657 and NJ541468) and on the recumbent of the Rothiemay RSC (NJ551487, four other stones upright). In 1921 The Right Revd G.F. Browne published an enthusiastic, if slightly eccentric, guide to North-East stone circles, *On Some Antiquities in the Neighbourhood of Dunecht House*. In it he claimed that the cup-marks on the Rothiemay recumbent represented the Pole Star, the constellation of the Great Bear (Ursa Major) and the brightest stars such as Arcturus, Bootes, Aldebaran, Capella, Vega and Altair. As ever, some individuals can produce the patterns they desire while ignoring the marks that do not fit the theory.

Equally strange but definitely real is the rock gong at Arn Hill Stone Circle (NJ53164564). Initially the site appears unpromising – the recumbent is the only stone still upright – but take a pebble, strike the huge saddle-backed stone in the right place, and it becomes clear why it is also known as the Iron or Ringing Stone. Here you can experience sounds as heard by our prehistoric ancestors. The gong featured in the 'Rock and Bones' episode of a 2007 BBC Radio Scotland series, *Scotland's Music*, written and presented by John Purser. At the time of writing the programme is still available on the BBC website.

A man at Retannoch believed his cows were bewitched. Janet Hepburn, his wife, cured them by driving them over the burn of Relashes and back again at midnight. (McPherson, *Primitive Beliefs*.)

INVERKEITHNY

Connoisseurs of ruined mansions will enjoy the Italianate house at Haddo (NJ619462), an easy walk along a track on the west side of the Keithny Burn. The decoration in one room features a pair of full-breasted female sphinxes. The usual rules about taking care apply while exploring the mostly roofless structures. The B9024 east of the village passes through a landscape overflowing with (mostly extensively damaged) prehistoric remains, including stone circles at Backhill of Drachlaw (NJ67294633), Greymuir Hill (NJ675452) and Harestanes (NJ664438), and a menhir at Crofts of Shielburn (NJ676463). The ruinous circle at Cairn Riv (NJ67444659) is the most intriguing. Once part of an immense cairn with a road or track leading to the circle at Backhill of Drachlaw, a number of high status finds were discovered when it was dismantled for building materials in the nineteenth century. All that remains now are two uprights, one a gobsmackingly huge boulder called the Carlin Stone, 'carlin' being an old word for witch.

FORGUE

On 18 January 2004 the *News of the World* reported that Alistair Halkett of the Bognie Arms Hotel had witnessed a 'feather-capped' spirit in the public bar, with other ghostly phenomena including door handles moving, footsteps in empty rooms, and objects moving of their own accord.

McPherson found a fascinatingly detailed example of a ritual surrounding a 'goodman's field' in the church records from 3 March 1650. Disease had struck a herd of cattle and so the farmers, Norman Leslie and James Tuicks, went to a piece of good land and repeated some words, promising that the land would remain untilled. They cast some stones over the dyke onto the field, thus signifying they were renouncing their claim to the land. The Kirk-Session clearly thought the men had dedicated the field to Satan, but it seems just as likely that they were attempting to placate a vengeful 'spirit of the land': if it accepted the gift of the field, it might stop killing the cattle. The power that this idea had over the men is clearly shown in the records: having been rebuked by the Session and ordered to plough the land, Tuicks was in front of the Presbytery two weeks later, confessing that because the cattle were still sick, the piece of land still remained unworked. In a later reference McPherson mentions a 'deevil's faulie' or 'black faulie' of about 4 acres on Boginspro Farm at Forgue that persisted until early in the nineteenth century. Eventually the Bognie farmer decided the powers of the invisible world had had long enough to cultivate the ground and so took the plough to it; there was no supernatural comeback.

A spectacular monument dated 1674 in the churchyard of Forgue kirk (NJ61084510) adds a thistle and bearded head to the usual angels, skull and hourglass, and there are more excellent carved symbols on other gravestones. The most bizarre site in the area is the Wild West town of Tranquility, at Drumblair near Glendronach Distillery. It comes complete with traditional Western saloon, bank, general store and undertakers. Oh, and gunfighters. See their website for details of their regular shootouts.

LARGUE

My eyes are seething in my head,
My flesh roasting also,
My bowels are boiling with my blood;
Is not that a woeful woe?
'The Fire of Frendraught', traditional ballad

The present Frendraught House (NJ62094189) stands on the site of the original castle in which took place one of the more mysterious events of Scotland's bloody history. Following a complex series of land disputes, skirmishes, assaults and killings among the local noble families, in October 1630 Sir James Crichton of Frendraught was given a protective armed escort to his home. The party, which included the son of the Gordon Marquis of Huntly, and Lord Rothiemay, was wined and dined and persuaded to stay for the night. When all were asleep the tower they were staying in was deliberately set alight, and most perished. The murder of aristocrats does not pass unnoticed, and a lengthy investigation ensued (involving the torture of servants) although no case could be made against the main suspects, Crichton and his wife. The traditional ballad quoted above became well known and firmly placed the blame on Lady Frendraught, possibly unfairly, as it is just as likely that the fire was set by one of the other fractious local families, such as the Leslies of Pitcaple. Whoever was responsible, the death of a Gordon son in a Crichton household poisoned relationships between the two families for generations, with the Crichtons eventually being eclipsed. Perhaps inevitably, the apparition of the supposedly regretful and white-clad Lady Frendraught is claimed to wander the house, although this is possibly due to her role in the ballad as a scheming murderess, always a popular turn in hauntings; surely those who perished horribly in the fire would be more likely to hang around?

In 1917 James Ritchie reported some of the other local traditions to the Society of Antiquaries of Scotland. The lady of the house took a moment's fancy to a passing Highlander, so her jealous husband promptly followed and killed the man and buried him under a large stone near the hill top. This may be a reference to the broken recumbent stone of the much-abused circle near the summit in the grounds at NJ61094285. The circle was also formerly known as 'The Covenanters Preaching Stones'. South-west of the House is Gallows Hill. The story here is that when a new gallows was erected, the workmen were not sure it would work properly, so they seized a poor packman who happened to be passing, and promptly proved the device was functioning to their satisfaction.

DRUMBLADE

The key local legends here link the fourteenth-century Robert the Bruce to the area's prehistoric monuments from thousands of years earlier. Bruce was taken ill at the Battle of Slioch against the Comyns (1307). His camp was supposed to have been on Robin's Height (NJ56443880), to the north of Slioch, and the OSA in 1799 described the hill once having large inscribed stones and entrenchments. Whatever these earthworks and stones were, they are long gone. The prehistoric round cairn and long barrow on Newtongarry Hill (NJ57624031) to the north-east, along with a third, now vanished tumulus, were said to have been built by Bruce's men as observation and communications posts, with the sick king giving orders from the camp. In later years one of the tumuli was named the Fairy Hillock, and was also supposed to have been a place of execution.

There are several carved gravestones in the kirkyard (NJ578403) and a skull can be seen on a slab inserted into a wall by Fourtrees (NJ58293957). The Chapel Well (NJ58583729) was a healing well associated with the now-vanished Nine Maidens' chapel and graveyard at Chapelton. The Ramstone boundary stone on the A96 was once regarded as a fairies' kiln. Leslie's Cairn on Play Hill (NJ60083634) marks the burial place of a suicide. *The Place Names of West Aberdeenshire* mentions that somewhere in the parish was a series of pits called Wolf Holes, generally supposed to have been used for trapping wolves, but more probably trenches dug to indicate a march or boundary. There was also a Buglehole or Boglehole, possibly referring to a bogle or hobgoblin.

In 1647 Isobel Wilson was accused of charming a cow belonging to John Findlay of Drumblade, and laying the sickness on his servant Margaret Hendrie. Margaret had stepped on the water used in the charm and the disease had been transferred to her; she was 'swollen so big that there was no hope of her life'. The case is in McPherson's *Primitive Beliefs*.

LOGIE NEWTON

The large white quartz stones in the kerbs of the cairns on Kirk Hill (NJ65943910) are dazzling in sunlight. A standing stone behind Mellan Cottages (NJ66293883) on the way up was apparently taken from one of the cairns, or near them, and erected here to mark the place where an urn containing human remains was found some time before 1871.

CLASHINDARROCH FOREST

This large high-level forest is liberally supplied with wells, many of which were claimed to have had healing properties: Caird's Well (NJ57413431); Thief's Well (NJ55413364); Slouch Well (NJ56033324); Whitestripe Well (NJ55593259); Todhole Well (NJ57403364); McClog's Well (NJ56103198); Deer Well (NJ57183240); Cold Well (NJ58323324); and Haining Well (NJ54363291). The most celebrated was Malsach or Melshach Well (NJ55443186). In the 1790s the OSA noted it was 'still in great reputation among the common people. Its sanative qualities extend even to Brutes ... it became customary to leave at the well part of the clothes of the sick and diseased, and harness of the cattle, as an offering of gratitude to the divinity who bestowed healing virtues on its waters. And now, even though the superstitious principle no longer exists, the accustomed offerings are still presented.' In 1908 an account was printed of a fertility ritual that apparently had taken place in the 1860s. On the first Sunday in May a keeper and an expert from Aberdeen went to the moor to investigate grouse disease. From a distance they saw several women with hands joined, dancing in a circle round the well. By using a spyglass they could see that the dancers' clothes were fastened high up under their arms, and a seated old woman was sprinkling their genitals and breasts with water from the well. Presumably these were married women hoping to conceive. The account is in McPherson's *Primitive Beliefs*.

GARTLY

South of the church is a piece of ground called Buried Men's Leys (NJ527342), which used to be thickly studded with cairns and is said to be the resting place of Highlanders who died in a skirmish after the BATTLE OF HARLAW. One mound was known as the Piper's Cairn. There is no way of telling whether the story is true, but as 'proof' the *NSA* in 1845 claimed that when the cairns were removed for building stone, a pair of brass buckles and two badly-decomposed dirks were found. Coombs Well at Whitelumbs (NJ52023230) was said to be a healing well.

The most intriguing extant monument in the area is the Drumel Stone, which is currently lying flat and easily-ignored in a field near Newnoth on the A97 (NJ51673061). Around 1823 it was moved about 20ft (6m) from its original position, and beneath it was found a truly strange collection of objects: a presumably prehistoric urn containing ashes, which was reburied at the spot; a piece of heavily decomposed tartan; and badly corroded silver and copper coins supposedly dating to the reign of Mary, Queen of Scots. If the description is accurate, when were the modern objects deposited? And by whom? And were they left under the stone so that the spot could be easily found again? At some point in the late nineteenth century the stone appears to have been lifted and used for the lintel in a new byre. In *Primitive Beliefs* McPherson relates how thereafter the steading door never remained closed and the cattle were constantly escaping. Once a replacement was installed and the stone was returned to the ground there was no further trouble. One of the contributors to the Modern Antiquarian website, 'BigSweetie' (Andy Sweet), tracked down a letter written to the *Scots Magazine* by Kathleen Davidson in November 1985. She regularly holidayed with her grandparents in the area in the 1920s and passed the stone daily. She was told the story about the lintel: 'The first night after the cows were shut in, they made a great rumpus. The farmer and my grandfather went out the next night to stand guard with guns. They never told what they heard or saw, but the stone was taken out and put back in the field.' The stone was relegated to its current ignominy around 1951.

LEITH HALL

The classic Aberdeenshire ghost book is *A Strange and Seeing Time*, written by Elizabeth Byrd in 1971. From 1966 she and her husband Barrie Gaunt rented the East Wing of the Hall, and between them and their guests they encountered a wide range of ghostly phenomena, including: apparitions (a Victorian lady, children playing, a man with a bandaged head and a formless grey mist); sounds (footsteps, a lady laughing, drums and bagpipes, the clinking of crystal, children giggling, party noises); smells (camphor and food); a sense of malevolent presence or of being watched (especially in the master bedroom of the second floor); environmental changes (flashes of light, and sudden temperature fluctuations); and poltergeist activity (doors slamming shut, small objects flying through the air, objects appearing out of nowhere). As a consequence the hall has become much visited by paranormal investigation groups.

The hall is owned by the National Trust for Scotland and until recently was open to visitors. However, on 20 May 2009 the NTS announced that Leith Hall was closed as part of a cost-cutting exercise across the charity. The NTS website states: 'A proposal is being progressed for the development of areas of the estate and the conversion of the house back to residential flats. The gardens and estate will remain open to visitors.' At least this means the dool or hanging tree is still accessible, although it is not clear what will happen to the two Pictish carvings, the Salmon Stone and the Wolf Stone, that are kept in a structure in the grounds.

KENNETHMONT

The Candy Stone (NJ53363036) is the sole survivor of a stone circle, now in the rear garden of Jeddah. South-west of Ardlair is a severely damaged RSC (NJ55272794) and a pair of standing stones (NJ55472784), one with a Pictish beast and the 'mirror' and 'tuning fork' symbols. A spring called Holywell once flowed nearby.

CLATT

The parish church (NJ53862599) has a damaged Pictish stone built into the kirkyard wall and a nineteenth-century burial vault which can be entered from outside the wall. A stone bearing both prehistoric cup-marks and a Dark Ages cross within a circle stands just south of Tofthills Farm (NJ55132657). It was found in 1879 and appears to have been part of a now-lost stone circle called the 'Sunken Kirk'. The name comes from the belief that the Devil/earth spirits had caused the stones to sink beneath the earth. Sunken Kirk legends are found throughout Scotland and Northern England. A number of cairns east of White Hill, including the only one now remaining, Jock's Cairn (NJ51922434), used to be regarded as the sepulchres of those slain at the nearby Battle of Tillyangus in 1571, when the Catholic Gordons defeated the Protestant Forbeses. The chalybeate Holy Well (NJ52312367) in the forest at the source of the Small and Gadie Burns has a heavy iron content and was once highly regarded medicinally. The RCAHMS Canmore website states: 'A silver coin will adhere to a vessel, due to the action of its minerals, if placed in it immediately water from this spring has been poured out.'

RHYNIE

The Old Churchyard (NJ49932647) at the south end of the village makes for a very satisfying visit, with a large number of eighteenth-century gravestones carved with symbols of mortality, a sculptured Gothic tomb recess with an adjacent stone coffin shaped to fit the corpse, and three fragments of Pictish stones – including what may be a representation of a dog or even a mask made from the skin of a deer's head. Several other Pictish stones have been found in the area. The most famous, the 'Rhynie Man,' a fiercely expressive bearded man, is in the council headquarters at Woodhill House, Aberdeen, but a cast can be seen in the vestibule of the school at Rhynie. A superb example still *in situ* is the large Craw Stone, standing in a field south-west of the graveyard (NJ49752635). The Salmon and Pictish beast are expressively carved. Two more incised stones, their carvings now all but invisible, flank the north-west entrance of the village square, and another pair of small standing stones guard the south-east gate.

The surrounding area has a good crop of antiquities: a pair of tall standing stones at Mill of Noth (NJ50332779), and extensively ravaged stone circles at Corrstone Wood (NJ51012711, one stone upright), Upper Ord (NJ48252696, two stones) and Wheedlemont (NJ47952660, two stones). Several rock outcrops around Templand (NJ47202722) are carved with cup-marks. The reduced Iron Age fort on Wheedlemont Hill (NJ47292605) is chiefly of interest because of its name – Cnoc Cailliche, the hill of the old wife or witch. The site of the demolished Old Kearn Church (NJ51452664) has a fine mausoleum. Gallows Hill Cairn (NJ47232773) is a substantial prehistoric mound re-used as a place of execution by the Gordons of Lesmoir. In 1651 Sir William Gordon of Lesmoir admitted that he had heard that a part of his home-farm was dedicated to the Goodman, and so was not worked; 'but he had a mind, by the assistance of God, to cause labour the same: Whereupon he was commended for his ingenuitie in declareing it, and exhorted to take paines shortly to have it laboured.' (*Presbytery Book of Strathbogie*.)

The restored Druminnor Castle (NJ51322640, private) is one of two castles – the other being CASTLE FRASER – where a story is told of an accidental massacre. In the sixteenth century a feast was held as part of an uneasy truce between the Forbes of Druminnor and their rivals the Gordons; the host indicated that if the guests made threatening moves he would stroke his beard as a signal for his cohorts to stab the visitors. During the meal he unintentionally made the gesture – and in seconds fifteen men were murdered. In *A Strange and Seeing Time* Elizabeth Byrd describes a visit to the castle in about 1968. Her psychic husband, Barrie Gaunt, picked up a murder scene in one of the bedrooms and an old crippled lady in the cellars, and correctly recounted obscure details about several of the Forbes relatives.

A curious report appeared in the *Glasgow Herald* on 22 August 1970. A number of people in Rhynie reported seeing a well-built man wearing a white ankle-length garment and heavy boots walking sedately through the village in the middle of the night. Along with another witness, Ian Howie, the proprietor of the Gordon Arms Hotel, followed the 'ghost' until it disappeared into vegetation at the church. Residents apparently also received anonymous phone calls describing strange rites allegedly carried out near the church. What exactly was going on is unclear, as the story just fizzles out.

In *Leopard* magazine (April 2004) David F. Clark reported seeing a nearly black big cat some years previously while driving north between Lumsden and Rhynie.

Everywhere around Rhynie the eye is drawn to Tap o' Noth, the hill that dominates the area for miles around. The impressive Iron Age fort on its summit (NJ48452930, reachable by a path from the car park on the A941) is one of the largest and highest in Scotland. It also has extensive sections of vitrified rock (see DUNNIDEER). A report from 1730 claimed that a taper placed in a well on the summit would reappear twenty-four hours later in a burn at the foot of the hill; this is a common folkloric motif, and is told about mountains throughout Scotland. There is now no well within the fort. (The story is from Macfarlane's *Geographical Collections for Scotland*, reprinted in Robertson's *Illustrations of the Topography and Antiquities of the Shires of Aberdeen and Banff*, 1847.) A large natural rock on the south slope is the Giant's Stone, part of the boulder-tossing contest between the giants Jock o' Noth and Jock o' Bennachie (see BENNACHIE). The eye of faith may be able to distinguish the giant's boot print on its surface. The information board in the car park contradicts the usual legend by stating that the monolith is associated not with a giant but with a saint.

North-west of Tap o' Noth, in the vast Forestry Commission plantation, the Cairn of Milduan (NJ47773011) provides an object lesson in the unreliability of place names and tradition. The bumps and lumps in the area were interpreted as the burial places of those killed at a battle in 1057, when Malcolm Canmore defeated and killed Lulach, stepson of Macbeth. The more prominent structures were seen as chiefs' sepulchres and the name

The summit of Tap o' Noth hillfort, with vitrified rocks in the foreground and around the trig point.

Milduan translated as 'Grave of a Thousand'. In truth, most of the features were stone clearance heaps, the 'chiefs' graves' were the remains of crofters' houses, and the Cairn of Milduan is actually a ruined kiln. The tradition seems to have evolved from the belief that these were the warriors' graves; there is no other evidence of the battle actually having occurred here. To the north, where the minor road follows the valley of Kirkney Water, is supposedly the site of willow trees planted by retreating survivors from the BATTLE OF HARLAW in memory of their fallen comrades.

Walking the forest track east from this road eventually brings you to lonely Wormy Hillock (NJ44983077), easily one of the strangest sites in this book. It consists of a bijou henge – with room for perhaps eight people to congregate – with a central platform linked by four low causeways to a well-defined bank; a prominent natural mound rises immediately to the north. Henges are thought to be meeting places for ceremonies and perhaps trade; quite how this cosy little space was used is a cause for speculation. There is some confusion as to whether the name 'Wormy Hillock' was thought to apply to the henge or the mound. The nearest thing to an explanation of the name is given in James Taylor's *The Cabrach* (1914) and *Cabrach Feerings* (1920): the old road that ran through this area was known as 'Wormy Howe' because it was created by a giant worm as it set out to do battle with a rival near Bennachie. Worms or wurms are a type of dragon found folklorically in Scotland, Northern England and Scandinavia; they are huge serpents lacking legs and wings, but otherwise well-equipped with traditional draconic attributes such as jaws filled with razor-sharp teeth, poisonous or fiery breath, and a voracious appetite for human flesh. Sadly the legend does not say if the two worms met, or what happened when they did. Presumably the shape of the henge prompted the belief that the worm had coiled up to have a nap here.

The bleak moors of Clayshooter Hill have a mound named Dead Wife's Cairn (NJ43852415), and, north-east of Smuggler's Well, two small huts which were probably sites for the illegal distillation of whisky (NJ42972388). *The Cabrach* notes that smuggling and illicit distilling

The henge of Wormy Hillock from the adjacent natural mound. The central platform can clearly be seen. The Worm, sadly, cannot.

were widespread in the area up until 1820, and that the approach of the dreaded exciseman was signalled by stretching a white sheet on a peat stack or a knoll. Thus warned, 'one of the distillers would seize the "pottie" and run with it, an essential condition being that he must run naked, why, no one seems to know'.

Five paces south-east of the triangulation pillar on the summit of The Buck, 2367ft (721m) above sea level at the junction of the three parishes of Cabrach, Kildrummy, and Auchindoir and Kearn, and on the border between Aberdeenshire and Moray, are carved three intertwined fish with their heads forming a triangle and their tales poking out in three directions. The letters 'W' and 'M' are on either side of the motif, with 'T(?) A' above and 'A' in the lower left, as well as some other graffiti which appears to be both less clearly incised and more recent. The carving is definitely not Pictish and is probably not medieval; it may be eighteenth or nineteenth century. But who did it and what does it mean?

AUCHINDOIR

The evocative roofless shell of the early nineteenth-century church near the A97/B9002 junction (NJ48322460) signposts you to the equally ruined medieval St Mary's Church (NJ47802455). Cared for by Historic Scotland, it has a sixteenth-century sacrament house, where the consecrated host or mass-bread was stored, with an abbreviated Latin inscription which translates as 'Here is the Body of Our Lord, with Mary, the Apostles, and Saints,' and a crucifixion above a skull – a reference to the place where Jesus was crucified, Golgotha, supposedly meaning 'Place of Skulls'. The magical graveyard hosts several skull-and-bones gravestones, a heraldic stone from 1580, and a nineteenth-century angel. A. Jervise gave the church's founding legend in the *Proceedings of the Society of Antiquaries of Scotland* in 1870: the church was originally to have been built at Glencairns south of Lumsden, but the Blessed Virgin Mary interceded – 'but for the warning voice of the Virgin, who appears to have been

'Squarehead' skull with symbols of death, St Mary's Church, Auchindoir.

a good judge both of locality and soil, the kirk would have been placed in an obscure sterile district'. A well dedicated to the Virgin, and visited as a cure for toothache, was somewhere west of the church. Immediately to the east is the very obvious Mote Hill, a medieval castle-mound on a striking position high above the river.

LUMSDEN

A sculpture trail on the south edge of the village showcases some of the work of the Scottish Sculpture Workshop, based in Lumsden. Some pieces are strange and delightful. The best is what appears to be a set of miniature steps leading to a polished flying saucer. Well, that's my interpretation.

7

UPPER DONSIDE

KILDRUMMY – STRATHDON – GLEN NOCHTY – CORGARFF

KILDRUMMY

St Bride's Chapel (NJ47251756) is the little-visited local gem. The present church is *ordinaire* but the raised circular mound of the graveyard is clearly ancient, and holds one of the best collections of carved gravestones and memorials in Aberdeenshire, several of them tucked away in the various burial enclosures. A slab with full-length effigies of a man and woman is hidden behind wooden doors in an arched tomb niche. The gravestones positively explode with skulls, winged souls, strange human figures and the Grim Reaper with his scythe. The short road to the church passes a prehistoric cairn marked by a lone pine.

The name of the solitary Lulach's Stone (NJ46761942) refers to the persistent tradition that Macbeth's stepson was killed by Malcolm Canmore in this area; the standing stone of course pre-dates Macbeth by at least 3,000 years, and the same tradition appears near INVERURIE and TAP O'NOTH. Lulach's Stone is also supposed to mark the site of a bull's hide filled with gold; treasure stones, unlike the actual riches, are plentiful in the area. Another widespread legend attaches to a spring on Craigs of Logie. The Nine Maidens' Well supposedly marks the spot where nine young women were killed by a savage boar. In one version of the tale Archencar or Ochonochar, a Pictish warrior and boyfriend of one of the girls, decapitates the animal, which in this account is a bear, and goes on to found the dynasty of the Forbes whose arms bear the ursine trophy. The tale of the Nine Maidens is a persistent motif throughout Scottish legend; variants include them being killed by a dragon or water monster. Stuart McHardy's *The Quest for the Nine Maidens* tracks the tale through English, Welsh, Norse and Classical mythology. As for the Craigs of Logie version, it may derive in part from the discovery of a Pictish carving of a boar on the site; the stone was still standing in the eighteenth century. The well, however, seems to be lost in the forestry; even the authoritative RCAHMS Canmore website gives two locations for it (NJ49391856 and NJ49871834). Further north Lord Arthur's Cairn (NJ51201980) is claimed to be the resting place for those carrying the coffin of Lord Arthur Forbes. Forbes was killed at the Battle of Tillyangus in 1571 (see CLATT).

KILDRUMMY CASTLE

(Historic Scotland. Open 1 April–30 September, daily 9.30 a.m.–5.30 p.m. Admission charge, guidebook, partial disabled access.)

A contrast to the tower houses so common in Aberdeenshire, this is a medieval courtyard fortress with a massive curtain wall and defensive towers, much ruined. Excavations in the east tower of the gatehouse uncovered two male skeletons, giving testimony to the castle's violent past: one had its skull smashed and the other had been beheaded. In 1306 Kildrummy was besieged by an English army; the legend is that it only fell through the treachery of

Happy skeleton, St Bride's Chapel, Kildrummy.

St Bride's Chapel, Kildrummy. Are these fellows lifting weights or beaming down radiance?

a blacksmith called Osbourne or Osbarn who set fire to the castle. When he claimed his reward – as much gold as he could carry – he received it as molten metal poured down his throat. A modern grotesque face of the unhappy Osbourne hangs in the visitor reception.

In *A Strange and Seeing Time* Elizabeth Byrd describes a déjà vu experience in Kildrummy Castle Hotel: on her arrival she knew she had been there before, and remembered how to navigate the corridors. She thought it might have originated in a forgotten precognitive dream. In the dining room her husband Barrie Gaunt psychically 'saw' a big dog by the fireplace and children celebrating a Victorian Christmas.

TOWIE

Another fine crop of symbols of mortality sprouts in the graveyard of Towie parish church (NJ43971296), which also has an upside-down iron lattice anti-bodysnatching mortsafe. Some distance to the east stands the Lang Stane (NJ48031394), looking like a tooth extracted from a giant's mouth. In legend it marks both the site of a battle and a pot of gold.

GLENKINDIE

The Treasure Stone just south of the road junction is yet another standing stone guarding a bull hide filled with gold (NJ43831375).

The Glenkindie Treasure Stone, supposed marker of one of several supernaturally-protected bull hides filled with cursed gold.

GLENBUCHAT

A natural pool of rainwater on the north side of the rocky summit of Ben Newe (NJ38171431) was given special veneration. In 'Guardian Spirits of Wells and Lochs' (1892) Walter Gregor notes: 'Everyone that goes to the top of the hill must put some small object into it, and then take a draught of water off it. Unless this is done the traveller will not reach in life the foot of the hill.' In 1890 Gregor found several pins, a small bone, a pill-box, and a flower, and through the twentieth century others reported seeing pins, coins and charms. Gregor also describes how Mrs Michie of Coull of Newe in Strathdon suspected someone was bewitching her cows, as the butter would not come. Peter Smith, 'a man of skill' from Towie, boiled up myrrh with some secret ingredients and gave the mixture to all the cattle. He also advised Mrs Michie to place water-wrack from the burn over the door of the cow-byre. Smith said he had the knowledge from his late wife, and before he died he had to pass it on to a woman. This passing of 'the power' to the opposite sex just before dying was a common procedure. This is from 'The Witch' (1889). In another article from the same year, 'Devil Stories', Gregor relates a story told him by William Michie of Strathdon:

> It was a common belief that the devil took the shape of a beast, often that of a dog, and made his way in that shape to any spot where a great crime was to be committed or some tragic thing to take place. J-R, farmer, in Milton of Glenbuck, was one Sunday morning strolling over his fields to view his crops, when a big black mastiff rushed past him at more than ordinary speed. The brute attracted the farmer's attention by his great sticking-out 'allegrugous' eyes. He followed him as fast as he was able, never lost sight of him, and saw him enter the door of the farmhouse of Drumgarrow [Drumnagarrow, NJ39061670], where two brothers lived. At that moment he heard a shot inside. One of the brothers was shot dead. A mystery hangs over the man's death.

BELLABEG AND STRATHDON

Easily-visitable in the grounds of the Colquhonnie House Hotel (NJ36521259) is a wonderful 24ft (7.3m) high totem pole created in 2003 by carvers from the Squamish Nation of British Columbia and several local artists. When the pole was erected it was blessed by being brushed with water from the River Don. Close by are the sparse remains of Colquhonnie Castle – which tradition insists was never completed, three Forbes lairds having supposedly died in succession during the building work. Again according to tradition, which of course is never in error, one of these chaps fell from the castle and so haunts the hotel as the Phantom Piper. The *Sun* for 16 October 2006 reported that an exorcism by two ministers failed to banish not merely the piper but also a Victorian lady and a poltergeist supposedly responsible for smashing glasses and moving furniture.

Bellabeg is dominated by the Doune of Invernochty (NJ35151296), an enormous castle motte or mound surrounded by a defensive network of ditches, dams and sluices, some of which can still be seen, as can the footings of a Norman church within the remains of the curtain wall on the summit. J.G. Phillips, in *Wanderings in the Highlands of Banff and Aberdeen Shires* (1881), relates a fairy encounter. Two men were walking past the Doune on Hallowe'en when they heard music. One, against the advice of the other, joined in the fairies' dance on the summit; twelve months had to pass before his friend could ascend the hill and rescue him from the revels. When returned to his family, the first man insisted he had only been dancing for a few minutes. There are dozens of versions of this tale throughout Scotland.

To the south, Strathdon parish church (NJ35541275) has another first-class set of carved tombstones. Towering over the other graves is the two-storey Mitchell-Forbes Mausoleum,

The totem pole at Colquhonnie House Hotel. The carvings include eagle, owl, salmon, boar, squirrel, a spear-carrying warrior and a woman in modern dress. The curvilinear forms are evocative of Celtic design.

a massive neo-Egyptian block that would be more at home in Glasgow's grand Necropolis than a quiet country churchyard.

Sometime in the early nineteenth century a coffin being carried over a burn in Strathdon suddenly became so heavy that the party came to a halt mid-stream. An old man asked if any of the mourners had shaved on Sunday; one admitted he had, and after he had placed his hand on the coffin it returned to its normal weight and the party proceeded as normal. When the schoolmaster Alexander Thomson was drowned in the great flood of 1829 his body was taken to a nearby cottage, but was refused entry until it was carried round the house. Despite this precaution the waters rose further and swept away the building – an event the owner blamed on the corpse having circled the grounds only once, rather than the regulation three times. Both tales were related in 1914 for the journal *Folklore* by David Rorie, who had been told them by some of the oldest inhabitants of the village.

Comedian and actor Billy Connolly owns Candacraig House, so the area regularly attracts attention from the national press. On 23 February 1998 the *Sun* claimed the house was haunted by a dog that climbed the staircase. A few weeks later on 15 March the *News of the World*, while describing the case of lorry driver Robbie Gray's unnerving night-time encounter with a big cat in an unnamed forestry plantation, reported that a pair of black panthers had been seen running together next to Candacraig. And on 13 July 2003 the *Sunday Times* noted that Connolly had installed a 9ft (2.75m) high 'pagan' stone in his garden, inscribed with his favourite saying: 'There's no such thing as normal.'

Two bizarre winged skulls that seem to belong to an alien species. Strathdon church.

GLEN NOCHTY

The Lost Gallery (NJ313158) is a wonderful art collection greatly enhanced by its remote location. Among the many outdoor sculptures is *Constellation* by Kenny Munro, a cup-marked monolith which clearly echoes the area's prehistoric rock art. On 25 August 2005 the *Sun* quoted gallery owner Peter Goodfellow as having once seen a UFO, 'a weird circular orange light which was moving about the sky'. There was a local tradition that a cateran was killed during a cattle raid on the area around Auchernach (NJ331159), and that his ghost haunted the place. The editors of *The Place Names of West Aberdeenshire*, in which the story appears, examined the evidence from a toponymic point of view and found it decidedly wanting.

CORGARFF CASTLE

> But when the lady saw the fire
> Come flaming owre her head,
> She wept, and kiss'd her children twain,
> Says, 'Bairns, we been but dead.'
>
> 'Edom o' Gordon', traditional ballad

(Historic Scotland, open 1 April–30 September 9.30 a.m.–5.30 p.m. daily; October 9.30 a.m.–4.30 p.m. daily; 1 November–31 March 9.30 a.m.–4.30 p.m. weekends only. Admission charge, guidebook, no disabled access. NJ25450867.)

Gaunt and isolated, the whitewashed walls and distinctive star-shaped bastion contain the Scottish equivalent of a Wild West frontier fort, a remote outpost in 'Injun country'. In 1571, following the Forbes massacre of Gordons at DRUMINNOR CASTLE, and then the BATTLE OF TILLYANGUS, the Gordons pursued their vendetta against the Forbes by attacking Corgarff. Only women and children were resident; Margaret, Lady Forbes, refused to surrender the castle so the Gordons burned it, killing at least twenty-four people, an atrocity commemorated in the ballad quoted above. Since then, the inevitable engine of folklore has geared up, with screams of the victims reported around the castle, particularly in the barrack room.

Up until the late nineteenth century a mound stood near the castle that allegedly marked the grave of Buachaill Mor, the 'Big Herd,' who seemed to have jokingly doubted the marksmanship of the soldiers garrisoned at Corgarff when it was a Government stronghold. As a result of his taunting, he was (accidentally) shot on the spot. A more recent monument that also seems to have vanished is a marker cairn to the east of the castle, to which bus driver George Allison would encourage visitors to add stones in the 1970s; the castle staff have no knowledge of it.

On 9 September 1980 the *Press and Journal* reported that three days previously an Australian couple travelling on the road near the castle at 6.45 p.m. saw 'a heavily built black lioness'.

CORGARFF

Walter Gregor excelled himself when it came to collecting stories from around Corgarff. In 'The Witch' (1889) he noted tales that were still being told about practitioners of magic. Jeanie Marae Alise of Badachallach was a noted witch who could help as well as harm. During a famine she created food for a starving man by shaping her apron into the form of a milk-churn, repeating the words: 'Froh [froth], milk, froh, milk, black stick, you an me, froh, milk,' and adding some mould brought from between the plough coulter and the sock. On a visit to a farmer friend she found both his son Duncan and his cow at the point of death. About

One of a pair of Asian monsters guarding the entrance drive to Corgarff Castle.

midnight she heard a voice asking, 'Will I tack the coo or Duncan?' She answered in favour of Duncan and the next morning the boy was up and about and the cow was dead. She could shape-shift into a deer or hare. When a farmer shot a mysterious hare with a sixpence marked with a cross on it, he found Jeanie lying wounded on her bed. She pronounced a curse on the man's wife, who soon died in childbed. When Jeanie's house caught fire she went into the smoke, and cried out, 'If a'm yours, give me three puffs an three blaws, an in the diel's name oot it goes'. Her gluttonous son, if refused milk by a farmer's wife, caused the herd to be dry for the next few months. Jeanie died doing a good turn; she was taking a man across a rain-swollen river by using a corn-riddle as a magical surfboard. In mid-stream the flood threatened to upset the pair and the man cried out, 'God save you, Jeanie'. She instantly disappeared with the riddle and was never seen again.

Another witch was Lizzie D., who clearly earned her living simply through having a threatening reputation. A farmer shot and wounded a hare, which turned out to be Lizzie, who walked with a limp thereafter. Much later she begged money from the man. Afraid of her he handed over a half-crown, a large sum. Subsequently all his enterprises flourished beyond expectation, so he kept Lizzie happy by gifting her two cart-loads of peats each winter. Wives who refused Lizzie curds, cheese, butter or milk found their labours unproductive and their cows dry; only when Lizzie had been placated by a present did things return to normal.

The old Laird of Skellater often employed a witch. On one occasion he bet on a crop-shearing contest between his men and those of a neighbouring laird; Skellater's reapers were losing so

Old Janet replaced one of them and turned three times against the course of the sun, saying, 'Black nickie, you and me; and di'el tack the hin-most'. The rival laird was standing behind his men with his face turned to the sun, so the Devil stole his shadow, and for the rest of his life the laird cast no shadow.

Magical counter-measures were much in vogue. Pieces of rowan placed secretly into the byre after sunset on Rood Day (2 or 3 May) prevented witches from taking horses for midnight gallops. When a mare was taken from the stable the first time after foaling, or when a horse was kept in a vulnerable open shed rather than a stable, a rowan cross was tied with red thread to the animal's tail. On Beltane eve (30 April) a similar charm was placed in each opening in the byre. Next morning these crosses were tied to the tails of the animals before being sent to the fields, and to drive them the herdsmen were given rowan wands or clubs, sometimes cut with a cross on the end. When a cow calved, the apotropaic item of choice was a mother's apron, which was placed over the horns or head of the animal for a short time, while an amulet was tied around the neck. The cow's first drink had to be water which had been warmed by having a live coal placed in it. All this protected the animal when she was at her most vulnerable. When witchcraft was the suspected cause behind a cow failing to give milk, a pair of the farmer's trousers was put over the cow's horns, and she would head straight for the witch's house and low at the door (Milly the Cow: Witchfinder General). Another ritual involved performing imitation milking on rowan pieces, then mock-milking the cow, both in the name of the Trinity, and finally putting fire in an old shoe and burning it below the cow, while repeating, 'May the Almighty smoke the witch in hell as I am smokin' the coo'. After a triple rub-down with holy water along the backbone from head to tail, the cow was ready to give milk.

Sometimes violence was called for. The accepted method was to conceal a silver pin within the finger and thumb of the left hand, pass between the sun and the witch in the morning, and then strike, drawing blood from above the eyes ('above the breath'). The witch's power was negated while the pin was still stained with the blood.

It was believed that protection was provided by 'getting the first word in' before a witch or supernatural being spoke. J.R., a farmer in Strathdon, returning home one wild cold night, met a child crossing the road at Dabrossach. He called out, 'Peer [poor] thing! Ye're far fae hame in sic a stormy nicht'. The child instantly disappeared and the man knew it had been a being of evil. In another article, 'Devil Stories', Gregor collected a much more light-hearted tale. A whisky smuggler called David Bertie, out on a night-time assignment, met a rider. At first he was scared that it might be the gauger (exciseman), but then he was relieved to see it was only a man with horns, hairy legs and cloven feet, reeking of brimstone.

Somewhere near the current graveyard at Corriehoul (NJ28320848) stood St Machar's Well, a place of pilgrimage for healing. Depositing a silver coin secured a cure. In 1613 the Kirk-Session of Elgin banned visits to the well on pain of a fine of ten marks. In 'Guardian Spirits of Wells and Lochs' (1882) Gregor tells how, during a time of famine, a priest appealed to St Machar and three salmon miraculously appeared in the well, but only after the housekeeper carried out a prescribed ritual: she had to circle the well three times at sunrise repeating the names of the Trinity, and draw a draught of water without looking into the well. Take away the Christian trappings and you have a fine example of folk magic. The three springs of Tobar Fhuar further west (NJ24701078) cured blindness, deafness and lameness respectively. Around 1840 a group of lads set out to possess the kettle of gold held by the well's guardian spirit under a large stone. After much effort they removed the Kettle Stone, and found – absolutely nothing. An old woman who met them later reminded them of the death curse that lay on anyone who tried to rob the spirit, and predicted they would soon lay beneath the ground. One of the lads, Gregor's informant, James Farquharson, was still thriving some fifty years later. Another well somewhere in the area, the Bride's Well, was visited by every bride the night before a wedding, to have their feet and upper part of their body bathed by the bridesmaids, a fertility ritual which ensured a family (for comparison, see the ritual at MELSHACH WELL).

The bride placed crumbs of bread and cheese into the water, a piece of sympathetic magic designed to keep her children from ever being hungry.

Some water spirits were less than benevolent. Gregor relates how a man, desperate to reach his sick wife but despairing because the Luib Bridge over the Don had been swept away in a flood, accepted an offer from a very tall individual to carry him across. In mid-river the kelpie, for such the stranger was, tried to drown the man, who only escaped after a fierce struggle. When he reached the bank the frustrated creature threw a boulder at him. Passers-by added stones to the boulder until it became known as the Kelpie's Cairn. These days the A939 crosses the Don on the very solid Luib Bridge (NJ26480879). A much-robbed cairn to the east at NJ26850908 may possibly be the Kelpie's Cairn, but it seems too far from the river.

A truly monstrous spirit inhabited Lochan-nan-Deaan (probably Lochan gun Doimhne, on the A939 Lecht road, NJ243140). The creature killed travellers and dragged them down into the bottomless waters. When the men of Strathdon and Corgarff tried to drain the pool to recover the bodies, 'there arose from its waters a diminutive creature in shape of a man with a red cap on his head. The men fled in terror, leaving their picks and spades behind them. The Spirit seized them and threw them into the loch. Then, with a gesture of defiance at the fleeing men, and a roar that shook the hills, he plunged into the loch and disappeared amidst the water that boiled and heaved as red as blood.'

In 'Notes on Beltane Cakes' (1895) Gregor describes how the spirit of the land had to be propitiated by travellers taking to the hills. One of two hillside wells had to be visited and a barley-meal cake left, marked on one side by an 'O'. On two occasions this was not done, and in both cases the people concerned – a man, and a woman called Elspet – lost their lives on the moors. T.D. Davidson, writing in *The Agricultural History Review* in 1955, noted a similar ritual at Corgarff: two pieces of land, on Torna-shaltic (allegedly Gaelic for 'Fire-hillock') and Tornahaish (tentatively translated as 'Cheese-Hillock'), were each year sprinkled with milk on the first day of April. This libation was to keep 'the evil one out of the hoose, the milk-hoose, the byre, an' the barn'.

There is a Fairy Hillock at the very head of Glen Ernan (NJ271129).

8

KINCARDINESHIRE

PORTLETHEN – STONEHAVEN – INVERBERVIE – LAURENCEKIRK

THE CROSSROADS

In his 1819 novel *A Legend of Montrose* Sir Walter Scott called this area the Moor of Drumthwacket. In the 1860s the landowner Sir David Stewart, clearly a Scott fan, changed the name of one of his farms from Banchory Hillock to Drumthwacket (NJ919002), one of several examples where Scott's popularity has reshaped Scottish geography and history.

PORTLETHEN

There are stone circles worth visiting at Craighead (NO91179772), Old Bourtreebush (NO90359608) and Aquhorthies (NO90189634), although the roar of the A90 can be distracting. James Crabb Watt's *The Mearns of Old* (1914) describes the area between Stonehaven, Maryculter and Aberdeen, as formerly 'dotted over with standing stones ... most of them are now buried like the bones or remains they are said to have burdened, or uphold crofters' houses or fence their fields or metal their roads ... Many such stones has the writer seen blown up by gunpowder'. Raised causeways can still be seen at the road near Causeyport (NO914987), remnants of the ancient Causey Mounth routeway that linked Stonehaven and Aberdeen, here crossing over the terrible bogs of impassable Portlethen Moss.

MUCHALLS

In *Ghosts of Today* (1980) Andrew Green recounts several experiences he was told about Muchalls Castle (NO893918, private). In the 1970s a visitor saw the apparition of a girl in an old-fashioned lime-coloured dress patting her hair into place, as if looking into a mirror. Maurice Simpson, the then owner, experienced an icy temperature in the same room, which had a history of hauntings dating back to 1906 when a guest saw a young woman in a green dress. The castle had its own Episcopalian chapel, destroyed in 1746 by the Duke of Cumberland on his way to Culloden – many Episcopalians were thought to be sympathetic to the Jacobites. A hill to the north-east is the site of the three succeeding chapels, located in a concealed spot for security. There is nothing to see on the ground now. On 23 June 2002 the *News of the World* reported that phantom footsteps echoed through Sandra Lappin's house in Muchalls, and that in 1982 at another house in the village she saw a ghostly hand.

In 2005 the ITV television series *Beyond Explanation* interviewed Tom Moir, who claimed he had seen three spaceships over Muchalls in 1971 when he was thirteen. The *News of the World* (27 January 2002) reported that locals 'say the area is rife with UFOs and strange lights in the sky,' and that people were blaming the irregular electricity supply on the aerial phenomena. As a gentle aside, it should be noted that this entire area is abuzz with helicopters serving the North Sea oil platforms.

KEMPSTONE HILL

Watt's *The Mearns of Old* tells of a tradition that a decapitated warrior ran the distance of 93 yards (85m) between the two standing stones on the summit (NO87678947 and NO87608942); the event took place during a battle long ago. He also says there were once five or six stone circles on the hill, which is one of the frontrunners for the unidentified Mons Graupius.

STONEHAVEN

Harbourside

The Tolbooth Museum (open April–September, Wednesday–Monday 1.30–4.30 p.m., partial wheelchair access, free). This sixteenth-century former prison appropriately holds a set of stocks and a crank machine, a punishment device which involved the prisoner turning a handle on a drum weighted with sand or water. Tightening the screw made the task harder – which is why prison guards are called screws. There is also a cup-marked stone and a model of the oldest known British land fossil, a 428-million-year-old millipede found at Cowie by Mike Newman. It is named *Pneumodesmus newmani* in his honour. In 1957 long cist graves and prehistoric human remains were found behind the Tolbooth. Much of central Stonehaven seems to be built on the dead – more ancient graves were found at the Market Cross and Mary Street. Five eroded carved heads adorn the front of the Marine Hotel. The human head is clear, and a lion, boar and stag can be made out.

High Street

Gordon J.N. Ritchie's *Stonehaven of Old* says that Cumberland House – so named because the Duke of Cumberland stayed there on his way to Culloden in 1746 – was also called the Green Lady after its resident ghost.

New Street

A splendid but strange painted relief carving of a pair of eagles fighting serpents, installed in an ordinary front garden wall. The lane wall up the slope at the junction with Victoria Street has two 'plague stones', one being the gravestone of a victim of the 'Pest' of 1608.

Mineral Well Road

The Victorian fountain of St Kieran's Well (NO86848684) stands somewhere near the site of a much-visited medicinal spring or holy well.

Dunnottar Woods

To get the best out of a visit here, try to pick up the 'Dunnottar Woodland Park' leaflet or George Swapp's booklet *Dunnottar Woods and House*. The delightful Dunnottar church (NO86318518) has numerous gravestones carved with skulls and other symbols of mortality. The most famous gravestone commemorates the Covenanters who perished in DUNNOTTAR CASTLE in 1685. The sight of a man lovingly restoring the lettering on the stone gave Sir Walter Scott the idea for his 1816 novel *Old Mortality*. Scott stayed at the manse opposite the church. In *Memorials of Angus and the Mearns* (1885) Andrew Jervise and James Gammack recall some of Scott's activities. He based the character of Meg Mucklebackit in *The Antiquary* on Kate

Moncur, on a Crawton fishwife he met, and studied John Thorn, a farmer from Fernyflat, who was a self-proclaimed expert in countering witches and fairies. While Scott was there Thorn was called on to remove enchantment from a cow at the manse. He boiled some of the animal's milk and made zigzag marks on the surface, which would cause equivalent wounds to appear on the body of a witch. In *Letters on Demonology and Witchcraft* (1830) Scott recorded: 'The late excellent Mr Walker, minister at Dunottar … gave me a curious account of an imposture … practised by a young country girl, who was surprisingly quick at throwing stones, turf, and other missiles, with such dexterity that it was for a long time impossible to ascertain her agency in the disturbances of which she was the sole cause'. This was presumably the 'clodding' at CRATHES.

Just south of the church a few miniscule blocks of stone by the roadside mark the site of St Ninian's Well, while to the north once flowed the Preenie Well where pins were deposited in exchange for healing water. The large Bronze Age cairn on steep Gallowhill was used as a place of execution. On 2 August 1700 thief John Reid was burned on the shoulder and bound to his accomplice John Duncan. They were marched to the gallows where Reid was forced to watch Duncan be hanged. He then had to dig Duncan's grave and bury the body before being banished on pain of death. To add insult to injury the doomster kicked him on the backside. In 1879 many human bones were found on the hill, probably the remains of numerous malefactors. Nearby in the Carron Burn is a pool called the Witches Hole or Deil's Kettle, while in the woods is the restored dome-shaped Shell House folly, and Lady Kennedy's Bath, a structure designed for *al fresco* aristocratic river bathing.

One of the great fire festivals of Scotland takes place in Stonehaven on New Year's Eve. Watched by a huge crowd, about fifty marchers swing burning fireballs above their heads while parading from the harbour to the Sheriff Court and back. At the end the brands are thrown into the harbour. The whole thing is a) a modern version of an ancient apotropaic fire purification ceremony, as once conducted at many places including CRATHIE; and b) tremendous fun.

McPherson's *Primitive Beliefs* notes that captains would pay a crone in Stonehaven old town to obtain a favourable wind. One sailor would throw his cap away into the winds of a gale, his sacrifice ensuring that the spirit of the air would look kindly upon him.

The human head on the Marine Hotel, Stonehaven. The four adjacent animals' heads are older and more eroded; they may have come from Dunnottar Castle. Where this head originated is quite unknown.

A slightly more recent human head, in the street behind the Marine Hotel.

Eagles battling serpents: a mystery sculpture in a garden on New Street, Stonehaven.

St Kieran's Well, overshadowed by the vast Glenury railway viaduct, Stonehaven.

An article by Derek Green in the *Ghost Club Newsletter* for Spring 2008 describes multiple encounters with a 'road ghost' in the summer of 1995. On two occasions the same driver 'hit' a white figure near the A90 between Aberdeen and Stonehaven. The first time there was an audible thud, but on stopping, no body was to be seen. In the second incident, some months later, an icy chill surrounded his car and an eerie presence stayed in the vehicle for several minutes. A few weeks previously the driver's mother had also encountered the figure, which this time came through the car windscreen before vanishing.

On 27 January 2002 the *News of the World* reported a sighting of two black big cats near a Stonehaven Farm earlier that month.

COWIE

A cliff-top walk from Stonehaven or a track from the golf clubhouse brings you to the roofless St Mary's Church, also appropriately known as St Mary-of-the-Storms (NO88428731), replete with gravestones carved with symbols of mortality, trade emblems and, in one case, a magnificent three-masted sailing ship. There was a corpse road down the coast, with funeral parties transporting coffins from Muchalls and Newtonhill. The health-giving Our Lady's Well below the kirk has vanished but the arch of an underground mort-house can be seen under one of the walls. One night, watchmen on the lookout for bodysnatchers saw 'something black' which moved then stood still. They fired and it fell with a thud. Investigation proved the guards had just shot a tombstone which had toppled and broken.

False painted window with lucky black cat looking out.
House gable opposite the caravan park, Cowie.

Words from beyond the grave. St Mary-of-the-Storms, Cowie.

On their way back to Cowie the watchers, to their embarrassment, met the coastguards who had seen the flash of gunfire and had mistaken it for the distress signal of shipwreck.

Local historian George Swapp told me of some of the traditions associated with the site. When St Nathalan (supposedly) founded the church in the seventh century he hid a cursed treasure between the chapel and the dell just to the south. Anyone who finds the gold will hang themselves. At the Reformation a Mr Raitt unroofed the church and used the slates for his own house. As divine punishment a 'rain of blood' appeared on his roof.

KIRKTOWN OF FETTERESSO

St Ciarán's Church (NO85298566) is the mirror of St Mary's, being roofless, ruined, and rich in headstones with *memento mori* symbols. In 1659 Jean Hunter was accused of enchanting a woman with a piece of fish roe; only when the husband threatened to burn her did she remove the charm.

ALONG THE A957 SLUG ROAD

James Grant's *The Mysteries of All Nations* (1880) describes a love charm from the 1820s. A Highland recruiting sergeant was prevented from wooing the daughter of Captain Bloomer of Ury House because of their class difference, so he consulted a wise woman called 'Lucky Lightfoot' (one suspects Grant made this name up). Lightfoot charmed a gold ring which was placed in Miss Bloomer's path, as if lost. Once she slipped the ring on her finger her heart was the sergeant's. The couple eloped to America, where the woman eventually became a proto-feminist journalist. The colossal Ury House (NO859878) is now a none-more-Gothic ruin.

One of the Roman camps on Raedykes (NO841902) is a candidate for the temporary headquarters of the legion that won the battle of Mons Graupius, which may have taken place on KEMPSTONE HILL to the east. West of the camps, Campstone Hill has two good ring-cairns and stone circles (NO83239066 and NO83309060) with other smaller cairns in the immediate area. The Lang Stane above Nether Auquhollie (NO82339080) is a standing stone with an inscription in Ogham, an ancient alphabet. Fetteresso Forest includes place names such as Red Beard's Well (NO765903, named after a notorious cattle thief), Elf Hill (NO798856), Elfhillock (NO801849) and Hill of Hobseat (NO757877), the last of which may refer to a hobgoblin.

DUNNOTTAR CASTLE

(Usually open daily, weather permitting, but times vary so see www.dunnottarcastle.co.uk or telephone 01330 860223. Admission charge, guidebook, no disabled access.)

Looking like the fossilised teeth of some great sea monster, the spectacular wave-girt peninsula and gaunt fortress of Dunnottar is deservedly popular. There may have been both a prehistoric fort and a Dark Ages church here. Access is via a narrow and steep pathway, which means the castle may be closed in bad weather. A torch is handy. The grimmest room is the Whigs Vault where 167 Covenanters were imprisoned in appalling conditions in 1685. Those that died are commemorated on the Covenanters' Stone at Dunnottar Church in STONEHAVEN. The drama of the setting almost begs for ghost stories, and several apparitions have indeed been sighted, including a young girl, a dog and a tall blond man. Convivial noises have been reported from the room in Benholm's Lodging.

The coastal path from Stonehaven passes the windswept War Memorial on Black Hill (NO87778488), a powerfully evocative structure built as an imitation ruined Greek temple, and the now inaccessible ancient settlement on the rock of Dunnicaer (NO88218464). Nobody really knows what Dunnicaer was, but several Pictish stones came from here in the nineteenth century.

KINNEFF

The redundant kirk (NO855749, open daily April-October), managed by the Kinneff Old Church Preservation Trust, is a real gem. It stands on the site of a previous church where the Honours of Scotland, the Scottish Crown Jewels, were hidden for eight years from 1652, and memorials and exhibition within tell this story. The Honours were smuggled out of DUNNOTTAR CASTLE under the noses of the besieging Cromwellian forces. The graveyard has several fine carved gravestones.

INVERBERVIE

Naked witches don't just appear in tabloid exposés; they also turn up in memorials (and then they get in the newspapers). Where the A92 enters Bervie from the north stands a memorial to Hercules Linton, who, not content with having a spiffing name, also designed the famous tea clipper the *Cutty Sark*, now based at Greenwich. A 'cutty sark' is the Scottish name for a short petticoat or shirt; In 'Tam o'Shanter', one of Robert Burns' most celebrated poems, the eponymous Tam encounters a group of witches dancing. The youngest and most attractive of the ladies is wearing the revealing garment, and after a particularly athletic leap Tam shouts out, 'Weel done "cutty sark"!' The witches immediately pursue Tam, who only escapes by crossing water just as the witch grabs his mare's tail. The poem's air of mystery clearly appealed to the shipowners, and a figurehead of the witch was commissioned. In 1997 a replica of this figurehead was unveiled as a new memorial to Bervie's most famous son. It shows the witch grasping the horse's tail; she is wearing the cutty sark – and her right breast is bared. There was something of a furore at the time. Some, of course, may say the more scantily-clad witches the better.

Charles Fort's compendium of strangeness, *New Lands*, mentions a story of an aerial object reported in the *Standard* on 16 December 1881. At 5 a.m. on 15 December Captain McBain of the steamship *Countess of Aberdeen* saw a large, bright light moving against the wind, 25 miles (40km) off the coast. Through glasses it seemed to be attached to what was thought to be the car of a balloon. The light was increasing and decreasing in size. After thirty minutes it faded from view, heading towards Bervie. The *Standard* suggested it was a fire balloon, which it may have been, but typically Fort was sceptical of this 'explanation'. On the evening of 27 December 1973 an intensely bright meteor passed over the coast at Bervie, when it was already brighter than the full moon. By the time it reached Clydeside it was too dazzling to look at directly. All witnesses agreed the head was deep green, with the tail being orange-red, showering red sparks. (*New Scientist*, 24 January 1974.)

Archibald Watt's excellent *Highways and Byways Round Kincardine* gives a family vendetta from 1570. A Rait from Hallgreen Castle argued over a girl with William Sibbald, brother of the laird of Keir, and killed him at Auchenblae. Three months later the laird and nine others murdered a Peter Rait of Tipperty and cut off his brother's hands. The Raits and their company, seventeen in total, intended to attack the Sibbalds, and to (literally) mask their intent gathered in disguise under the pretence of performing the play *Robin Hood and the Abbot of Unreason*. Such plays had been banned by the killjoys of the Reformation so it is possible the illegality of this gathering was what brought them to the attention of the authorities. The legal process dragged on, eventually returning several Not Guilty verdicts. Nothing more was heard about the blood feud. Hallgreen Castle (private), at the southern end of Bervie by the shore, is supposedly haunted by a servant girl.

Even more bloodthirsty is the tale of the Sheriff's Kettle. The basic story is that around 1420 the unpopular John Melville, Sheriff of the Mearns, was decoyed to a false hunting session, murdered by several lairds, flung into a large cauldron, boiled (in some versions while still alive) and converted into soup. Each of the four main conspirators then took their horn spoons from their belts and supped at the liquid (it is not recorded whether any of them quipped, 'Hmm, tastes like pork'). The barons concerned were pursued by church and court, and, depending on the version cited, barricaded themselves in their lairs, were punished, or repented and performed good works. The whole cannibalistic horror was said to be the lairds taking the king at his word when he impatiently cried, 'Sorrow gin the Sheriff were sodden – sodden and supped in his brew!' A likely story. Various commentators have debated the truth of the tradition; G.H. Kinnear's 1895 *History of Glenbervie* summarises all the learned arguments pro and con, and cautiously suggests the murder was real but not the soup-making. The Sheriff's Kettle is a rather dull hollow on a minor road between Inverbervie and Easter Tulloch (NO777723). The spot later became a refuge of brownies or goblins, as shown in the name of the nearby farm, Brownie-leys.

ARBUTHNOTT

The Grassic Gibbon Centre (open April-October, daily 10 a.m.-4.30 p.m., excellent disabled access, admission charge) commemorates local man James Leslie Mitchell, who under his pen-name found lasting fame with a trilogy of novels known as *A Scots Quair*. Lewis Grassic Gibbon's work is steeped in the mundane toil and tragedies of a Mearns farming community, and hence may not be thought of as fertile ground for the mysterious. But he has his moments. In *Sunset Song* (1932) the central character Chris Guthrie uses a pair of standing stones as her personal open-air sanctuary from the grimness of everyday life. Chris' father angrily catches her reading at the stones – and his reaction makes her realise he is afraid of the megaliths. At the end of the novel one of the stones is dedicated as a memorial to the dead of the First World War.

Gibbon also satirised the local monuments. An effigy of an armoured knight inside the splendidly medieval church of St Ternan (NO80167465) is thought to be Hugo de Arbuthnott, who allegedly gained the lands here through slaying a wild boar in the Den of Pitcarles. In Gibbon's version he becomes 'Cospatric de Gondeshil, him that killed the gryphon,' and the whole story is told in the form of a standard knight-kills-dragon tale. Symbols of mortality and immortality decorate some of the gravestones.

JOHNSHAVEN

The church at Benholm (NO80446925) contains one of the more extraordinary monuments in Aberdeenshire: the wall memorial to Lady Mary Keith who died in 1620 aged four. She was the daughter of Lady Margaret Ogilvie and George Keith, 5th Earl Marischal and one of the most powerful men in the country. In the 'basement' of the multi-tiered 'house' the skeleton of Death (with knobbly knees and Frankenstein-monster-like great boots) confidently handles a pair of outsize darts which pierce the torsos of the richly-costumed countess and earl, the latter holding a gun. There is also an ornately carved pre-Reformation sacrament house, a marble monument decorated with cherubs and winged souls, and, in the graveyard, the usual collection of skulls and crossbones. The building is in the care of the Scottish Redundant Churches Trust and is open daily during daylight hours from April to October.

In *Evil Scotland* Ron Halliday describes the case of 'Ann', who in the 1990s experienced a living hell after using a Ouija board. Her new home was visited by the sounds of children and a dog, apparitions, black mist, invisible guests and infestations of maggots. Objects disappeared and turned up several days later. The fire alarm and cooker switched on and off. Doors slammed shut and locked. Her eldest daughter was pushed off her bed and scratched. Halliday comes to no conclusion about the events.

ST CYRUS

The dunes and cliffs of St Cyrus National Nature Reserve provide a suitable backdrop to the beach-side Nether kirkyard (NO74506390). The collection of carved stones is of exceptional quality, with wings sprouting from the hearts of the deceased, and a unique scene showing a renowned bone-setter called Alexander Webster setting the arm of a patient while his wife and two children look on. There is a small anti-bodysnatching watch-house and several burial enclosures. Near the south-east corner is the grave of George Beattie, who blew his brains out at this very spot because his betrothed dumped him for a wealthier man after she received an inheritance. A herdsman discovered the body propped against the wall close to the stile. The girl's name was William Gibson (her parents had wanted a son) from MORPHIE. Before his suicide Beattie enthusiastically treated his friends to a meal and calmly wrote down his reasons for dying in his *Statement of Facts, Supplement to Statement of Facts, Additions to Supplement and the Last*, which became a local bestseller, turning the graveyard into a place of pilgrimage.

In 1847 James Walker of Nether Warburton, just outside the present reserve, discovered a cave filled with bones. It was later identified as a Neolithic midden containing remains of ox, sheep, pig, deer, badger, sea birds and shellfish. When workmen were clearing the cave the roof collapsed, blocking the entrance. And now no one knows exactly where the cave is.

On 9 June 2007 the *Daily Express* reported that a family of three narrowly escaped death on 7 June when a lightening bolt struck the road to the nature reserve, ripping up the tarmac and gouging an irregular trench 20in (50cm) wide and 12in (30cm) deep. The trio had been caught in a thunderstorm and were making their way back to the car when the lightning hit.

In 1630 a commission was granted to several local gentlemen to 'apprehend and try Patrick Tod for witchcraft,' but there are no details of what happened.

A bequest in the will of John Orr from 1844 provides each year for four local brides to receive a dowry – but they have to qualify as the eldest, the youngest, the shortest and the tallest, and so are carefully documented and measured by the local minister. The dowry used to be substantial but the investment has reduced and now brides receive an engraved glass vase instead.

A few hundred paces east of the A92/B9120 junction a descent at the road bridge brings you to the gorge and waterfall of the Den of Finella (NO772664), where Queen Finella supposedly leapt to her death (see FETTERCAIRN). The cave is allegedly a secret tunnel to Lauriston Castle.

MORPHIE

The magnificent Stone of Morphie (NO717626) sits next to the road through the farm where George Beattie's ill-fated romance took place. The 11ft (3.4m) tall monolith was once used as the core of a grain stack, and in that guise was blown down – along with the stack – by a hurricane in about 1850. Six years later, digging prior to re-erection unearthed a skeleton. Folklorically, it marks the grave of the mythical Danish leader Camus.

The stone's surface bears the fingerprints of the local kelpie, who was also enslaved by the laird to build the now-vanished Morphie Castle. This kelpie lived in Ponage Pool in the North Esk and achieved lasting fame in the poem John o' Arnha', a kind of Kincardineshire

'Stand aff, ye fiend, and dread my wraith / Or soon I'll steek your een in death: / Not you nor a' the hounds o' hell / Can my undaunted courage quell.'

    John Findlay takes on the Devil. From George Beattie's *John O'Arnha'* (1883 edition).

version of Tam o'Shanter written by the tragic George Beattie. John Findlay, John o'Arnha', was a boastful and authoritarian Montrose Town Officer whom Beattie knew well. The poem was turned into a play and performed at the Theatre Royal in Montrose in 1826, with the principal actor wearing Findlay's own red coat. The action concerns the fearless John who works his way up the supernatural food chain, besting the kelpie, a group of witches, and finally Old Nick himself.

MARYKIRK

The *OSA* describes St John's Well at Balmanno as curing rickety children and sore eyes in great numbers, only requiring pins, needles, and rags in return. This well appears to have vanished. The mound called Witch Hillock in Inglismadie Forest (NO64406732) is a prehistoric burial mound. The signposted Capo long barrow (NO63326645) is an immense 262ft (80m) long, one of the largest in Scotland.

LAURENCEKIRK

Aristocratic eccentrics: where would we be without them? Lord Gardenstone enthusiastically developed eighteenth-century Laurencekirk while maintaining a fondness for pigs. One followed like a dog during perambulations around his town. At first the animal shared his bed, but when it grew up to be a big pig it slept on a couch formed from his lordship's clothes. He was depicted carrying a pig on the pub sign of the now-demolished Gardenstone Arms.

The town was apparently named after Laurence, the seventh-century Archbishop of Canterbury who was said to have visited the Mearns. Watt's *The Mearns of Old* gives the tradition that St Margaret supposedly came on pilgrimage here in the eleventh century, disguised as a canon, 'and thus violating the proprieties of her sex and country, she is said to have been repulsed by the holy men'. The eighteenth-century church out of town at Garvock (NO74457047) has a sailing boat incised on its south-east corner, and several good carved gravestones. St James's Well, once the site of miracles at the annual pilgrimage, is 100 paces north-east (NO74517052). In 1862 drainage work on the bogs at Bent to the north-west revealed bones of horses, cattle, red deer, roe deer, oxen, dogs – and a human skeleton. The site was probably a 'well-eye' in the quicksand which had claimed its victims over many years.

FETTERCAIRN

East of the village there once stood a castle often visited by royalty, and the thriving burgh of Kincardine, the county capital of Kincardineshire. By the seventeenth century economic and geographical factors were at work. The burgh ceased to be the county town, eclipsed by Stonehaven. The market, St Catherine's Fair, was transferred to Fettercairn. The royals gave up their holiday home, which was ruinous by 1646. Other than the paltry remains of the castle (NO67127511, close to the Victorian mansion, private), the only visible sign of Kincardine's former existence is a graveyard containing just one small tombstone. Someone should put up a sign reading *Sic transit gloria mundi* (Thus passes the glory of the world).

In AD 995 King Kenneth II was killed somewhere in the Fettercairn area, probably by his own men, and possibly through the treachery of a revenge-motivated noblewoman named Finella (or Fenella, Finnguala or Fimberhele). From these bare bones – and the early chroniclers either provide nothing more or disagree with each other about the meagre details – a full-blown myth has developed, most notably in Andrew Wyntoun's rhyming pseudo-history *Orygynale Cronykil of Scotland* written about 1410, and elaborated by later writers who could not resist its combination of low cunning and high technology. Finella invited Kenneth to feast and hunt at Fettercairn, where she constructed a richly-furnished tower in which stood a bronze statue of the king with a golden apple in his hand. Flattered by this image of himself which no doubt exaggerated his manly qualities, Kenneth touched the apple, and before you could say 'hair-trigger booby trap' he was struck through with quarrels from the crossbows hidden within the statue. Depending on who you read, Finella then a) fled to Ireland, aided by her co-conspirator – and Kenneth's successor – Constantine III; b) fled to the coast where, cornered, she threw herself in the gorge near ST CYRUS; c) was captured, and burned along with her castle; d) escaped by walking over the treetops (because, obviously, she was a witch). Candidates for Finella's home include the medieval earthwork called Green Castle (NO66887648) and the prehistoric fort of Green Cairn (NO63347228). Strath Finella runs into the Glen of Drumtochty, the road between Clatterin' Brig and Auchenblae.

The prospect of imminent death in battle concentrates the mind. During the Civil War in 1648 the lairds of Middleton and Balbegno, two neighbouring estates at Fettercairn, made a pact that the first to die on campaign would return and tell the other about the afterlife. Balbegno was killed, and Middleton was captured at the Battle of Worcester. Imprisoned in the Tower of London, he was visited by his friend's spectre, who had no inside information on the Other Side, but did correctly predict that Middleton would escape in three days, and that the monarchy would be restored. The story appears in several works, notably John Aubrey's *Miscellanies upon Various Subjects* (1696) and Robert Wodrow's *Analecta: or Materials for a History of Remarkable Providences*, written in the 1720s. Wodrow was told it by the son of a man who heard Lord Middleton relate it at dinner, while Aubrey picked it up from Sir William Dugdale who got it from the Bishop of Edinburgh. It sounds like Middleton – fond of a drink or two – was also fond of repeating the story, which may have grown in the telling.

Watt's *Highways and Byways* describes several local traditions. Tod Hillock (NO636725) was also known as the Executioner's Knoll, nearby being a small croft called Taed's Nest or hangman's dwelling. A probable prehistoric mound just east of Fettercairn (NO653736) was called Randal's Knap, after Randal Courtney, an Irish soldier hanged here in 1743 for stealing a watch and other articles from the laird of Caldhame. The original Gannochy Bridge over the North Esk was erected in 1732 by wealthy farmer James Black. His neighbours persuaded him to build it by dressing up as the ghosts of those drowned during the flood of 1731, urging him to prevent further tragedies. The reality was that Black lived on the Edzell side of the river but had fallen out with the Edzell kirk, so attended the Fettercairn alternative. He built the bridge to avoid the inconvenience of crossing the river on horseback. In 1773 the Fettercairn congregation wanted John Barclay as their minister but the heritors (landed gentry) installed their preferred candidate, Mr Foote. When he arrived a great wind damaged many crops, the parishioners viewing 'Foote's Wind' as divine wrath. After a long dispute and several rejected petitions to the Synod, General Assembly and the king, the congregation seceded and set up their own church at Sauchieburn.

Fettercairn church (NO651736) has some good gravestone carvings, including Adam and Eve depicted with the First Man wearing shorts. St Ringan's Cairn on Redstone Hill (NO65497944) appears to have been built as a base for a Pictish cross slab. The *Ordnance Survey Name Book* for 1863 states that Smart's Cairn (NO69377772) is associated with the slaying of a huge serpent or dragon, but gives absolutely no more details.

GLEN DYE

This is the Cairn o' Mount road, one of the key routes over the mountains to Deeside. Edward I of England came this way in 1296 during the Wars of Independence. The remote route was a target for bandits and robbers (a ravine north of the car park and Bronze Age cairn is still called Thieves' Bush). In medieval times there was a 'hospitium', a hospital or traveller's rest at the junction of the Water of Dye and the Spital Burn. This was later replaced by an inn. In 1613 the three Erskine sisters travelled from Stonehaven to this Muir-alehouse to purchase poisonous herbs from the resident witch Janet Irving. A murderous aristocratic plot had been hatched to bring their brother, Robert Erskine or 'Johnne of Logy', to his inheritance. Robert thought they had not bought enough poison, so later went to meet the witch himself. The deadly herbs were steeped in ale which was then force-fed to their nephews – John Erskine, the young Laird of Dun, and his brother Alexander. The boys speedily sickened and died horribly, the eldest actually turning black. Robert, Isobel and Annas Erskine were convicted and beheaded in Edinburgh, while the 'more penitent' Helen was banished. A commission was issued to arrest Janet Irving but there is no record of whether she was apprehended. The details are in John Hill Burton's *Narratives From Criminal Trials In Scotland* (1852).

McPherson's *Primitive Beliefs* places Glendye as the home of Colin Massie the warlock, who attended magical conventions on the back of a huge black boar, and had a hare-woman as a witch-mother.

AUCHENBLAE

The legendary lore of this area is bound up with a Roman missionary, St Palladius, who supposedly worked here between AD 431 and 450, very early in the history of Scottish Christianity. As with all Dark Ages saints, Palladius was a miracle worker, causing a spring to gush forth to supply water for the baptism of his pupil, St Ternan, a local boy later active on Deeside. And also as with all Dark Ages saints, Palladius' biography is deeply dubious. In one version he died in the church he founded here; in another, he never visited Kincardineshire and his relics were simply brought here from his grave in Galloway by St Ternan; alternatively, the Auchenblae Palladius is not the emissary from Rome, but a Scottish or Irish holy man called Paldoc or Paldy, a follower of St Ninian. Until recently the annual market was known as Paldy's or Paddy's Fair. In 1978 the Catholic Church, recognising the doubts about Palladius' very existence, excised him from the official list of saints.

There was some kind of shrine here which would have attracted pilgrims, although the details are scant. In 1494 Archbishop William Sheves of St Andrews came on pilgrimage and placed Palladius' bones into a silver casket (if indeed the relics were those of the saint, and not some handy bones the Archbishop said were Palladius'). At the Reformation the silver reliquary was trousered by one of the reformers, James Wishart of Pitarrow, no doubt for entirely worthy reasons, and not because it was worth a fortune.

The much-restored medieval Paldy's Chapel, now roofless, stands next to the present church (NO72627842). A small burial vault has long been pointed out as the place where Palladius' relics were kept, although it is more probably a tomb recess. Two stones in the north-wall exterior wall have cup-markings and there are several good carved gravestones. The stone-lined pit of Paldy's Well (NO72607833) is close by in a private garden. The current church holds a superb Pictish stone, one of the best in the county.

The first church here was positioned by supernatural guidance. The original site was atop Knock Hill to the north-east, but each night the builders' work was demolished by unseen spirits, and a voice chanted:

> Gang farther down,
> To Fordoun's town.

Chambers' *Popular Rhymes of Scotland* notes that a new site was then chosen by the throwing at random of a mason's hammer.

A very large cairn west of Luther Water at NO72367802 was called Katie's Cairn because it supposedly marked the spot where Katie the witch was burnt. This is probably the same cairn described as the Witch Knap in Watt's *Highways and Byways*, in which it was placed just east of the burn. Every schoolboy knew to contribute a stone to the cairn when passing – or else the witch would get them. The cairn evaporated during the stone-hungry years of the mid-nineteenth century. Another vanished cairn, at Bogburn (NO70428165), was termed Dead Man's Cairn in folkloric memory of the place where several Highland caterans were repelled and killed.

A persistent tradition, unsupported by any documentary or archaeological record, insists that a medieval monastery existed in the Glen of Drumtochty, giving rise to place names such as Friar's Glen, Priest's Well and Abbot's Face. The beautiful Victorian neo-Gothic Church of St Palladius has a large statue of the eponymous saint and benefits greatly from its woodland setting (NO707798). A ghostly Green Lady appears on the main front staircase of Drumtochty Castle (NO699800, private), but, for some reason, only in the month of May.

GLENBERVIE

The fragments of St Michael's Church (NO76708043) shepherd a fine flock of carved gravestones, including several winged souls wearing wigs. *Thrummy Cap*, a ghostly tale by local poet John Burnes, is set in a haunted ale-house next to the graveyard. Getting up in the middle of the night for a drink, poor Thrummy encounters two skeletons defeating a third at football, so he joins in to even the odds. One of the ghosts then tells Thrummy that, in return for his sense of fair play, he will be rewarded if he removes a stone in the wall and takes what is concealed within to the laird. The hidden papers free the laird from a complicated lawsuit over his estate, and Thrummy is rewarded with fifty guineas. The poem can be found in G.H. Kinnear's *History of Glenbervie* (1895). Kinnear also relates that St Conan's Well (NO77428109) was used as a wishing well on the first Sunday of May, with visitors throwing three pins over their shoulders. McPherson's *Primitive Beliefs* mentions that a drover returning through the glen above Glenbervie saw the apparition of Adam Strickland, who had sold his shadow to the Devil.

DRUMLITHIE

The irregularly-shaped Court Stane (NO77487946) is one of those standing stones which attracts folkloric flotsam. The name could come from the site of the feudal court of the Barony of Mondynes (which may mean there was a stone circle here – for a similar usage, see OLD RAYNE); or perhaps it was emblematic of the authority of a Steward or Thane. More theatrically, it is said to mark where Duncan II was killed in 1094. In 2004 the stone was a bright white, courtesy of a tradition of unknown purpose maintained by the estate. In recent years the paint has not been renewed and the stone has reverted to its native grey.

The miniature steeple on High Street has a bell that summoned weavers to their work and indicated meal times. The locals are used to the taunt that the steeple has to be taken inside on a rainy day.

9

THE CAIRNGORMS

BEN AVON – BEN MACDHUI – LAIRIG GHRU – CAIRNTOUL

Here we venture into the upper lands, where every site can only be attained by those skilled in mountaincraft. The Cairngorm plateau is the nearest that mainland Britain comes to an Arctic environment, a windswept tundra both tranquil and deeply threatening. The best articulation of the joys and extremes of the peaks is Nan Shepherd's 1977 *The Living Mountain* – a beautiful book, poetic, self-aware, occasionally mystical as it attempts to gauge the effect of mountain walking on the mind and soul. She describes trekking as creating a trance-like state – 'I have walked out of the body and into the mountain'. There are trenchant observations on the way the weather and the landscape can alter perception. Mist can bring on 'mountain panic' (see below), things seem closer or further away, ground levels appear to be at the same height even if they vary widely, distances collapse into each other, and ravines disappear (a particularly dangerous illusion). In other words, in the mountains, things may not be what they seem.

And not just in the mountains …

On 19 February 1983 the body of a young climber was recovered from the Cairngorms. At the morgue Angus and Ethal Clunas identified the body as their son Stephen, as did the Clunas' son-in-law Fraser Ross. But the 24-year-old Stephen had actually gone birdwatching and had spent the weekend at a hotel. He only learned about the incident when a friend heard the report on a radio, and was reunited with his parents on the day set for the funeral. The dead man, who was barefoot, was wearing the same design of sweater, parka, underwear and gold watch as Stephen. His identity remained unknown. (Source: *Fortean Times*, Autumn 1984.)

BEN AVON

A mystery body was found on the south face of Ben Avon on 19 September 1938. The man had been dead for two months and had no identification on him. What he did have was gear, not for camping in the Cairngorms, but for strolling down a city street. His dark suit was complemented by a bowler hat, a walking stick, and an attaché-case containing pyjama trousers, two collars, a toilet roll, scissors and matches. Shaving gear was set out, and it seemed he had been about to shave by a stream when somehow he was struck dead. As far as I know the case is still open. (Source: *Sunday Post* 18 July 1976.)

BEN MACDHUI

I was returning from the cairn on the summit in a mist when I began to think I heard something else than merely the noise of my own footsteps. For every few steps I heard a crunch, and then another crunch as if someone was walking after me but taking steps three or four times the length of my own. I said to myself this is all nonsense. I listened and heard it again but could see nothing in the mist. As I walked on and the eerie crunch, crunch sounded behind me I was seized with terror and took to my heels, staggering blindly among the boulders for four or five miles nearly down to Rothiemurchus Forest. Whatever you make of it I do not know, but there is something very queer about the top of Ben Macdhui and I will not go back there myself I know.

So wrote Norman Collie, professor of organic chemistry at University College London and hugely experienced mountaineer, in *The Cairngorm Club Journal*. The episode he was referring to took place in 1891 but he did not go public until 1925. The revelation prompted a flurry of interest in mountaineering circles and the popular press, with more reports coming to light. Part of the debate was over whether there was – or wasn't – an existing but unrecorded body of belief in 'something' on the mountain among the local people. If there was, none of the assiduous nineteenth-century folklorists such as James Grant, Walter Gregor or Alex Maconnochie had picked it up. In 1949 Seton Gordon stated in *Highways and Byways in the Central Highlands* that the Marquess of Ailsa had told him he had heard of the spectre when staying at Castle Grant in the 1890s. But Collie's 1925 bombshell was the 'event horizon' for the Big Grey Man phenomenon – as with the Loch Ness Monster less than a decade later, once the cat was out of the bag it proved difficult to find 'authentic' early accounts because anyone speaking about it may have been influenced by the publicity. Although Collie did not see anything, the 'entity', if such it was, became known as the Fear Liath Mor or the Big Grey Man of Ben Macdhui, and remains a staple in paranormal literature.

When it comes to analysing the 'something very queer' on the mountain the two outstanding works are *The Big Grey Man of Ben Macdhui* by Affleck Gray (1972) and Andy Roberts' 'The Big Grey Man of Ben Macdhui and Other Mountain Panics', published in 1998 in *Fortean Studies Volume 5*. Gray collected a vast corpus of sightings and other strange phenomena, and carefully considered – and usually rejected – the various 'explanations' that had been put forward, from Caledonian Yetis to space visitors. Roberts' incisive essay pared away the cases that were irrelevant, peripheral or semi-fictional, and ended up with a small number of episodes that he identified as including key elements of the core phenomenon on or near Ben Macdhui: an apparent giant figure, whether seen or not; a sensation of 'presence'; the sound of footsteps; and a sensation of utter terror so strong as to make the mountaineer flee blindly across dangerous terrain.

Gray's cases that met most or all of these criteria included:

Around 1903: a second-hand account of Dr Henry Kellas and his brother, who fled in panic after sighting a 'giant figure' that followed them.

1904: Hugh Welsh and his brother had an eerie sensation of not being alone, and heard strange footsteps.

Sometime before 1924: a mountain-experienced friend of Dr Ernest A. Baker felt a terrifying presence that caused him to flee to low ground.

1943: Alexander Tewnion heard loud footsteps and saw a 'strange shape' coming towards him which so scared him he fired three shots from his revolver at it, then fled in panic. Tewnion's account, in which he vouched for the 'reality' of the figure – and it was certainly 'real' enough for him to shoot it – appeared in the *Scots Magazine* in 1958. In 1966 Tewnion wrote to Affleck Gray, stating: 'To this day I am convinced that I saw something but I am equally convinced that something was only a towering wisp of mist which I imagined to be a menacing ghost.'

1945: Peter Densham heard crunching noises and was then seized by a blind terror so strong he almost ran into a ravine: 'I tried to stop myself and found this was extremely difficult to do. It was as if somebody was pushing me.' After managing to deflect his course – which saved his life – he continued fleeing for several miles.

Both Gray and Roberts agree that the BGM is not a corporeal being – that is, there is no actual monster stalking the summits. The intense interest that the BGM has attracted has thrown up other mysterious phenomena in the area. Mountaineers have mentioned hearing singing and voices, or glimpsed distant figures, or seen the Brocken Spectre, an eerie spectacle where sunlight casts your distorted shadow onto mist or cloud, creating an apparently independent – and monstrous – figure. Other strange experiences may not have been recorded, either because the witnesses did not want to come forward, or because the experiences do not conform to the template that now exists for a 'BGM encounter'.

The general notion is that the BGM is a combination of an extreme environment and human psychology. Distorted perceptions, a sense of not being alone, and noises that sound like footsteps, are reported elsewhere in the mountaineering literature, although usually without the overwhelming terror. Encountering such phenomena, even when we know they have an explainable source, can generate feelings of unease which can trigger something deeper. Roberts quotes a Jungian analyst who discusses how the immensity and sublime savagery of the mountain landscape can overwhelm the 'heroic ego'. When we discover how pitifully small and irrelevant we are, the only response is an emotional one – panic.

Of course, this is just another notion, not a solution – mountain panic is not easily subject to strict scientific scrutiny. There may be as yet undetected environmental anomalies around Ben Macdhui that impact on human brain chemistry. In his book *The Goblin Universe* paranormal researcher F.W. Holiday suggests that the BGM was a member of the 'Phantom Menagerie', creatures that exist in an other-world and occasionally intersect with our own dimension. The BGM may be the *genius loci* or 'spirit of place' of the mountain. There are many more ideas, but all rest on the interpretation of a small number of cases; interestingly no very recent sightings have been reported – have the increasing numbers of hillwalkers banished the spectre from either (or both) our minds and the mountains?

If the Earl of Fife had had his way, Ben Macdhui would have been the highest mountain in Britain, not the runner-up to Ben Nevis. A monument covering the 100ft (30m) difference was planned, but never executed.

LAIRIG GHRU

This 18 mile (30km) high-level pass through the Cairngorms between Deeside and Rothiemurchus is a well-trod but still challenging route. Seton Gordon's *Highways and Byways in the Central Highlands* tells of Alexander 'Sandy' Davidson, a very experienced mountain man who became lost during a heavy snowstorm. He determined to follow a small burn to low ground, but was so tired he could not tell which way the stream was flowing. He therefore threw snowballs into the water – and they appeared to float in an upwards direction! He realised the fatigue was making him hallucinate, so he followed the snowballs as they went 'uphill', and eventually reached safety. In *The Secret of Spey* (1930) Wendy Wood described hearing a voice 'of gigantic resonance' one snowy day in the pass. She searched the area in case it came from an injured climber, but soon developed a sense of being followed – and heard the footsteps of someone taking long strides – so she departed hurriedly. In many respects this is an echo of the Ben Macdhui reports.

The most bizarre encounter in the pass was recorded by Sir Hugh Rankin, Baronet, whose obituary in the *Daily Telegraph* (2 May 1988) described him as 'an extraordinary character whose eccentricity was remarkable even by the rarefied standards of the baronetage'. Variously a Communist and atheist, and former President of the British Muslim Society, by 1944 he was a practising Buddhist. Sometime before 1959 he and Lady Rankin were cycling through the pass by the Pools of Dee (NH973009) when they encountered a large man dressed in a long robe and sandals. This, they recognised, was the Bodhisattva of the Cairngorms, one of the five 'Perfected Men' who live in the mountains of the world and meet once a year in a cave in the Himalayas. The Presence, as Rankin described the man, spoke in what may have been Sanskrit, and ethereal music played throughout the encounter.

BRAERIACH

50 Strange Stories of the Supernatural, published in 1974, contains the story 'The Grey Man of Braeriach' by Doddy Hay. It tells of how on 21 May 1935 two Scouts became separated from their party on the mountain's summit in zero-visibility mist; when they returned they were accompanied by a huge bearded man wearing a full-length loose grey cloak and carrying a long crook with a ram's-horn handle. This benevolent shepherd-like figure was witnessed by the two leaders and twenty-two Scouts before he moved off into the mist, but was invisible to the two boys he had rescued. Subsequent investigation showed that at a certain place both lads had felt a horrible sensation, 'like a cold hand grabbing the back of your neck.' Because of this feeling they had stopped in their tracks and returned to the camp. The spot where this occurred was, it transpired, a few paces from a yawning chasm. The two leaders both refer to the mysterious figure as the Grey Man of Braeriach, a being well-known in the area.

The book's editor, John Canning, notes that he sometimes changed names and locations in his contributors' stories to avoid pain or embarrassment to surviving relatives, and it is possible that Hay's story was originally called 'The Grey Man of Ben Macdhui'. The team leaders are named as Scoutmaster Colin MacDougall and his assistant Davie Bruce, and the missing pair as Sandy MacAllister and Billy Gilchrist, although all these could be pseudonyms. The other stories in the volume all purport to be non-fiction or, at worst, folk legends, and there is nothing in the book's context or Hay's text that suggests this particular tale is fictional. All of Hay's other works – many of which derive from his exciting life, including being a test-pilot for ejector seats – are non-fiction. Of course, 'The Grey Man of Braeriach' could be a flight of fancy, or a retelling of a mountaineer's fireside yarn, but just possibly it is a record of an unusually benevolent encounter with the BGM.

CAIRN TOUL

In the 1890s a stag was shot and wounded on the Great Moss on Cairn Toul. A ghillie wanted to save the trouble of carrying the corpse off on a pony so he drove the wounded animal in front of him. The stag kicked out, caught the gun with its hoof, and shot the ghillie dead. Queen Victoria once asked her ghillie about the meaning of the mountain named in Gaelic 'Bod an Deamhain'. The bowdlerised reply was that it was 'The Devil's Point', by which name it is still known today. The literal translation is 'The Devil's Penis'. Both episodes are in Ronald Turnbull's *The Cairngorms*.

GLEN DERRY

In 1914 George Duncan and James A. Parker travelled down the glen in a horse-drawn dog-cart after ascending Ben Macdhui. A mile below Derry Lodge, at the Black Bridge, Duncan looked troubled and fell silent. At dinner that evening he told Parker he had seen the Devil: 'a tall figure in a black gown waving his hands towards me.' Duncan went back several times to the spot to see if the trees or other factors had caused an illusion, but he could not recreate the figure. The case is in Norman Adams' *Haunted Valley*.

DEESIDE

Both the ruined Bynack Lodge (Glen Tilt, NO00058555) and Gelder Bothy (Glen Gelder, NO25718999) are reputed to be haunted, their remote locations possibly contributing to the sense of a 'haunted house'.

BIBLIOGRAPHY

PSAS = Proceedings of the Society of Antiquaries of Scotland.

HISTORY, ARCHAEOLOGY AND GENERAL

Aberdeenshire Council *The Historic Kirkyards of Aberdeenshire A Survey Report* (1998)

Adams, Norman *Hangman's Brae: True Crime and Punishment in Aberdeen and the North-East* (Black & White Publishing; Edinburgh, 2005)

Alexander, William *Notes and Sketches Illustrative of Northern Rural Life in the Eighteenth Century* (David Douglas; Edinburgh, 1877)

Allan, Norman *The Kirk at Alvah 1792-1992* (Banff, 1992)

Andrews, William (ed.) *Bygone Church Life in Scotland* (William Andrews & Co.; London, 1899)

Apted, M.R. *The Painted Ceilings of Scotland 1550-1650* (HMSO; Edinburgh, 1966)

Bath, Michael *Renaissance Decorative Painting in Scotland* (NMS Publishing; Edinburgh, 2003)

Brotchie, T.C.F. *The Battlefields of Scotland, Their Legend and Story* (T.C. & E.C. Jack; Edinburgh, 1913)

Browne, G.F. *On Some Antiquities in the Neighbourhood of Dunecht House Aberdeenshire* (Cambridge University Press; Cambridge, 1921)

Bryce, Ian B.D. and Alasdair Roberts 'Post-Reformation Catholic Symbolism: Further and Different Examples' in *PSAS*, Volume 126 (1996)

Bryson, Alexander 'Remarks on a Bone Cave near the Mouth of the North Esk' in *The Edinburgh New Philosophical Journal*, Volume XLIX (1850)

Buchan, David *The Ballad and the Folk* (Routledge; London, 1972)

Buchan, David S.C. *St Combs My Buchan* (The Pentland Press; Edinburgh, 1993)

Burton, John Hill *Narratives from Criminal Trials in Scotland* (Chapman and Hall; London, 1852)

Cameron, Archibald Cowie *The History of Fettercairn: A Parish in the County of Kincardine* (J. & R. Parlane; Paisley, 1899)

Cameron, David Kerr *The Cornkister Days: A Portrait of a Land and its Rituals* (Penguin; Harmondsworth, 1986)

Chambers, Robert *Domestic Annals of Scotland from the Reformation to the Revolution* (W. & R. Chambers; Edinburgh & London, 1874)

Clark, Ronald W. *Balmoral: Queen Victoria's Highland Home* (Thames & Hudson; London, 1981)

Coles, Fred R. 'Report on Stone Circles of North Eastern Scotland' in *PSAS*, Volume 37 (1902-3)

Cooke, G.A. *Topography of Great Britain or, British Traveller's Pocket Directory. Vol. XXV: Scotland – Middle Division* (Sherwood, Neely & Jones; London, 1820)

Defoe, Daniel *A Tour Thro' the Whole Island of Great Britain* (Penguin; Harmondsworth, 2005 – first published 1724-1726)

Dinnie, Robert *An Account of the Parish of Birse* (Birse Community Trust; Finzean, 1999 – first published 1865)

Edwards, D.H. *Modern Scottish Poets: With Biographical and Critical Notices Tenth Series* (Brechin Advertiser; Brechin, 1887)

Farquharson, Donald Robert *Reminiscences of Cromar and Canada* (The Planet Publishing House; Chatham, Ontario, n.d.)

Fojut, N. and Love, P. 'The defences of Dundarg Castle, Aberdeenshire' in *PSAS*, Volume 113 (1983)

Forbes, H.O. 'Dolmens in Scotland' in *Antiquity*, Volume 3 (June, 1929)

Fraser, Amy Stewart *The Hills of Home* (Routledge & Kegan Paul; London, 1973)

Garner, Harold Wallace *Congan: A Celtic Saint of the Isles, the Highlands and Aberdeenshire in Historical Perspective* (Timoleon; Banff, 2007)

Geddes, Jane *Deeside and the Mearns: An Illustrated Architectural Guide* (RIAS; Edinburgh, 2001)

Gilfillan, George (ed.) *The History of a Man* (Arthur Hall, Virtue, & Co.; London, 1856)

Godsman, James *Glass, Aberdeenshire. The Story of a Parish* (Alex P. Reid & Son; Aberdeen, 1970)

Gordon, Seton *The Cairngorm Hills of Scotland* (Cassell & Co.; London, 1925)

——————— *Highways and Byways in the Central Highlands* (Macmillan; London, 1949)

Grant, David *A Feughside Fairy Tale and the Sounin' o' the Kirk* (Robin Callander; Finzean, 1980)

Gray, John *A Barony and a Realm* (Peterhead, n.d.)

Groome, Francis H. (ed.) *Ordnance Gazetteer of Scotland: A Survey of Scottish Topography, Statistical, Biographical and Historical* (Thomas C. Jack; Edinburgh, 1882–1885)

Henderson, B. 'Slains Castle' in *Transactions of the Buchan Field Club* Volume XVIII Part III (1979)

Henderson, John A. *History of the Parish of Banchory-Devenick* (D. Wyllie & Son; Aberdeen, 1890)

——————— *Annals of Lower Deeside, Being a Topographical, Proprietary, Ecclesiastical, and Antiquarian History of Durris, Drumoak, and Culter* (D. Wyllie & Son; Aberdeen, 1892)

Henry, Robert James, A.S. McPherson and Alastair E.D. Paterson *Macduff and its Harbour 1783-1983* (E.A. Porterfield; Macduff, 1983)

Jack, Rosalind A. *Maud: A Glimpse into the Past* (Rosalind A. Jack; Maud, 1986)

Jackson, Robin 'The Horn of Leys: Fact or Fiction?' in *Leopard* magazine October 2004

Jervise, A. 'Notices respecting the Castle of Craig and the Old Kirk of Auchindoir, etc., in Aberdeenshire' in *PSAS*, Volume 8 (1868-70)

Jervise, Andrew and James Gammack *Memorials of Angus and Mearns: An Account Historical, Antiquarian, and Traditionary* (David Douglas; Edinburgh, 1885)

Kinnear, G.H. *History of Glenbervie* (the author; Montrose, 1895)

Lawson, John Parker *Historical Tales of the Wars of Scotland, and of the Border Raids, Forays, and Conflicts* (A. Fullarton & Co., Edinburgh, London and Dublin, n.d.)

Littlejohn, William *Stories of the Buchan Cottars before the Year 'One'. Being Sketches of Life and Character in a Buchan Parish in Aberdeenshire in the Olden Times* (Milne and Hutchison; Aberdeen, 1929)

Livingstone, Sheila *Confess and be Hanged: Scottish Crime and Punishment through the Ages* (Birlinn; Edinburgh, 2000)

Lyons, A.W. 'Further Notes on Tempera-Painting in Scotland, and Other Discoveries at Delgaty Castle' in *PSAS*, Volume 44 (1909-10)

Macdonald, James, Donald MacKinnon and C.E. Troup *The Place Names of West Aberdeenshire* (Spalding Club; Aberdeen, 1899)

Mack, A. *Field Guide to the Pictish Symbol Stones* (The Pinkfoot Press; Balgavies, 1997)

MacGillivray, William *The Natural History of Dee Side and Braemar* (printed for private circulation; London, 1855)

Marner, Dominic 'The Sword of the Spirit, the Word of God and the Book of Deer' in *Medieval Archaeology* Volume 46 (2002)

McConnochie, Alex Inkson *Deeside* (James G. Bissett; Aberdeen, 1985 – first published 1893)

——————— *Bennachie* (Lewis Smith & Son; Aberdeen, 1897)

——————— *The Book of Ellon* (Victoria Hall Committee; Ellon, 1901)

McKay, Margaret & Bill *A United Parish: Auchaber, Forgue, Inverkeithny and Ythan Wells* (no publisher; 2001)

McKean, Charles *Banff and Buchan an Illustrated Architectural Guide* (RIAS; Edinburgh 1990)

Michie, John Grant *History of Logie-Coldstone and the Braes of Cromar* (D. Wyllie & Son; Aberdeen; 1896)

Milne, James *Twixt Ury and Don, and Round About* (Dufton Scott & Son; Inverurie, 1947)

Ministers of the Respective Parishes, the *New Statistical Account of Scotland* Volumes 12 & 13 (William Blackwood; Edinburgh and London, 1845)

Penny, Cecilia (ed.) *Stuartfield: Our Place* (Stuartfield Millennium Group; Stuartfield, 2000)

Peterkin, Alexander (ed.) *The Booke of the Universall Kirk of Scotland* (Edinburgh Printing & Publishing Co.; Edinburgh, 1839)

Phillips, J.G. *Wanderings in the Highlands of Banff and Aberdeen Shires, with trifles in verse* (Banffshire Journal; Banff, 1881)

Pococke, Richard *Tours in Scotland 1747, 1750, 1760* (The Scottish History Society; Edinburgh, 1887)

Pratt, John B. *Buchan* (Lewis & James Smith; Aberdeen, 1858)

Reid, Hugh G. *Past and Present of Social and Religious Life in the North* (Edmonston; Edinburgh, 1870)

Ritchie, Gordon J.N. *Stonehaven of Old* (Stonehaven Heritage Society; Stonehaven, 1989)

————— *Stonehaven of Old Volume 2* (Stonehaven Heritage Society; Stonehaven, 1995)

Ritchie, Sandy *Stories from New Deer and St Kane's* (W. Peters & Sons; Turriff, 1989)

Robertson, George *A General View of Kincardineshire, or, the Mearns: Drawn Up and Published by Order of the Board of Agriculture* (R. Phillips; London, 1810)

Robertson, Joseph (ed.) *Illustrations of the Topography and Antiquities of the Shires of Aberdeen and Banff* (The Spalding Club; Aberdeen, 1847)

Roughead, William *Twelve Scots Trials* (William Green & Sons; Edinburgh, 1913)

Rowley-Conwy, Peter 'Great Sites: Balbridie' in *British Archaeology,* Issue 64 (April, 2002)

Scott, Patrick W. *The History of Strathbogie* (Patrick W. Scott; Aberdeen, 1997)

Shepherd, Ian *Gordon – An Illustrated Architectural Guide* (The Rutland Press; Edinburgh, 1994)

————— *Aberdeenshire: Donside and Strathbogie – An Illustrated Architectural Guide* (The Rutland Press; Edinburgh, 2006)

Shepherd, Nan *The Living Mountain* (Aberdeen University Press; Aberdeen, 1977)

Simpson, W. Douglas 'The Castles of Dunnideer and Wardhouse, in The Garioch, Aberdeenshire' in *PSAS,* Volume 69 (1934-5)

Sinclair, Sir John, Ian R. Grant, Donald J. Withrington (eds) *The Statistical Account of Scotland 1791-1799. Vol XIV Kincardineshire and South and West Aberdeenshire; Vol XV North and East Aberdeenshire; Vol XVI Banffshire, Moray and Nairnshire* (EP Publishing; Wakefield, 1982)

Slade, H. Gordon 'The House of Fetternear: A History and a Description' in *PSAS,* Volume 103 (1970-71) 'Craigston Castle, Aberdeenshire' in *PSAS,* Volume 108 (1976-77)

Slater, James *'Bonnie Portsoy' A Village History* (Banff and Buchan District Council; n.d.)

Smith, John S. and Stevenson, David (eds) *Fermfolk and Fisherfolk: Rural Life in Northern Scotland in the Eighteenth and Nineteenth Centuries* (The Mercat Press; Edinburgh, 1992)

Smith, Robert *Deeside (25 Walks)* (HMSO; Edinburgh, 1994)

————— *Buchan – Land of Plenty* (John Donald; Edinburgh, 1996)

————— *A Queen's Country* (John Donald; Edinburgh, 2000)

————— *The Road to Drumnafunner: A Journey through North-East Scotland* (Birlinn; Edinburgh, 2007)

Spalding, John *The History of the Troubles and Memorable Transactions in Scotland, from the Year 1624 to 1645* (T. Evans; London, 1792)

Spence, James *Ruined Castles: Monuments of Former Men in Vicinity of Banff* (Edmonston and Douglas; Edinburgh, 1873)

Stewart, James *Deeside Tinkers* (McKenzie Quality Print; Dyce, 2007)

Stirling, A.M.W. *Fyvie Castle, Its Lairds and their Times* (John Murray, London; 1928)

Swapp, George D. *Dunnottar Woods and House 1782-2008* (Stonehaven Heritage Society; Stonehaven, 2008)

Taylor, James *The Cabrach* (*Banffshire Journal*; Banff, 1914)

————— *Cabrach Feerings* (*Banffshire Journal*; Banff, 1920)

Taylor, James 'Pitsligo: Castle, Church and Famous Laird' in *Transactions of the Buchan Field Club* Volume XVIII Part IV (1989)

Taylor, James & Liz *The Vanishing Laird: Lord Pitsligo* (Visual Image Production; Fraserburgh, n.d.)

Turnbull, Ronald *The Cairngorms* (Pevensey Press; Newton Abbot, 2002)

Urquhart, Christine *Mither o' the Meal Kist: A Pictorial History of Fordyce* (Turriff, n.d.)

Watt, Alexander *The Early History of Kintore: Extracted from Old Records and Charters* (Published by, and for the Behoof of The Widow; Kintore, 1865)

Watt, Archibald *Highways and Byways Round Kincardine* (Gourdas House; Aberdeen, 1985)

Watt, James Crabb *The Mearns of Old: A History of Kincardine from the Earliest Times to the Seventeenth Century* (William Hodge & Co.; Edinburgh and Glasgow, 1914)

Watt, V. J. Buchan *The Book of Banchory* (Oliver & Boyd; Edinburgh, 1947)

Watt, William *A History of Aberdeen and Banff* (William Blackwood & Sons; Edinburgh and London, 1900)

Windsor, Duke of *A King's Story: The Memoirs of H.R.H. The Duke of Windsor* (G.P. Putnam; New York, 1951)

Wyness, Fenton *Royal Valley: The story of the Aberdeenshire Dee* (Alex P. Reid & Son; Aberdeen, 1968)

MYSTERIOUSNESS

Adams, W.H. Davenport *Witch, Warlock, and Magician* (J.W. Bout; New York, 1889)

Adams, Norman *Haunted Scotland* (Mainstream Publishing; Edinburgh, 1998)

———— *Haunted Valley: Ghost Stories, Mysteries and Legends of Royal Deeside* (Tolbooth Books; Banchory, 1994)

———— *Scottish Bodysnatchers: True Accounts* (Goblinshead; Musselburgh, 2002)

Allen, Greg Dawson 'The Pursuit of Witches' in *Leopard* magazine (October, 2002)

Anderson, Duncan *Scottish Folk-Lore, or, Reminiscences of Aberdeenshire from Pinafore to Gown* (J. Selwin Tait & Sons; New York, 1895)

Anderson, James 'Sketches of the Life of Adam Donald' in *The Bee, or Literary Weekly Intelligencer* December 21, 1791

Anson, Peter F. *Fisher Folk-Lore* (The Faith Press; London, 1965)

Balfour, Bernard Maitland *Secrets, Stories, Skeletons and Stones* (Cranstone House Publishing; Aberdeen, 1993)

Banks, M. Macleod 'Folklore of the Net, Fishing-Line, Baiting and the Boat on the North-East Coast of Scotland' in *Folklore*, Volume 50, No. 4 (December 1939)

Banks, Mrs M.M. & M.M. 'Scottish Lore of Earth, Its Fruits, and the Plough' in *Folklore*, Volume 50, No. 1 (March 1939)

Baring-Gould, S. *The Lives of the Saints* (John C. Nimmo; London, and Longmans, Green, & Co.; New York, 1898)

Barrett, Michael *A Calendar of Scottish Saints* (The Abbey Press; Fort Augustus, 1919)

Beattie, George *John O' Arnha', A Tale: To which is added the Murderit Mynstrell and Other Poems* (Alexander Burnett; Montrose, 1883)

Black, William George *Folk-Medicine; A Chapter in the History of Culture* (The Folk-Lore Society/Elliot Stock; London, 1883)

Brand, John *Observations on Popular Antiquities: Chiefly Illustrating the Origin of Our Vulgar Customs, Ceremonies and Superstitions* (F.C. & J. Rivington *et al*; London, 1813)

Briggs, K.M. 'Some Late Accounts of the Fairies' in *Folklore*, Volume 72, No. 3 (September 1961)

'Buchan Horseman, A' *The Horseman's Oath* (Scottish Country Life Museums Trust; 1972)

Buchan, David (ed.) *Folk Tradition and Folk Medicine in Scotland: The Writings of David Rorie* (Canongate; Edinburgh, 1994)

Buchan, David D. 'A Lughnasa Piper in the Northeast of Scotland' in *The Journal of American Folklore*, Volume 81, No. 321 (1968)

Buchan, Peter *Annals of Peterhead, from its Foundation to the Present Time* (P. Buchan; Peterhead, 1819)

———— *Witchcraft Detected and Prevented; or, the School of Black Art Newly Opened* (P. Buchan; Peterhead, 1824)

———— *The Peterhead Smugglers of the Last Century or, William and Annie, in Three Acts* (P. Buchan; Peterhead, 1834)

Burne, Charlotte Sophia *The Handbook of Folklore* (Sidgwick & Jackson; London, 1914)

Byrd, Elizabeth *A Strange and Seeing Time* (Robert Hale; London, 1971)

Chambers, Robert *Popular Rhymes of Scotland* (W. & R. Chambers; Edinburgh and London, 1841)

Clark, David F. 'Track of the Big Cat?' in *Leopard* magazine April 2004

Coburn, Sue *Fyvie Castle Unexplained* (Sue Coburn; 2006)

Combe, George *The Phrenological Journal and Miscellany Volume I* (The Proprietor; Edinburgh, 1824)

Crombie, James E. 'First-Footing in Aberdeenshire' in *Folklore*, Volume 4, No. 3 (September 1893)

Dalyell, John Graham *The Darker Superstitions of Scotland: Illustrated from History and Practice* (Waugh and Innes; Edinburgh, 1834)

Davidson, T.D. 'The Untilled Field' in *The Agricultural History Review* Volume 3 Part 1 (1955)

Davidson, Thomas 'Plough Rituals in England and Scotland' in *Agricultural History Review* Volume 7 Part 1 (1959)

Farquharson, J. and Macintosh, H. 'Notes on Beltane Cakes' in *Folklore*, Volume 6, No. 1 (March, 1895)

Fenton, Alexander and David Heppell 'The Earth Hound – A Living Banffshire Belief' in *Folklore Frontiers*, No. 34 (1998)

Fisher, Adrian *Mazes and Labyrinths* (Osprey Publishing; Botley, 2004)

Frazer, Sir James George *The Golden Bough: A Study in Magic and Religion* Macmillan and Co.; London, 1933)

Goodare, Julian 'The Scottish Witchcraft Panic of 1597' in Goodare, Julian (ed.) *The Scottish Witch-Hunt in Context* (Manchester University Press; Manchester & New York, 2002)

Gordon, Patrick *A Short Abridgement of Britane's Distemper: From the Yeare of God M.DC.XXXIX to M.DC.XLIX* (The Spalding Club; Aberdeen, 1844)

Grant, James *The Mysteries of all Nations: Rise and Progress of Superstition, Laws Against and Trials of Witches, Ancient and Modern Delusions Together with Strange Customs, Fables, and Tales* (W. Paterson; Edinburgh And Simpkin, Marshall, & Co.; London, 1880)

Grant, John *Legends of the Braes O' Mar* (Alexander Murray; Aberdeen, 1910 – first published 1861)

Green, Andrew *Ghosts of Today* (Kaye & Ward; London, 1980)

Green, Derek 'Spectral Highways of Scotland' in *The Ghost Club Newsletter* (Spring, 2008)

Gregor, Walter *Notes on the Folk-Lore of the North-East of Scotland* (Folk-Lore Society; London, 1881)

———— 'Stories of Fairies from Scotland' in *The Folk-Lore Journal*, Volume 1, No. 1 (January, 1883)

———— 'Stories of Fairies from Scotland' in *The Folk-Lore Journal*, Volume 1, No. 2 (February, 1883)

———— 'Kelpie Stories from the North of Scotland' in *The Folk-Lore Journal*, Volume 1, No. 9 (September, 1883)

———— 'Some Old Farming Customs and Notions in Aberdeenshire' in *The Folk-Lore Journal*, Volume 2, No. 11 (November, 1884)

———— 'Fishermen's Folk-Lore' in *The Folk-Lore Journal*, Volume 2, No. 12 (December, 1884)

———— 'Notes and Queries: Unspoken Nettles' in *The Folk-Lore Journal*, Volume 2, No. 12 (December, 1884)

———— 'Some Folk-Lore of the Sea' in *The Folk-Lore Journal*, Volume 4 (1886)

———— 'Bread' in *The Folk-Lore Journal*, Volume 7, No. 3 (1889)

———— 'Devil Stories' in *The Folk-Lore Journal*, Volume 7, No. 4 (1889)

———— 'The Witch' in *The Folk-Lore Journal*, Volume 7, No. 4 (1889)

———— 'The Scotch Fisher Child' *Folklore*, Volume 2, No. 1 (March, 1891)

————— 'Guardian Spirits of Wells and Lochs' in *Folklore*, Volume 3, No. 1 (March, 1892)

————— 'Some Scottish Folklore of the Child and the Human Body' in *Folklore*, Volume 6, No. 4 (December, 1895)

Grinsell, Leslie *Folklore of Prehistoric Sites in Britain* (David & Charles; Newton Abbot, 1976)

Gurney, Edmund, Frank Podmore and Frederic W.H. Myers *Phantasms of the Living* (The Society For Psychical Research/Trubner & Co.; London, 1886)

Guthrie, E.J. *Old Scottish Customs: Local and General* (Hamilton, Adams & Co.; London; and Thomas D. Mortson; Glasgow, 1885)

Haddow, Angus H. *Dowsing for Patterns of the Past – The Stone Circles of Aberdeenshire* online at www.equinoxe.org.uk/ (retrieved 09 April 2009)

Halliday, Ron *Evil Scotland* (Fort Publishing; Ayr, 2003)

Hay, Doddy 'The Grey Man of Braeriach' in Canning, John (ed.) *50 Strange Stories of the Supernatural* (Century Books; London, 1974)

Henderson, G.D. *Mystics of the North-East* (Third Spalding Club; Aberdeen, 1934)

Henderson, Robert *Scottish Keeriosities* (St Andrew Press; Edinburgh, 1995)

Hickey, Sally 'Fatal Feeds?: Plants, Livestock Losses and Witchcraft Accusations in Tudor and Stuart Britain' in *Folklore*, Volume 101, No. 2 (1990)

Holiday, F.W. *The Goblin Universe* (Xanadu; London, 1986)

Hutton, Ronald *The Triumph of the Moon: A History of Modern Pagan Witchcraft* (Oxford University Press; Oxford, 1999)

Jackson, Robin 'The Horn of Leys: Fact or Fiction?' in *Leopard* magazine (October, 2004)

Jones, Richard *Haunted Houses of Britain and Ireland* (New Holland Publishers; London, 2005)

Kirby, B.S. *Kirby's Wonderful Eccentric Museum; or, Magazine Including all the Curiosities of Nature and Art, from the Remotest Period to the Present Time* Volume VI (B.S. Kirby; London, 1820)

Lorenzen, Coral E. *Encounters with UFO Occupants* (Berkley Medallion; New York, 1976)

MacDonald, A. 'Midsummer Bonfires' in *Folklore*, Volume 15, No. 1 (March, 1904)

————— 'Some Former Customs of the Royal Parish of Crathie, Scotland' in *Folklore*, Volume 18, No. 1 (March, 1907)

————— 'Sacred Wells' in *Folklore*, Volume 19, No. 4 (December, 1908)

————— 'Scraps of Scottish Folklore, I' in *Folklore*, Volume 21, No. 1 (March, 1910)

Mackinlay, J.M. (1893) *Folklore of Scottish Lochs and Springs* (William Hodge; Glasgow, 1893)

Maclagan, R.C. 'Ghost Lights of the West Highlands' in *Folklore*, Volume 8, No. 3 (September, 1897)

Maclellan, Malcolm 'Facing the Future' in *Scotland in Trust* magazine (Spring, 2009)

Maxwell-Stuart, P.G. *An Abundance of Witches: The Great Scottish Witch-Hunt*, (Tempus; Stroud, 2005)

McAldowie, Alex M. 'Personal Experiences in Witchcraft' in *Folklore*, Volume 7, No. 3 (September, 1896)

McHardy, Stuart *The Quest for the Nine Maidens* (Luath Press; Edinburgh, 2003)

McPherson, J.M. *Primitive Beliefs in the North-East of Scotland* (Longmans, Green & Co.; London, 1929)

Michell, John *The New View Over Atlantis* (Thames & Hudson; London, 1986)

Michie, John *Deeside Tales* (John Adam; Aberdeen, 1872)

Milne, Graeme *The Haunted North: Paranormal Tales from Aberdeen and the North East* (Cauliay Publishing; Aberdeen, 2008)

Milne, John *Myths and Superstitions of the Buchan District* (Rosalind A. Jack; Maud, 1987 – first published 1891)

Mitchell, Arthur 'Vacation Notes in Cromar, Burghead, and Strathspey' in *PSAS*, Volume 10 (1872-74)

Morris, R. & F. *Scottish Healing Wells: Healing, Holy, Wishing and Fairy Wells of the Mainland of Scotland* (Alethea Press; Sandy, 1982)

Owen, Robert Dale *Footfalls on the Boundary of Another World* (J.B. Lippincott & Co.; Philadelphia, 1872)

Peterhead Tourist Initiative *Peterhead Stories and Legends* (Peterhead Tourist Initiative; Peterhead, n.d.)

Pickup, Gilly 'John Anderson: The Wizard of the North' in *Leopard* magazine (September, 2005)

Podmore, Frank *Apparitions and Thought-Transference: An Examination of the Evidence for Telepathy* (Walter Scott; London, 1894)

Rannachan, Tom *Psychic Scotland* (Black & White Publishing; Edinburgh, 2007)

Rennie, Billy 'The Horseman's Word' in Aikey Fair Committee, *Aikey Fayre 1994 Souvenir Booklet* (Banff & Buchan District Council; 1994)

Ritchie, James 'An Account of the Watch-Houses, Mortsafes, and Public Vaults in Aberdeenshire Churchyards, Formerly used for the Protection of the Dead from the Resurrectionists' in *PSAS*, Volume 46 (1911-12)

————— 'Notes on some Stone Circles in Central Aberdeenshire' in *PSAS*, Volume 51 (1916-17)

————— 'Relics of the Body-Snatchers: Supplementary Notes on Mortsafe Tackle, Mortsafes, Watch-Houses, and Public Vaults, Mostly in Aberdeenshire' in *PSAS*, Volume 55 (1920-21)

————— 'Folklore of the Aberdeenshire Stone Circles and Standing-Stones' in *PSAS*, Volume 60 (1926)

Roberts, Andy 'The Big Grey Man of Ben Macdhui and Other Mountain Panics' in Steve Moore (ed.), *Fortean Studies Volume 5* (John Brown Publishing; London, 1998)

Robertson, Stanley *Exodus to Alford* (Balnain Books; Inverness, 1988)

Rorie, David 'Scottish Amulets' in *Folklore*, Volume 20, No. 2 (June, 1909)

————— 'Stray Notes on the Folk-Lore of Aberdeenshire and the North-East of Scotland' in *Folklore*, Volume 25, No. 3 (September, 1914)

————— 'Migratory Stones in Banffshire' in *Folklore*, Volume 34, No. 2 (June, 1923)

Rust, J. *Druidism Exhumed* (Edmonston & Douglas; Edinburgh, 1871)

Scott, Sir Walter *Letters on Demonology and Witchcraft* (Wordsworth/The Folklore Society; Ware & London, 2001 – first published 1830)

Society for Psychical Research *Journal of the Society for Psychical Research* Volume 8 (1897-98)

Stewart, William Grant *The Popular Superstitions and Festive Amusements of the Highlanders of Scotland* (Aylott And Jones; London, 1851)

Stuart, John (ed.) *The Miscellany of the Spalding Club Vol I.* (The Spalding Club; Aberdeen, 1841)

————— *Extracts from the Presbytery Book of Strathbogie* (The Spalding Club; Aberdeen, 1843)

Thiselton-Dyer, T.F. *British Popular Customs Present and Past: Illustrating the Social and Domestic Manners of the People: Arranged According to the Calendar of the Year* (George Bell & Sons; London 1911)

Tibbets, Charles J. *Folk-Lore and Legends: England and Scotland* (Gibbings & Co.; London, 1894)

Urlin, Ethel L. *Festivals, Holy Days, and Saints' Days: A Study in Origins and Survivals in Church Ceremonies and Secular Customs* (Simpkin, Marshall, Hamilton, Kent & Co.; London, 1915)

Walker, William *The De'il at Baldarroch, and Other Poems, in the Scottish Dialect* (printed for the author; Aberdeen, 1839)

Wright, E.M. *Rustic Speech and Folk-lore* (Oxford University Press; London, 1913)

FICTION

Gibbon, Lewis Grassic *A Scots Quair: Sunset Song* (Pan; London, 1982)

MacDonald, George *Phantastes* (Gollancz; London, 1971 – first published 1858)

————— *Lilith* (Gollancz; London, 1971 – first published 1895)

Stoker, Bram *Dracula* (Wordsworth Editions; Ware, 1993 – first published 1897)

————— *The Mystery of the Sea* (Sutton Publishing; Stroud, 1997 – first published 1902)

————— 'Crooken Sands' in *Dracula's Guest and Other Stories* (Wordsworth Editions; Ware, 2006)

NEWSPAPERS AND MAGAZINES

Banffshire Journal: 19 September 2006; 10 October 2006; 17 January 2007; 07 February 2007; 14 March 2007; 28 March 2007; 04 April 2007; 12 June 2007; 27 June 2007; 31 October 2007; 12 December 2007; 15 July 2008; 21 October 2008; 03 February 2009

Buchan Observer: 13 January 2009

Daily Express: 09 June 2007; 31 October 2008

Daily Mail: 23 March 2001; 03 March 2003; 17 February 2004; 27 October 2006

Daily Mirror: 02 May 2002; 30 May 2005; 27 August 2008; 30 October 2008

Daily Record: 15 June 1991; 15 January 2002; 29 October 2003

Daily Telegraph: 02 May 1988

Evening Express (Aberdeen): 22 July 1996; 8 August, 2007; 19 June 2008

Financial Times: 16 November 2002

Fishing News: 03 July 1987

Fortean Times: No. 42 (Autumn 1984); No. 50 (Summer 1988); No. 96 (March 1997)

Hartlepool Mail: 12 January 2009

Herald (Glasgow): 22 August 1970; 19 March 2001

New Scientist: 24 January 1974

New Statesman: 03 March 1995

News of the World: 27 October 1996; 15 March 1998; 19 July 1998; 20 June 1999; 11 June 2000; 03 September 2000; 07 January 2001; 17 June 2001; 20 January 2002; 27 January 2002; 23 June 2002; 16 March 2003; 18 January 2004; 07 September 2008

Press and Journal: 9 September 1980; 14 April 2004; 11 August 2004; 18 June 2008; 23 June 2008; 05 July 2008; 26 August 2008; 20 October 2008; 17 November 2008; 13 January 2009; 20 January 2009; 07 February 2009; 23 February 2009

Scotsman: 18 November 1999; 29 November 2001; 22 June 2004; 01 December 2006; 14 May 2008

Sun: 23 February 1998; 10 January 2003; 25 August 2005; 16 October 2006

Sunday Mail: 08 June 2003

Sunday Post: 18 July 1976; 07 May 1978; 24 January 1993

Sunday Times: 13 July 2003; 31 December 2006

The Times: 14 January 2003

RADIO PROGRAMMES

Scotland's Music, Programme 1: 'Rocks and Bones' written and presented by John Purser, BBC Radio Scotland, 07 January 2007

WEBSITES

Aberdeenshire Museums: www.aberdeenshire.gov.uk/museums/

Aberdeenshire Sites & Monuments Record: www.aberdeenshire.gov.uk/archaeology/smr/

Angus Council: www.angus.gov.uk/history/

Banff & Buchan Arts Forum: www.bbaf-arts.org.uk/sites/bbaf/home/home.html

Big Cats in Britain: www.bigcatsinbritain.org

The Book of Deer Project: www.bookofdeer.co.uk/

Cairness House: www.cairnesshouse.com

Deveron Arts: www.deveron-arts.com

The Modern Antiquarian: www.themodernantiquarian.com

Monymusk: www.monymusk.com

Oldmeldrum Golf Club: www.oldmeldrumgolf.co.uk

Royal Commission on Ancient and Historical Monuments in Scotland (Canmore): www.rcahms.gov.uk

Survey of Scottish Witchcraft: www.shc.ed.ac.uk/Research/witches/

Tranquility Wild West Town: www.geocities.com/tranquility_wildwesttown/

UFOInfo: www.ufoinfo.com.

INDEX